T. Rowe Price

T. Rowe Price

The Man, The Company, and The Investment Philosophy

CORNELIUS C. BOND

WILEY

Library of Congress Cataloging-in-Publication Data is Available:

ISBN 9781119531265 (Hardback)
ISBN 9781119531289 (ePDF)
ISBN 9781119531319 (ePub)

Cover Design: Wiley
Cover Image: Photograph by Bachrach

Printed in the United States of America.

V10008036_020519

"They come and they go — with brief torrents of publicity and a moment or two of glory on the Lipper sheets. But few money managers, very few, stand the test of time. One of the handful that has is the Sage of Baltimore, 77-year-old T. Rowe Price, Jr."

"Why T. Rowe Price Likes Gold," Forbes, October 15, 1975

Contents

Foreword

Thomas Rowe Price, Jr. developed the "Growth Stock Philosophy" of investing in the 1930s. His innovative ideas captured the imagination of a *Barron's* editor who asked him to write a series of articles, published by the magazine in the spring of 1939. Adhering to this philosophy, he successfully invested his clients' money at his new firm for sixteen years. By 1950, his success gave him the confidence to introduce his first mutual fund, the T. Rowe Price Growth Stock Fund, consisting of large well-established growth companies. Ten years later, he started the New Horizons Fund to invest in emerging growth companies earlier in their life cycle. The Growth Stock Fund ultimately produced the best performance record through its first ten years of any U.S. equity mutual fund, with the objective of growth, income secondary. New Horizons had the best performance for its first five and ten years of any U.S. equity mutual fund. This is according to *Investment Companies* by Arthur Wiesenberger, the source for mutual fund performance data at that time.

The firm that bears his name has grown to become one of the largest companies in the business of actively managing money in the United States, with more than $1 trillion in assets under management as of March 31, 2018.

The T. Rowe Price Group today still operates under many of the basic tenets of the Growth Stock Philosophy, including a focus on the longer term, a strong emphasis on fundamental research, and the belief that knowing and respecting management are key factors in buying the shares of any company. In 2017, the firm continued its long record of outstanding performance with 81 percent of all mutual funds beating their respective Lipper averages on a total return basis over ten years, according to the firm's 2017 annual report.

An important contributor to this book is Robert (Bob) E. Hall, who worked with me at T. Rowe Price Associates for more than ten years, during which he was chairman of the Investment Committee of both the Growth Stock Fund and the New Era Fund. He later joined Brown Capital Management and co-founded the Small Company Fund. According to Bob, this fund has been run since inception under the tenets of Mr. Price's Growth Stock Philosophy. In 2015, Morningstar awarded Bob and his team the title of Domestic Stock Fund Managers of the year. The Morningstar announcement mentioned that the fund's performance was in the top ten percent of all U.S. mutual funds for the previous three, five and ten, years – and since Morningstar was launched in 2011, as measured by Morningstar's five-star rating.

It is apparent that this philosophy of managing money is as valid today as it was when Mr. Price introduced it eighty years ago. It will be discussed in detail in the following pages. Its deceptively simple concepts are based on common sense or "horse sense," as his grandmother used to say. Mr. Price, however, was hardly an amateur investor and had more than a usual level of investment common sense. Little has been written about how this modest, ethical man managed to build one of the largest U.S. companies in the business of managing mutual funds. Yet his record of stock market performance over his long career places him among the top money managers of the twentieth century.

He also had an amazing ability to forecast the long-term trends in society, politics, and the economy that impacted the stock market. His analysis of these trends allowed him to take positions at favorable prices well before other investors became aware that a change had occurred. He believed that a serious investor should consider these long-term trends from time to time and adjust his investments accordingly. Mr. Price issued his last detailed forecast in 1965, in which he foresaw the coming runaway catastrophic inflation that did, in fact, occur in the 1970s. He started the New Era Fund to produce excellent results in this environment, wherein gold went up more than twenty times and mortgage rates exceeded eighteen percent. A suggested outlook for the next decade, based on the use of Mr. Price's long-held ideas and concepts as well as the author's inputs of current data and major changes, is discussed in detail, and brought up to date, in Chapter 16.

A memorial in the November 21, 1983, issue of *Forbes* stated: "[Price] never achieved the influence of the late Benjamin Graham because, unlike Graham, Price was not an articulate man." He hated to give speeches and was not good at delivering them. He was impatient with reporters who failed to quickly understand his ideas. His writings, however, were clear and well thought out.

One of my first assignments as a young analyst at what was then T. Rowe Price and Associates was to interview the management of Hewlett-Packard in Palo Alto, California. I had used the company's reliable, well-built electronic instruments as a Princeton undergraduate engineer, working in the university labs, and, later, working for Westinghouse Electric Corporation as an electrical engineer. Fortunately for me, my contact had been called out of town and the legendary David Packard took his place as a pinch hitter. Having built one of the great growth companies in the world, he explained to me how he did it, sitting in his functional, simply furnished open office.

Being an engineer himself, he used his original pencil-drawn charts to demonstrate what he had learned when he looked back over the company's growth from its inception in 1939, twenty-one years before. Each product started slowly, grew rapidly, and tapered off in maturity, ultimately declining in old age.

Mr. Packard learned from these charts that the key to building a successful company (which Mr. Price would call a "growth company") was to introduce new products on a regular basis over time. This continual need for new products opened Packard's eyes to the extreme importance of productive research. He also realized that Hewlett-Packard had to generate enough profits to pay for growth in facilities, inventories, and personnel to cover the costs of physical growth. After this analysis, he substantially increased spending for research. It emphasized to him where top management should be spending much of its time.

In fact, I later learned that Mr. Price had first called his new theory of investing "the life cycle method of investing." He had also realized, from his experience at DuPont, that if new products weren't continually introduced, the whole company would follow its natural life cycle and quickly sink from growth into maturity.

Although the growth of a company in any one year can appear to be trivial, the magic of compound growth over the long term can produce astonishing investment returns. A little more than seven percent compound growth (seven cents on every dollar) doubles sales and earnings in ten years. A fifteen percent growth, typical of Hewlett-Packard in the

1960s, doubles sales and earnings in just five years. This is the real secret of investing in growth stocks.

One of the world's most successful investors, Baron Nathan Rothschild, is said to have called compound interest "the eighth wonder of the world."

In this book, I describe how Mr. Price recognized companies that produced superior growth over long periods of time, tell the story of how his company grew, and provide an insight into Thomas Rowe Price, Jr., the man.

Acknowledgments

F irst, I would like to thank the many individuals at T. Rowe Price, both active and retired, whom I interviewed for this book. They were uniformly professional and pleasant, a hallmark of the firm's personality when I joined it nearly sixty years ago. I also thank the others who gave me advice, helped with the editing, and answered critical questions during the course of writing this book.

I am indebted to Mr. Price's son, Thomas Rowe Price III, who reviewed some of the early family history in the book and explained a little about the farm where Charles "Charlie" W. Shaeffer and Mr. Price developed plans for the company's future.

I have mentioned Bob Hall in the foreword; he was my major contributor, friend, and support, particularly when problems arose that might have ended the project.

George A. Roche was also a major contributor and friend throughout, sharing commonsense advice as well as his insight into the thinking of Mr. Price, with whom he was close, particularly in Mr. Price's declining years.

Austin George, who graduated from Princeton a year before I did and joined the firm in 1959, also a year before me, was the fourth member of our small informal group who saw the project through from beginning to end and added thoughtful input, particularly on the early days of the firm and from his position as head of equity trading.

Joseph A. Crumbling, Chief of Staff, Office of the President and CEO, patiently stewarded the project through the alleys and byways of the company's administrative structure and is owed special thanks.

After his many years as a T. Rowe Price research analyst and portfolio manager, thanks to Preston Athey for his patient and thorough editing of the book after its initial completion, with his in-depth knowledge of the firm and the people mentioned in the book.

A special thanks to Jim Kennedy, who got behind the book project at its inception and provided excellent advice along the way. Jim retired as CEO and president of T. Rowe Price halfway through the writing of the book. He was succeeded by Bill Stromberg, who was also a great help, particularly in the writing of the epilogue, which is about the Price firm of today.

Truman Seamans' amazing recall of his 70 years at the epicenter of Baltimore business was a great help in understanding the people and organizations that made it all work.

I also want to acknowledge Theresa Brown, who transcribed hours of my dictation and worked through the difficult task of interpreting my handwriting to produce a first draft.

Karen Malloy was the first statistician for the New Horizons Fund and came out of retirement to develop the statistics found in Chapter 17, which required many hours of compiling ancient financial data.

Kate Buford also edited the book, having written biographies herself. She managed to maintain her calm and good advice despite my less than deferential remarks when I found some of my "best" passages on the cutting room floor.

Steve Novak put his skills as a former analyst for Naval Intelligence and his passion for genealogy and biographical research to good use in performing a great deal of the research and fact checking, as well as developing the annotations for the book.

I am indebted to Richard (Rich) Wagreich, who, with his background at Goldman Sachs and the Federal Reserve, and his experience at T. Rowe Price, helped me with many of the economic statistics used in the book.

Also, my unofficial editor, Stephanie Deutsch, devoted many hours in instructing me in the fine art of the biography. She is an excellent biographer in her own right.

A special thanks to Ann O'Neill, a long-time resident of Glyndon and expert in its history.

All that said, any errors in this book are mine alone.

Finally, but most importantly, I am grateful to my wife, Ann, who reorganized our lives for the last five years to allow me the time to devote to this book.

■ Part One ■

THE BEGINNING

■ Chapter One ■

THE HOUSE ON DOVER ROAD, 1898–1919

A soft orange glow from oil lamps could be seen through the first-floor windows of the house at 4801 Dover Road in the small town of Glyndon, Maryland. The flickering light illuminated the branches of the trees dancing to the force of the cold northeast wind. At this early hour, the lamps provided the only light on the street. It had been raining the day before and puddles remained on the hard dirt surface of the street, bordered by wooden sidewalks.

A rooster prematurely announced the dawn as the soft whinny of a horse came from the stable behind the house. Suddenly the sound of a slap on a wet baby's bottom emanated from the interior of the home. It was March 16, 1898, and Thomas Rowe Price, Jr. let out his first cry as his father, Dr. Thomas Rowe Price – the only doctor in town – brought him into the world. He was swaddled in a warm blanket and placed in the arms of his mother, Ella Stewart Black Price, who settled back for a well-earned rest.

The above account is as imagined by the author after visiting the original house in which Mr. Price was born and following discussions with several local residents, one of whom was delivered by Mr. Price's father and another of whom is an active member of the historical society.

Mr. Price's mother, Ella Price, born 1869. TRP archives; photo owned by
Mrs. Margaret Moore, wife of Dr. Moore, Mr. Rowe Price's nephew.

Mr. Price's father, Dr. Thomas Price, born 1865. TRP archives; photo owned
by Mrs. Margaret Moore.

Every summer Rowe's future paternal grandfather, Dr. Benjamin F.
Price – also a physician – and grandmother, Mary A. Harshberger Price,
enjoyed the beach at Ocean City, Maryland. That is where Thomas
Price met Ella Black following his graduation from medical school.

It was love at first sight for both of them. They were married in 1893 and moved into a new house on Dover Road, a wedding gift from Ella's new husband.

Dr. Price's original home, where he delivered all of his children; built 1893; photographed in the nineteenth century. TRP archives; photo owned by Mrs. Margaret Moore.

It was a large house for the time, with three floors and a square tower on the side, in keeping with the Victorian style of architecture. On the first floor were a large dining room, a living room, and a kitchen in the back overseen by the cook. A handsome staircase led up two flights of stairs to the bedrooms and a large sleeping porch for hot summer nights. Also on the first floor were Dr. Price's office and a small laboratory off the office where he concocted his medicines. Friends who came to call would enter through the front door and chat with him in his office. Patients would enter and leave through a back door if they needed a physical examination or treatment in his examining room. In those situations, one did not want to advertise serious illness, as the odds of recovery were much lower than today.

Medicine bottles used by Dr. Price. Author's photo.

In the spacious backyard, shaded by tall oak trees, were a carriage house, a barn, and a stable where Dr. Price had two horses, buggies, harnesses, and a cow for milk. In lieu of indoor plumbing, the family used a generously sized outhouse with different-sized cutouts for different ages. The large front porch was close to the sidewalk and had a comfortable swing. On warm nights the Prices, as well as their neighbors, would sit on the porch and gossip with those who were strolling down the sidewalk. Often singing could be heard from the other houses nearby, with a piano as an accompaniment.

There was plenty of space for Rowe, his older sister, Mildred, and his younger sister, Gahring, who would arrive five years later, as well as his maternal grandfather, Samuel Black, and his grandmother, Margaret Catherine Grubb Black. These grandparents lived with Dr. Price and his family from the time Rowe was two until their deaths in 1910.

Samuel Black had a significant influence on the young, impressionable Rowe. He was a successful entrepreneur involved in real estate – the major investment opportunity for most people at the turn of the century – as well as home construction throughout Baltimore County. His assets in the 1870 census were listed as $70,000 ($1.7 million in 2018 dollars). Today, one is conservative in listing assets for the census taker and this was also likely true at that time. Moreover, Black continued to be an active real estate developer for many more years and didn't retire completely until he moved in with his son-in-law. In the 1930s, when Rowe was first describing his Growth Stock Philosophy, he would say,

Mr. Samuel Black, Mr. Price's grandfather, born 1824. TRP archives; owned by Mrs. Moore.

Mrs. Margaret Black, Mr. Price's grandmother, born 1830. TRP archives; photo owned by Mrs. Moore.

"to find a fertile field to invest in you didn't have to go to college, you only needed what my grandmother called horse sense."

Glyndon was a lovely rural town 20 miles northwest of Baltimore with a winter population of about 300. In the summer months, it more than doubled in size, as people fled Baltimore's heat, seeking relief in the relative coolness of the country. The town was perched 750 feet above sea level, considerably higher than nearby Worthington Valley. This elevation helped to cool the air, particularly in the evening, making for better sleeping on hot nights.

According to *Glyndon: The Story of a Victorian Village,* the town was founded and named in 1871 when the track of the Western Maryland Rail Road (which became the Western Maryland Railway in 1910) from Baltimore stopped there rather than proceeding on to Reisterstown, where the city fathers had refused to have the railroad enter its city limits. The railroad caused the town to grow. It was easy for visitors to come out from Baltimore on day trips and for the men of the community to commute into Baltimore for work. And grow it did, for the next forty years, into large grassy neighborhoods of stately homes with gables, wide verandas, and big sleeping porches.

To the small population of year-round residents and the wealthy summer crowd were added two camps that were famous locally. They ultimately became well known nationwide and likely would have an important influence on the values of young Rowe. The largest and best known, Emory Grove, was named after John Emory, a Methodist Bishop born in Maryland in 1789. One of the founders of Methodist theology, he rode through the state on the circuit, preaching the Christian gospel. Education was also very important to Emory. He was one of the founders of Dickinson College and Wesleyan College, and Emory University in Georgia is named for him. The camp occupied 160 acres of rolling wooded land. Intended as a quiet retreat away from the "madding crowd," it was far from quiet. With accessibility provided by its own railroad stop, the camp grew significantly in popularity. The beauty of the setting, and the frequent appearance of famous preachers such as Billy Sunday, drew thousands over summer weekends. In June 1895, it was reported that 10,000 people came to Emory Grove to hear another well-known preacher of the time, Eugene B. Jones, speak. For those who required at least modest comfort, there were four hotels and more than 700 tents for the rest. The days were given to religious services and teaching, and many nights to the singing of hymns. It is no accident that Rowe and his sisters would grow up as Methodists. On other nights, the younger set took over with parties, games, and much laughter. Although winter evenings were quiet for the Price family, the Grove provided a lot of social activity in the summer. Rowe was acclaimed in his high school yearbook as being a good dancer, presumably based on the practice he got at the Grove.

Close to the Price house was the temperance summer camp run by the Prohibition Party. Mandating total abstinence from alcohol and its "evil" effects, the camp was set up on 18 acres and everyone lived in tents. There was a natural bowl formation on the property, making it an excellent amphitheater where thousands could listen from the grassy slopes. Many good orators spoke there, including members of the Prohibition Party, which ran candidates for U.S. president and was an active third party in the early 1900s. Other entertainment included concerts, poetry, and lectures on many subjects. As Prohibition declined in popularity later in the 1920s and was finally repealed in 1933, the camp adopted the entertainment and educational model of the more famous Chautauqua assembly in New York State. Rowe's father never allowed alcohol or wine in the house.

To paint a picture of life in Glyndon at the time, below are excerpts from *Glyndon: The Story of a Victorian Village*, in which one of the authors, Jean Wilcox, describes an average day in the summer around the turn of the century:

> *Days followed a carefree pattern. In the morning we were up early to have breakfast with Papa before he took the 8:05 train to the city and work. Then came the day's chores. The children filled the oil lamps; the mothers canned fruits and vegetables or possibly worked in their flowerbeds.*
>
> *Everybody in the town retired to the second floor from 2 until 3:30 p.m. The shutters were closed and the streets were deserted and quiet. [Later] the young people played croquet on the front lawns or tennis, while the mothers strolled the boardwalks or met on each other's porches to talk or rock. The town's lively air was largely due to the fact that each street took on a social atmosphere in the afternoon*

The Big Event of the afternoon was the walk to the Western Maryland Station to meet Papa who came home on the 5:50 train from Baltimore with other working husbands and fathers. Most of Glyndon turned out at the station every day.

After supper, we amused ourselves with parlor games or recitations.

Glyndon was an active center for sports of all kinds. An ardent Glyndon tennis player was Edmund C. Lynch, whose family summered in the town around the turn of the century. Later one of the founders of Merrill Lynch, he was thirteen years older than Rowe. Though there is no indication that they knew each other well, Eleanor Taylor, an elderly Glyndon resident who had been delivered by Dr. Price some ninety-two years earlier, recalled that Rowe and Ed often crossed racquets on the grass courts during summer afternoons. Rowe greatly enjoyed the sport and would be an active player until his later years. Lynch, and his later success at Merrill Lynch, may have had some influence in steering Rowe into finance.

One of Samuel Black's grandsons, Rowe's first cousin, was S. Duncan Black, the founder of Black & Decker. Begun in 1910, the company would become one of the leading worldwide electric tool manufacturers for the home improvement market. Growing businesses was apparently in the genetic makeup of the Black family.

Dr. Price's career path differed from that of his father-in-law, whose singular interest was business. Rather than heading to medical school right after high school, Dr. Price taught school for several years, as had his own father, before deciding to go to the University of Maryland's medical school. He graduated in 1891, at the age of twenty-six, and moved to Glyndon to establish his practice.

Helping his clients achieve financial health would be very important to Rowe and a fundamental reason he founded his company. Money was also important to him, but in moderation, so that he and his family could enjoy a comfortable life. He would never drive an expensive car or live in a very large house.

Dr. Price was a good, traditional country doctor, according to Eleanor Taylor. He treated his patients wherever they got sick, often traveling in the evening to distant farms in all kinds of weather. He was fond of telling the tale that after his last call on cold, dark nights, he would often snuggle down into the blankets in his buggy, wrap the reins around the whip handle in its socket, cluck to his horse to begin the trip back, go to sleep, and wake up when the horse stopped at the door to his Dover Road stable. Over the years, Dr. Price became highly recognized in his profession. He was appointed surgeon to the Western Maryland Rail Road that serviced Glyndon, and was also named the Health Officer for Baltimore County, an important honorary post and one that his father had been granted years before. He was a director and then treasurer of the Glyndon Permanent Building Association, an organization of volunteers that provided financing for homes in Glyndon before banks came to the area, and an elected board member of Emory Grove. According to Eleanor Taylor, he was a gentleman, quiet and highly professional. He reportedly had a competitive side that he passed along to his son. According to Mildred's son, Rowe, he had the biggest sled in town, which could outrun any other on its long runners. Dr. Price also did well financially. By 1918, he listed his holdings as 73 acres, three homes, a tenant house, a stable, sheds, two barns, three cars, and a truck.

Rowe's mother, Ella, was a strong-willed woman and the youngest of seven children. Like her husband, she was well respected in the community and a founding member and the first vice president of the Woman's Club of Glyndon. Originally, this group reviewed books for discussion and was involved in various social activities locally, but as it grew in membership it became committed to more important civic issues. In 1902, the club was responsible for bringing electricity to Glyndon. Later, it created street signs and instituted garbage collection. One could speculate that Ella Price was likely a strong mover behind these activities, given her reputation for drive and getting things done. When a fire destroyed the meeting room of the Woman's Club in the Methodist Church of downtown Glyndon in 1932, Dr. Price would buy the old two-room schoolhouse to provide a permanent home for the club. It took some courage and the urging of a very determined wife to make such an investment in the depths of the Great Depression.

Rowe was sent off to elementary school at Glyndon School (the same schoolhouse Dr. Price would later buy) at the age of five. As was true until he got to college, he was the youngest member of the class. It was fairly easy for him to walk the mile or so, or to ride the trolley, which ran down Butler Road (Dover Road had become Butler Road by then, which it remains today) in front of his house. His older sister,

Mildred, accompanied him. Glyndon School was a red brick two-room structure with a cedar shake roof and a large bell tower. The interior of the school was grim, with practical brown paint decorating the walls. The rope to the bell hung below the tower and it was fun to pull on the rope when you were asked, but woe to the child who pulled it out of turn. In general, the classes were well disciplined and quiet, at least in the upper grades. Rowe went to first and second grade in the room on the north side; the other, larger room was for the third through the sixth grades. There were two teachers, with the upper-grade teacher also acting as principal. The alphabet and reading were taught in the first two grades; the multiplication tables weren't taught until the fifth grade. The teachers were strict and a firm rap on the knuckles could be expected if one forgot the product of two numbers. Writing was learned by long practice with handbooks and scratchy straight pens that were dipped into inkwells planted on the desk.

Mr. Price's first school, Glyndon Elementary School, built 1887. Glyndon Historical Society.

In 1909 Rowe graduated from elementary school and entered Franklin High School in Reisterstown. Under the supervision of his sister Mildred, they made their way to and from school by electric trolley. In his sophomore year, there was a school-wide tennis tournament consisting of fourteen students; Rowe finished second. His years of practice on the grass courts of Glyndon had stood him in good stead. His high school nickname was Doc, suggesting that he intended to

Mr. Price's older sister, Mildred Price, born 1895. Photo owned by Mrs. Margaret Moore.

follow in his father's footsteps. In his first year there were more than sixty students in his class. By graduation, this had been whittled down to twenty-three. In later years, Rowe would proclaim that he was "not much of a student," but he certainly had the willingness to work and the ambition to do at least well enough to get through and graduate in a class with a 60 percent attrition rate.

He was well liked at Franklin, a bit of a cutup, and the humor editor of the yearbook. The comments under his yearbook photograph read, "His legs are long, he is very tall and ever has a good word for all," and "It is only his tender years that have saved him from being reprimanded for his pranks at school. His specialty is teasing the girls." The editor (most of the editorial staff were girls) added, "A day spent at school without Rowe would be a day lost," and "When he was on the program [Rowe was a member of the Franklin Literary Society] we all looked forward to being highly entertained."

He was only sixteen when he graduated from Franklin, and his parents decided to send him to the Friends School of Baltimore as a postgraduate student, presumably, to ensure that he got into a good college. Founded by the Quakers in 1784, the school when Rowe attended it was located at 1712 Park Avenue, next to the Friends Meetinghouse (today it is located on Charles Street). Friends remains one of the oldest private high schools in the country. The classes were also small, typically with twelve students, which allowed for a strong interaction with the teachers. At the end of the year, in 1915, Rowe did not finish at the head of the class, according to "T. Rowe Price: A Legend in the Investment Business," the *Baltimore Sun*, October 22, 1983, but did well enough to be one of three who were accepted at Swarthmore and the only one of them to graduate from the college.

Swarthmore was an easy choice. His sister Mildred was already enrolled there, it was relatively close to Glyndon, and it had small classes and an excellent academic reputation. It was founded in 1864 by the Quakers, although students of other religions were accepted. In 1906 it formed its own administration and was no longer directly managed by the Quakers. In 1915 many of the qualities of the Quaker church, such as austerity and simplicity, still remained. As a school, it would have seemed like Friends School: the student-to-teacher ratio was only eight to one and the overall Quaker philosophy was similar.

When Rowe first traveled to Swarthmore to enter college that fall, he probably took the train from Baltimore to Philadelphia, from which he would have continued on another train some eleven miles up the Main Line. Mildred would either have come with him or would have met him at the station on the edge of the campus.

The Pennsylvania climate could be harsh, so the school was a cold and bleak place in the winter. The original hot-water radiators were no match for the wind and snow. Heavy sweaters and jackets were the norm, worn daily both inside and out. But on his initial arrival on that autumn day, it was an easy walk through beautiful stands of oak, sycamore, and elm to the lower campus. His arrival is as imagined by the author after a visit to the Swarthmore campus on a bright sunny day early in the fall semester:

Rowe and Mildred walked through the trees from the station to the Magill Walk, lined with oak trees, up the grassy slope to Parrish Hall, built on the top of the hill. They passed small groups of students picnicking and gossiping about their summer and the year about to begin. The bright dresses of the women were splashed with sunlight, adding color to the scene. Parrish Hall, where they signed in for the new school year, was a large building made of locally quarried gray stone. Other than white paint outlining the windows and doors, Parrish Hall, true to its Quaker heritage, was completely unadorned, with none of the Victorian curves and embellishments so popular elsewhere in the early twentieth century. A broad porch supported by white wooden columns extended across a portion of the facade. Students were gathered there, in lively conversation, filling out papers and class requests.

Rowe arrived at Swarthmore with the full intention of becoming a doctor. Not surprisingly, the major reason, according to Mildred's son, Rowe, was due to Dr. Price's strong, unrelenting sales pitches over many years. As the only son, Rowe bore the full brunt of his father's campaign for him to become a physician. It is not certain why he decided not to follow the family tradition. With customary modesty concerning personal matters, he would attribute his change of heart to poor marks. Whatever the reasons, he switched to chemistry in his junior year. Possibly he felt that such courses were an important part of

Mr. Rowe Price, Swarthmore College junior yearbook, 1918. Swarthmore College.

a premed degree and essential subjects for a budding doctor, so credits here might have helped if he later changed his mind and decided to go to medical school. Or perhaps it was to help his relationship with his father. Chemistry was also then one of the major technologies of the future at the dawn of the twentieth century.

Despite the large offering of subject matter at Swarthmore, Rowe did not take a single course in either economics or business. When he left college, he was a chemist by training and believed that chemistry would be his career. Although he was referred to as "the electrician" in his Franklin High School yearbook, Rowe never fully developed an interest in the science of electricity at Swarthmore. But in the summer of 1916 he did electrical work at Emory Grove and was paid the large sum of $18.85.

Mr. Rowe Price, Swarthmore College senior yearbook, 1919. Swarthmore College.

A comparison of Rowe's graduation pictures from Franklin High and Swarthmore College shows a clear physical maturation in his college years. Active in athletics, he was the manager of both the football and swimming teams. It was in lacrosse, however, that he excelled. Not only was he on the varsity team in his senior year, for which he won his letter, but, based on reports in the school paper, he became a star player toward the end of the season. He was also active outside of sports. He was a photographer on the yearbook staff, played a major role in the school play, was president of the junior class, and joined the Delta Upsilon fraternity.

By his senior year he had come into his own and was considered to be one of the "big men on campus," in a phrase of the time. In that era, it was not unusual for a number of students to drop out before completing four years of college. Rowe most likely felt a sense of accomplishment to graduate in 1919, because, as he told us "juniors" at the firm, he was the only student of the three that had been accepted from Friends that year to graduate.

In his later years, Rowe would not appear particularly religious. He did go to church and would later become a Presbyterian, but it would not be a major part of his life. Still, in an interesting way, the adult Rowe would seem to incorporate the values of the "Quaker Way," and such qualities were certainly part of his family upbringing. He believed in hard work. He was never ostentatious. He believed in the value of women in the workplace. As advocated by Quakers, Rowe would practice all of his life the exercise of both mind and body, and he would be an independent thinker of the first order.

Perhaps most importantly, integrity – beginning with his own personal integrity – would be a guiding principle of the firm that he would form many years later, at a time when integrity would be in short supply in the financial world. As a Securities and Exchange Commission lawyer would comment later to Walter Kidd, one of the founders of T. Rowe Price, "T. Rowe Price and Associates was the gold standard" when it came to its conduct toward its clients.

Chapter Two

LESSONS LEARNED, 1919–1925

The following fictional account describes how Rowe might have been introduced to his first job, shortly after graduation from Swarthmore. It is based on photographs of the plant, an interview with Ralph Mehler of the nearby town of Sharpsville Historical Society in Pennsylvania, and the author's experience working at Westinghouse Electric at its oldest plant, then located on Turtle Creek in Pittsburgh. The basic facts are accurate, such as location of the plant, its size, and the principal characters. Only the words of the conversations are completely made up.

Rowe and his fraternity brother Lindsay Cornug stepped off the train into the summer heat of western Pennsylvania in 1919. They had arrived in Leechburg, a small town of four thousand souls planted on the banks of the polluted Kiskiminetas River. The town earned its living by building products made of the steel produced in large quantities in Pittsburgh, thirty-five miles to the west. The men's immediate destination was the Fort Pitt Enamel and Stamping Company.

The air was thick and humid with an industrial haze and a faint smell of sulfur.

The two young men looked at each other. Rowe rubbed a tear from his eye. For a moment, he could not figure out why he was crying. Then he realized it was from the chemicals and other pollutants in the air. It was certainly very different from the clear blue skies and tree-shaded campus at Swarthmore.

They found the company right on the river. It was early afternoon and the hot sun generated a metallic smell from the slowly moving dark waters. The company consisted of several buildings; the office was a simple wooden structure painted white. When they opened the door, they entered a large room with employees busily typing and operating large adding machines behind big desks and counters. Seeing the two new arrivals, a young man hurried over with an outstretched hand.

"Hi, I'm Charlie Bischoff. Remember me? The guy that hired you two!" Even in these industrial surroundings, he was the consummate salesman who had so impressed the two young men. He was well dressed, with a tie and high collar. He also sported a striped blazer and a ring bearing the Princeton seal, class of 1916

"Welcome to Fort Pitt," he said. "Let me show you around."

Rowe and Lindsay were assigned to desks in a small chemistry lab in the rear of the enameling building, behind hot molten tubs of zinc. This was where the enamel was heated preparatory to being coated on sheet steel in a continuous process. It was very warm and the noise was intense. They stowed their bags under their desks, rolled up their sleeves, and began to explore the new equipment. Rowe noted that the large blowers that brought in fresh air and removed the fumes from the laboratories at Swarthmore were absent here. Open windows had to suffice.

Rowe was hired as a chemist and would be exploring fresh surroundings far from Glyndon. He would also hope to be learning about how the subjects he had learned in class were actually applied in a real business. But within a month, the company's fortunes took an abrupt turn for the worse. The factory workforce went on strike. Financing from the bank ceased, putting the company near bankruptcy. With production shut down, Rowe and Lindsay's jobs disappeared. They were soon on the train heading east.

Rowe had just learned some important, if costly, lessons that would stand him in good stead when he ultimately began to invest in companies for himself, and later for clients. He experienced first-hand how important strong finances are, particularly when business conditions suddenly change for the worse. He learned about the importance of good labor relations. He learned about the danger of working for a small company without a proprietary product in a competitive industry. Finally, he had been convinced to take the job based on a very good sales pitch delivered by a master salesman. He had not done the research to find out the facts for himself.

Fort Pitt Enamel and Stamping Co., PA

Mr. Price was employed here for his first job as a chemist after graduation from Swarthmore.

Rowe's next job was as an industrial chemist at the DuPont plant in Arlington, New Jersey, which produced plastic products. Even then, DuPont was a large company. With a thousand employees, the Arlington plant was much bigger than the close-knit group of twenty-eight at Fort Pitt. DuPont was known for its research and development of new innovative chemical products. It appeared to be an ideal place to work for a young chemist just getting started, perhaps a bit like going to work for IBM as a young computer scientist in the 1960s or for Google as a software engineer in the 2000s. The company also enjoyed a very healthy balance sheet. Its labor relations were excellent.

Located beside the marshy Passaic River, Arlington had a population of about two thousand. There was not much for a young man of twenty-two to do after work in the 1920s. Rowe said later that it was at DuPont that he began to read financial publications such as the *Wall Street Journal* and *Barron's*. He found that he was more drawn to them than he was to the latest news concerning new chemical products and processes in thick technical chemical journals. Such financial news media exposed him to a whole new world. He became fascinated by how companies were built, the new products that could form large businesses, and how all of that was financed in the stock and bond markets.

These publications would also have alerted him to the fact that all was not well in the financial and business world. The stock market began to fall sharply in 1921, reflecting deteriorating business conditions – particularly in financially leveraged industries like automotive and real estate. Even the mighty DuPont found itself embarrassed financially in the downturn as its profits nosedived. Pierre S. du Pont, the company's president, had bought a personal stock position in General Motors in 1914. GM was being built at that time primarily from acquisitions engineered by the charismatic William C. Durant, into the largest automaker in the U.S. Pierre du Pont was invited on the General Motors board in 1915.

After World War I, John Jakob Raskob, DuPont's treasurer, convinced the DuPont board to invest $25 million of the company's capital into General Motors stock. This was based on the significant opportunity for profits that he saw from General Motors' leading position in the exploding automobile market. The investment would also help cement DuPont's position as a major supplier of plastic products and paint, not only to General Motors, but to the auto industry as a whole.

For several years, General Motors and its stock did prosper. DuPont became its dominant paint supplier and also developed a number of plastic products for the auto industry. By 1920, General Motors accounted for 50 percent of DuPont's earnings.

Unfortunately, things began to unravel during the short recession of 1920–21. Industrial production declined 30 percent, the stock market fell by almost half, and automobile sales as a whole dropped 60 percent. The General Motors Corporation plunged into a deep loss. Durant, although a visionary with the persuasive power to have put together a General Motors, could not run the resulting conglomerate. In 1920, in a radical move, Durant resigned as CEO of General Motors and Pierre du Pont became president. His brother, Irénée, succeeded him as the president of DuPont.

As a relatively inexperienced chemist who was among the last to arrive at DuPont, it was not surprising that Rowe was laid off in these trying conditions. He spent the summer of 1921 back home in Glyndon. It was a time to reflect on his short, traumatic business career. In two years, two very different companies had employed him. In both cases, he had been laid off. The first time was due to financial problems following labor issues; the second time was due to a sharp decline in business as a result of a recession.

More fundamentally, Rowe discovered that while his interest and enthusiasm for a career in chemistry had waned, growing businesses and the people who ran them fascinated him. He had also discovered the world of finance, particularly the stock market. It seemed to him that it might be possible here to make a reasonable living and, at the same time, to enjoy what he was doing. This was a heady discovery for a young man in his twenties who had been pursuing a profession simply out of the necessity to earn a living.

However, there were no stockbrokers in the immediate family, and at that time stockbrokers were commonly looked upon with some suspicion by businessmen and professionals. Real estate, his grandfather's major asset and business, was a tangible asset that one could touch and see. But even his grandfather might not have supported a move into the stock brokerage business. Real estate increased in price because of supply and demand, which was easy to understand. Investing in stocks seemed to many then – and does still today – to be more like gambling, with stock prices moving up and down for mysterious, emotional reasons. For most people, there was nothing tangible about a stock. Few had an understanding of the actual worth of the companies that these stocks represented.

Years after Mr. Price's death, Steve Jobs, the principal founder of Apple, which today is among the most valuable companies in the world, would tell the Stanford graduating class of 2005: "The only way to do great work is to love what you do. If you haven't found it yet, keep looking. Don't settle. As with all matters of the heart, you'll know when you find it." Rowe believed, despite the probable misgivings of his family, that he had found it.

At the end of the summer in 1921, Rowe probably began to comb the few want ads in the financial sections of the local papers. The Dow Jones Industrial Average continued to decline until August 24, when it tumbled to a low on light volume. After Labor Day, brokers came back to their offices and, for no apparent reason, suddenly began to buy stocks again. The market rose sharply and the want ads finally began to appear again for brokers. When the economy begins to recover, salesmen are often the first to be hired. Salesmen of stocks can generate profits quickly in a rising market. Commissions were then the major compensation for brokers, so the financial risk of hiring them was low.

With only enthusiasm and youth and no experience to recommend him, Rowe was not a top candidate to enter the brokerage business. After what must have been considerable searching and rejections, according to the 1983 *Baltimore Sun* article, he was finally offered, through a distant relative of his mother, a position as a stockbroker in a small Baltimore stock brokerage firm where his mother had a small account.

It didn't take Rowe long, however, to realize that he really didn't enjoy selling stocks. In fact, as reported in *The History of T. Rowe Price Associates, Inc.*, he "intensely disliked it," but remained enormously interested in the business of finance, how the stock market rewarded long-term investors in fine companies like DuPont, and how they were built. But this was not to be his job at Smith, Lockhart, despite their promises to the contrary. It was not how the firm made money. Buying and holding the stock of a great company, no matter how good this might be for the client, did not represent any income for Smith, Lockhart. Their income was primarily from the commissions from buying and selling stocks, as was generally true for brokerage firms at that time.

Most stocks then were bought and sold on a fixed commission basis and at prices quoted on an open exchange like the New York Stock Exchange. Transactions involving small companies were based on prices published in the so-called "pink sheets" that were then published weekly (on pink paper). Such purchases or sales generated a much bigger reward for the broker.

The best way to maximize a brokerage firm's profits was to sell shares of stock in companies for which the firm – usually in a syndicate of other firms - was raising capital. Here, the profits were even higher because the firm sold the shares at a very handsome predetermined commission at no risk to its capital because it didn't have to buy the stock in the market. Moreover, the total dollar profits were large because of the size of the transaction. Rowe loathed the intense pressure that was brought to bear on the stockbrokers to sell stocks to clients in these offerings, whether or not it was good for the client. As Rowe cynically wrote, "I observed that in many instances, the salesmen who made the biggest earnings were the ones who were least conscientious about their clients' best interests," as recorded in *The History of T. Rowe Price Associates, Inc.*

Although Rowe did not support such practices – and others that were even more suspect – he did prove to be a good investor. By late spring 1922, the young man had accumulated enough money to take a three-month trip to Europe with a friend. He sailed on what he called a cattle boat that June and enjoyed a good vacation in a Europe still suffering from the aftereffects of World War I. The dollar went a very long way and three months was a luxurious time to learn about a new environment, to mix with the people, and to enjoy the food.

Travel would become one of his favorite hobbies. He would later tell us in the firm that, when married, he and his wife even enjoyed traveling in the passenger cabins of freighters to Asia and other far-off ports during the depths of the Depression. But travel was also important to Rowe in developing his ideas about business. He was a keen and exceptional observer and evaluator of people and their cultures. He learned from his travels how the world really worked, how different countries had very different personalities, and how these personalities would help or hinder their success in business and war. He put all this to good use when he developed and then published his own strategies for successful investment. When he was asked, late in his career, for an article in the October 1980 issue of *Baltimore* magazine ("We're Off to See the Wizard"), what the keys were to his success, he replied, "Growing up on a farm [where he learned about human nature], travel, and hard work."

When he returned to Baltimore in September, Rowe, to his surprise, found Smith, Lockhart in bankruptcy; the partners would be charged with defrauding their customers and head to prison. The company had for many years followed a practice of selling stocks to their customers on an installment basis. The company would buy the stock, collect a down payment, and use the shares as collateral until the transaction was paid off. In the meantime, they collected their full commission and a very good rate of interest. The shares would only be transferred to the customer's account after they were fully paid for.

This way of doing business had gone off the tracks during the sharp stock market decline in 1921. As their collateral declined, many clients didn't or couldn't make their payments. The firm ran short of cash and fell into a classic pyramid scheme, similar to that made famous much later by Bernie Madoff. Instead of actually buying the shares of stock for their customers, Smith, Lockhart would collect the cash from the client for purchases, but would actually use this money to pay off prior purchases made for other customers. False accounting covered up all these phony transactions. This scheme ended when the firm finally ran out of cash to cover all of its losses in the declining market and couldn't borrow any more. These illegal activities cost the small firm's customers some $2.5 million ($34,200,000 in 2018 dollars).

Now, Rowe, at twenty-four, and only three years out of college, had experienced three jobs with very different companies. Two of the three had actually gone out of business. Again, he learned important lessons. Despite these unfortunate experiences, he remained fascinated by the world of finance and became even more convinced that this was what he wanted to do for the rest of his life. He did realize that he still needed to do far more research on the finances and the business dynamics behind the next company that he was going to work for.

When he joined the firm of Jenkins, Whedbee & Poe early in 1923 as a bond salesman, he took note of these prior lessons. It was a small, extremely conservative bond house, the exact opposite of Smith, Lockhart. The partners were wealthy. They had no need to take risks to make more money, or to stay long hours at the office. Conservation was their goal, not expansion.

High-quality bonds are much less volatile than stocks because they trade relative to interest rates, not on emotion. Overall interest rates generally move slowly up or down. In an economic expansion, interest rates rise and bonds trade lower. If, for example, a $100 face-value bond pays $3, it is said to yield 3 percent. If interest rates went up to 4 percent, the price of the same bond would drop to $75 to keep pace with the interest rate change. At $75, it would yield the new market rate of 4 percent while still paying $3. The reverse typically happens in a recession. When capital is not needed to finance expansion, interest rates decline and bond prices rise, reflecting the lower interest rate.

The actual return to the wealthy investors of Jenkins, Whedbee & Poe was usually just the interest on the bond. The clients generally bought their bonds at their original face value and held them to maturity. There was no difference in price between the original face value of the bond and the price at which it was redeemed, even though there might be considerable price fluctuations in between. The clients only expected regular interest payments. They did not want excitement or risk of their capital.

Though the income from trading quality bonds at the time was less than trading in stocks, the job was financially secure, and Rowe was still in the financial services industry. More importantly, he was introduced to another new world, the business of bond financing and bond trading. It is not widely known, but the bond market is, and was then, much larger than the stock market. Trading can also be quite profitable because most bond transactions are done on a markup basis. Bonds that are sold to customers are either already owned by the firm and are sold from their inventory, or bought in the market by the firm and resold. As with trading over-the-counter stocks, the customer has only a vague idea what the current market is for the bonds he or she is buying, or what his or her broker might have paid for them.

Rowe likely knew little about bonds prior to being hired by Jenkins, Whedbee & Poe, other than from his reading of financial publications. It is doubtful that he had learned much about them at Smith, Lockhart. In fact, bonds would have seemed to offer little interest to a young man fascinated by the stock market and growing businesses. He probably took the job because it was the only way he could stay in the financial world. His résumé did not yet have enough depth and there was no one who could credibly recommend him. As it turned out, a thorough knowledge of bonds and their associated credit ratings was to become important to his career: Analyzing corporate financials and balance sheets of a company is essential in determining the worthiness of its bonds. The same analysis is critical to understanding the underlying financial health of a corporation and its long-term viability.

The job for which Rowe was hired was the selling of bonds. High-quality bonds, though, had none of the issues he so disliked in selling equities at Smith, Lockhart. That type of bond provided the income that the customer wanted, and the firm simply made money on the markup of the sales price to the customer over cost to the firm. Because the firm did very little trading, there was no conflict of interest between the customer and the firm. Rowe's principal responsibility was to determine that the bond was of a suitable quality (initially this would have been with the help of the firm's partners and staff), to interact with the client in making sure the bond's maturity schedule fit with his or her goals, and that there was proper diversification in his or her portfolio.

Rowe found that he was adept at conveying the benefits of such a product, particularly in one-on-one situations or in small groups. Though he did well and learned a lot about bonds, Jenkins, Whedbee & Poe proved to be even more ultraconservative than he had initially thought and perhaps a bit boring. "The partners were men of wealth and integrity," he stated in September 7, 1951, bulletin "The Firm's Goal and How We Plan to Attain It," "but they lacked ambition and offered little opportunity." With bonds being their total focus, there was not much chance to rub shoulders with people involved in the far more exciting equity market. The bull market in stocks that began in 1921 was continuing to move upward. Many of Rowe's friends who were stockbrokers were undoubtedly doing far better financially than he was. He increasingly began to feel that the slow pace at Jenkins, Whedbee & Poe was quite constraining.

By 1925, he was casting about once more for a change – not because the company was going out of business or because he was being let go. Now he wanted to expand his horizons, take on more challenges, and learn more about the broader financial business. He had gained a good reputation with a respected firm and that made him much more marketable. As he would describe in his bulletin "The Firm's Goal and How We Plan to Attain It," he "had an opportunity to study the various investment houses in the city and selected Mackubin, Goodrich, and Company as the one that possessed most of the things I wanted in an employer."

He wanted a firm where the owners were not all wealthy, but were interested in expansion. He wanted a solid financial base with a diversified product line and a good reputation in the business community. He wanted to work for an individual he could respect and who could be his mentor.

Chapter Three

MACKUBIN, GOODRICH & CO., 1925–1927

Rowe joined Mackubin, Goodrich & Co. in 1925. A relatively small financial firm in Baltimore, it was quite different from Jenkins, Whedbee & Poe. He would spend his next twelve years there and form his basic investment beliefs.

George Mackubin started the firm as George Mackubin & Co. in January 1899, after he borrowed $300 to buy a seat on the Baltimore Stock Exchange. G. Clem Goodrich, sixteen years older, joined as its second partner eleven months after the firm opened its doors. John C. Legg, whose name the firm still carries today, was hired a year later as the "board boy." His job was to keep the prices for the stocks being traded up to date on the large blackboard at the front of the public trading room. Five years after he was hired, John Legg was made a partner, the rapid rise an indication of his ability and the respect that he earned from others.

Mackubin's father was a wealthy lawyer and his mother a direct descendent of Martha Washington. An outgoing man, Mackubin ran the firm in an aggressive way, but was fair and respected by his employees. He believed in focusing on a few industries and companies and researching them very carefully. The oil and gas business around Houston, for example, caught his fancy. To find out what was really going on there, he would camp out for weeks in the hot, humid, mosquito-ridden oil fields near the Gulf of Mexico. He thus got his information directly from the drillers and the oil exploration teams in the field rather than from the front office. Soon after he was hired, Rowe reportedly found himself on a trip down to the oil fields with Mackubin and his son. Mackubin would be a founder of the Houston

Natural Gas Corporation in 1928 and ultimately made millions of dollars for the firm's clients due to the appreciation of the company's stock. He also made money for the firm from the commissions on the capital raised in its many bond and stock offerings. As Houston Oil, the company was sold to the Atlantic Refining Company for $198 million in 1956 ($1.76 billion in 2018 dollars).

This kind of thorough, hands-on research before investing, investing in rapidly growing industries, holding the equities over a long period of time, and focusing on a few outstanding companies were key lessons for Rowe. It was a unique approach for the time, and later became part of the basis for his Growth Stock Philosophy.

Clem Goodrich's background was quite different from Mackubin's. His father had been a Presbyterian minister in Hagerstown, Maryland. Perhaps because of this upbringing, he was more taciturn and even-tempered. He had a reputation in Baltimore as a man who could be trusted. Before he joined Mackubin to form Mackubin, Goodrich & Co., he had been the manager of the Baltimore Clearing House, a company that moved checks and securities between banks.

The third partner, John Legg, always addressed as "Mr. Legg" except for a few close friends, was tall, athletic, and known to be aloof, opinionated, and tough. He had none of the money or social connections of George Mackubin. His education stopped at high school. His father

Mr. John C. Legg, mentor to Mr. Price and then managing partner of Mackubin, Goodrich. Photo owned by Mr. William Legg and family.

was the police commissioner of Baltimore. He could be difficult to get along with, but he was, by the sheer force of his personality, the dominant presence at the firm. In the mid-1920s, when Rowe joined, he was in charge of day-to-day operations. He was the man who "made things happen," in the words of his grandson, Bill Legg, and effectively was the managing partner, even though this was not his official title at the time.

Joseph Ward Sener, Jr., who later became managing partner and vice-chair of the board, remembers running into Mr. Legg on the street shortly after he was hired.

"Where's your hat?" demanded Mr. Legg.

"I beg your pardon?" Sener replied.

"You don't have a hat on. Let me tell you, a gentleman would just as soon be seen on the street without his trousers as he would without a hat." Sener purchased a fine fedora that same day, even though it cost a week's wages."

The different personalities and interests of these three men were probably what gave the firm the strength and ability to survive and prosper in the tumultuous years prior to 1922. A fire had totally destroyed Baltimore's financial district in 1904. The stock market went into free fall and closed its doors at the onset of World War I on July 31, 1914, and did not reopen for four months. The sharp recession of 1921 created its own financial challenges.

One example of the firm's expertise was Goodrich's skill at shorting. Despite his conservative background, Goodrich had a feel for the market and greatly enjoyed short-term trading. He might sell $5,000 of a stock short ($73,380 in 2018 dollars) in the morning and close out his position in the afternoon, making perhaps $500 ($7,338 in 2018 dollars) on borrowed money on a good day.

Shorting is a stock trading strategy used when the trader believes a stock will decline in value. To execute a "short," the trader tells his stockbroker to short 100 shares of a stock that he believes will go down. He never actually owns these 100 shares. His broker borrows them from a third party and then immediately sells the 100 shares for $10 per share. The broker credits the $1,000 from the sale to the trader's account. At that moment everyone is even. The trader has borrowed 100 shares. The broker quickly sold these shares for $1,000, which is in the trader's account. The trader owes the third party the shares, but he has the $1,000 in his account to buy them back at the market.

If the stock goes down to $5 per share, the trader might decide to "close out" his trade. He calls his broker, who buys the 100 shares that he owes to the third party for $500 at the market. His broker then returns the 100 shares that he borrowed to the third party. After deducting the $500 required to buy the shares in the market, at $5 per share from the $1000 in his account, the trader has a very nice profit of $500. Too bad he didn't buy more.

The problem about shorting comes if the stock goes up instead of down. The upside is infinite. A trader can end up losing far more than the money he thought he was dealing with when he entered the transaction. In the same example, suppose the stock tripled to $30 per share. The trader decides that enough is enough and tells his broker to close out the trade. The broker buys the 100 shares of stock in the market for $3,000. He sends the 100 shares back to the third party that he borrowed them from. The third party has been getting any dividends that might have been paid in the interim and his stock has gone up 300 percent. He is quite happy. The trader, on the other hand, had to pay $3,000 to buy back the stock and he only had $1,000 in his account. After paying his broker the difference and a commission on both buying and selling, the trader realizes that he has lost more than $2,000 due to the stock's increase, or twice the amount he used to buy the original 100 shares.

In such short trading, the smart speculator was careful to place limit orders so the trade is closed out if the loss becomes excessive. One of Goodrich's favorite companies to trade was General Motors, a company well known to Rowe because of its relationship to DuPont. Its volatility in the 1920s made it attractive because of the opportunity to profit from the big swings in price.

It must have been exciting for the twenty-seven-year-old to sit next to Goodrich in his small office at the Baltimore Stock Exchange and watch as he traded short-term fluctuations in the market. He undoubtedly used charts and the so-called "technical" tools which helped the savvy trader to guess which way a stock was going and by how much. All publicly traded stocks are charted today by a number of services, and the same technical formations below, and many more, are still monitored by the traders.

Usually, charts are produced by plotting the price of the stock on the vertical axis, and time on the horizontal axis, with daily trading volume in shares shown in these charts on the lowest horizontal axis. Such charts create patterns that have meaning for the skilled trader. For example, a trader might note that a stock abruptly moved up on significant volume. During this upward move, "gaps" were created when a stock rose several points without a trade. Such gaps are almost always "filled," even if it takes years to do so. That is the rising stock will often eventually retreat back to the price of the stock at the bottom of the gap. The difficulty is figuring out how long this might take

Stock chart of "gaps." TSR Trading Setups Review.

Another common formation is a "head and shoulders." A stock might rise in price, then stay at a constant price for a number of days, then rise again, stay for one or two days, and then collapse back to near the price

Stock chart of "head and shoulders." TSR Trading Setups Review.

of the stock before it began the second up move to form the "head" of the formation (see chart.). If the stock should fall back through its "neckline" – the line that goes from one shoulder to the next – through the "head," the stock will often fall by the difference in stock price between the top of the "head" and the "shoulder." For Goodrich as a stock trader, such a formation would have been a classic example of a shorting opportunity.

A final example of a stock formation, which is often noted in publications such as the *Wall Street Journal*, is a "resistance" level (see chart). These are prices where a stock has traded for a long period of time at good volumes. Usually such resistance levels have been tested several times, as the stock falls back to this level, only to recover. A stock can move up from such a resistance level for many years. With bad news, it could come back to it. A trader might bet that the resistance will hold and place a buy order at this resistance level.

Stock chart of "support and resistance levels." TSR Trading Setups Review.

Such techniques are controversial and risky. Watching Goodrich make mistakes, as all traders do, would have confirmed Rowe's belief in buying and holding. Few individuals have been able to make money consistently by short-term trading. Most of those who seem to be able to do it successfully for a short time are almost always wiped out over the long term. In later years, however, Rowe was rarely without a chart book, just for "a final check," before buying or selling.

Later, Rowe described this approach succinctly, as reported in *The History of T. Rowe Price Associates, Inc:* "The majority of people think of common stocks as something to buy or sell for speculative profits. They believe it is necessary to guess the ups and downs of the stock market to be successful. We do not think it is a good approach. The greatest American fortunes were the result of investing in a growing business and staying with it through thick and thin."

The market does seem to have a life of its own, which can be mesmerizing to watch. Trading can slow down to a crawl as traders feel its pulse. Then there will be a sudden increase in activity – often based just on a rumor – and it will swing up or down with heavy volume. It's almost like watching a large school of fish that, for seemingly no reason at all, will turn on a dime and swim in perfect unison with flashing fins in an entirely different direction.

In 1925, when Rowe first walked between the impressive white marble columns and opened the large, dark mahogany doors of Mackubin, Goodrich & Co. at 111 East Redwood Street, the bull market of

Bond offices of Mackubin, Goodrich, circa 1925. Legg, Mason corporate archives. All rights reserved. Copyright @ Legg, Mason

the twenties was well on its way upward. The Dow Jones Industrial Average had more than doubled to 135 from its low in 1921 just four years before; Mackubin, Goodrich & Co. was rapidly expanding from its base of 30-plus employees. Although its emphasis was on building up its stock brokerage business, the firm was hiring employees for its bond business as well.

The firm was then best known for its expertise in fixed-income securities. When the stock market was closed for four months in 1914, in order to keep the young firm going, the partners made their first foray into real estate by financing and selling mortgages for the Roland Park Company, which had just begun to develop neighborhoods in Baltimore's northern suburbs. By the beginning of 1925, the overall mortgage market, interest-bearing mortgage notes, and mortgage bonds had become an important part of their business.

Rowe was likely hired by the firm because of his successful experience at Jenkins, Whedbee & Poe as a fixed income salesman. It is quite possible that Mr. Legg himself was involved in hiring Rowe, as he soon became his mentor.

As the firm prospered in the long bull market, Rowe's compensation would have risen with his increasing experience and capability as a bond analyst and salesman.

Eleanor Price, born 1904; Goucher senior yearbook, 1926. TRP archives.

About this time, he met a pretty, dark-haired Goucher College student named Eleanor Baily Gherky. She was six years younger than Rowe, but that didn't seem to matter a bit. The winter of her senior year, on December 18, 1925, he gave her an engagement ring, and they were officially engaged on December 26. They were married September 18, 1926, at her family's summer home in Ocean City, New Jersey.

Mr. Rowe Price, circa 1926. TRP archives.

When the couple returned from their delayed honeymoon to Europe in August 1927, they rented a small house at 11 Talbot Road in Baltimore. The city life would have appealed more to Eleanor than did Glyndon, where Rowe had lived as a bachelor prior to their marriage. There was more to do in Baltimore and she had a number of friends and classmates from Goucher who lived nearby. For Rowe, the Baltimore house was not far from his office and near where many of his clients lived. It might have been difficult for him, however, to leave the Glyndon area and his close-knit family, which had been such a focal point of his life up to then.

Eleanor's family lived in what was known as the West Diamond Street Townhouse Historic District of Philadelphia. The area indeed featured many beautiful Victorian townhouses and catered to a new class of entrepreneurs growing rich on the important inventions of the late nineteenth and early twentieth centuries. Her father, William D. Gherky (sometimes spelled Gharky), was born and raised in Portsmouth, Ohio. In high school he became interested in telegraphy, which was just being introduced. This technology allowed an operator skilled in Morse code to send messages instantly over long distances to others, using wires. At the age of eighteen, in 1886, Gherky left high school to become a telegraph operator for the railroads. Two years later, he was employed by the Edison Electric Company in New Jersey to build a brand-new pilot plant to mass-produce electric light bulbs.

Mr. Gherky, Eleanor Price's father, born 1868. TRP archives.

Edison Electric was where many of the major inventions that would so affect the twentieth century were being developed. Edison's seminal patent for the first long-lasting electric light bulb that could be economically manufactured would be resolved, after years of legal haggling, in 1898, the year after Gherky arrived at the company. The plant that Gherky was hired to set up was an experimental facility that took the raw concepts developed by the engineers and transformed them into practical manufacturing processes and machinery for the large factory that would mass-produce the first Edison light bulbs. It was up to Gherky and his crew to iron out the manufacturing and engineering problems on a small scale before the large factory was built that would bring electrical illumination to the world.

This plant was located in Menlo Park, New Jersey in the huge Edison Electric complex. Coincidently, it was near Menlo Park, California, where many of the inventions of the twentieth and early twenty-first century were first dreamed of and produced in the plants of Hewlett Packard, Apple, Facebook, and the like. The Edison Electric facility was populated by men such as William K.L. Dickson, who developed one of the first motion picture cameras; Reginald Fessenden, who developed a new way to insulate electric wires, without which electricity could not be brought inside; and – the most famous of them all – Nikola Tesla, who today has an electric car named after him. Tesla was a consummate inventor, involved in many fields of technology. Later, at Westinghouse Electric Corporation, working directly for George Westinghouse, Tesla developed the technology of alternating current, which is necessary to transmit electricity over long distances – a technology that Gherky would put to good use later in his own facility.

It was as if all the entrepreneurs in today's Silicon Valley were crowded together on a single large campus in New Jersey – a heady environment for a young, technically inclined man from Ohio.

There are interesting parallels between Thomas Edison and William Gherky. Edison was also from Ohio and was interested in technology, particularly the telegraph, at a very early age. Did Edison, who was thirty-nine in 1888, and the twenty-year-old Gherky actually meet? Did Edison relate to him and personally hire him? We aren't sure of the answer, although Gherky's obituary in the *New York Times* states that he was "a former research assistant to Thomas A. Edison." It was certainly an impressive promotion for the young Gherky to suddenly rise from the job of telegraph operator to running one of the most important projects at the Edison Company.

Gherky did not stay at the Menlo Park labs long. Perhaps his inexperience caught up with him. By the end of the year, he was transferred to the engineering department of the Edison United Manufacturing Company. After another year, he left for the Field Engineering Company in New York in 1890 and began what became his life's work: designing and building electrical transportation systems and the associated electrical distribution equipment. Gherky constructed subway and cable systems for this company in the cities of Detroit and Buffalo. One of his most famous projects, in terms of publicity, at least, was designing the lighting for the first Broadway play to use electrical lighting, *Little Lord Fauntleroy*.

In 1892, Gherky moved to Philadelphia, where he installed the city's trolley line and the associated electrical systems. He went out on his own in 1911 and organized the Railway Track-Work Company, which made electrical railroad equipment, and formed the General Grinding Wheel Corporation. Throughout his career, Gherky not only designed systems, but was also an inventor, holding important patents for manufacturing processes, electrical equipment, and telephonic equipment.

These activities made Gherky a wealthy man. When he died on January 17, 1937, his estate was worth $389,710 (about $6.65 million in 2018 dollars). Like Samuel Black, Rowe's grandfather, he was an entrepreneur. He and Rowe were certainly close, as Gherky entrusted his son-in-law to manage his assets.

Eleanor, by all reports from those who knew her best, was devoted to Rowe and shared his passion for travel and, at the same time, understood his long working hours. She organized Rowe's personal life in an efficient behind-the-scenes manner, as she had been brought up to do as a woman of her time and social position. Her dinner parties were carefully planned, with everyone having a place card, even if Rowe was just having supper with his junior associates. The food was always excellent and beautifully served, the silver freshly polished and glittering, and the cook and butler working effectively together. She would allow Rowe to dominate the conversation while she remained in the background, thoughtful and considerate to those around her, as I can attest as a guest at several of these dinners.

They both kept daily diaries, but hers reflected the social side of their life. It mainly contained the names of friends, the specific parties they went to, what was served, and the specific rooms they had stayed in at various clubs and hotels where they might return. She was a generous supporter of Goucher College, served as chairwoman of the board, and often ran local fundraising campaigns for the school. As Ann D. Hopkins, who worked with Eleanor on several such projects, reported, she was a good organizer and always got the job done effectively and efficiently. If someone was lagging a bit, she would often pick them up in her car, without any fuss or embarrassment, and help them keep the fundraising appointments that they had accepted but were slow in delivering. Hopkins found that Eleanor was always very cordial and natural to be with.

Eleanor was quite interested in gardening, although more from a supervisory perspective. She let Rowe get his hands dirty digging around the roses that became one of his most important hobbies. She was president of the local garden club and also active at the state and national level. Her keen, active interest in projects outside the home must have reminded Rowe of his own mother. Thus, by the standards of that time, she was an ideal partner for a man whose major focus was business. An independent woman, she managed their social life in addition to her community involvements, to allow her husband more time to build the business.

Their major disappointment was that there were no children. She finally took matters into her own hands, although Rowe certainly did not object, and went to an adoption agency in New York City. On June 28, 1937, they adopted their first child, Richard (Dick) Baily Price. Two years later, they returned to adopt Thomas Rowe III.

Growing up in the Price household was sometimes difficult for the two boys, according to Tom and a good friend of Dick's. Like many successful men, particularly of that time, Rowe was a distant father. The boys complained that when they took a vacation, Rowe would take briefcases full of business reading material in which he buried himself for much of the day. He was a tough disciplinarian, but fair. The same friend of Dick's tells a story about weeding their large yard. Rowe enlisted his sons for the job and told them that he would pay them fifty cents an hour, a good wage for children in the 1950s. Something came up, and both boys forgot about the job. A week later, in an attempt to teach them a lesson about honoring their commitments, Rowe gathered them into his study and said that because they had not done the work that he had requested, he had to do the job himself. They owed him eight dollars. He collected this sum over time by deducting it from their allowance. Yet despite these issues, both sons loved and respected their father. Young Tom would name his son after his father.

Eleanor was devoted to her sons. She would often pad their allowance to pay for toys and other items that they desperately wanted. She gave the love and affection that business too often kept Rowe from providing. As Tom said, his father "did not try to push us into business. He would have liked it, but he wanted us to do what interested us, and he could see [we] really didn't have the interest." In the year before he died, according to Tom, his father finally opened up to him. "We had more love and warmth," he said, "than all the times we had had together. That's because he let his defenses down. He was able to be a real human being."

Chapter Four

THE GREAT BULL MARKET AND THE CRASH, 1927–1929

For almost a decade, from 1915 through the end of 1924, the Dow Jones Industrial Average had moved very little. The deep bear market of 1921 had traumatized investors, and there was little interest in buying stocks. However, 1925 was a good year, with a rise of about 20 percent in the Dow Jones, but 1926 was flat. The Dow made up for this in 1927, when from the beginning of the year it began to march steadily upward with a firm step and little retreat. This momentum was supported by a good economy, with the Federal Reserve index of industrial production rising more than 50 percent. Corporate earnings were rising even faster, as were stock dividends. Interest rates were low. By late 1927, business was becoming very exciting at Mackubin, Goodrich.

The late 1920s were also a fun time for many in the United States, with the Jazz Age, flappers, and – due to Prohibition – speakeasies. The scientific discoveries and inventions of the late nineteenth century were yielding many important new products. The first mass-produced automobiles were appearing on the road and airline transportation over short distances was becoming commercially feasible. The miracle of radio was coming to the average home and there was talk that even moving pictures might soon be transmitted over the air. Nothing seemed impossible in this new era of innovation.

Britain went back on the gold standard in 1925. As Chancellor of the Exchequer, and with no economic experience, Winston Churchill arbitrarily priced the currency in terms of gold at pre–World War I levels. This significantly overpriced the pound in world markets. British exports declined sharply and in spring 1927 the three other

43

most-developed world economies at the time – France, Germany, and the U.S. – reluctantly decided to pursue an easy money policy to bail out Britain. Many economists credit the subsequent powerful bull market of the late 1920s to this action.

In late 1927 the stock market rally did begin in earnest and stocks accelerated their advance. By December, the market had increased 69 percent from its lows. All of a sudden it seemed that making money was easy and not particularly risky. People began to notice the new automobiles in the driveways of those of their neighbors who were investing in the stock market. In 1928 came the even more expensive large additions on these neighbors' houses as the market gained increased momentum. Greed, driven by envy of the new riches of others, can often contribute to the second phase of a strong bull market.

When the Prices returned from their honeymoon in the fall of 1927, they found that the stock market was continuing the strong rally that had begun before they left and Mackubin, Goodrich was prospering in the ebullient upswing. If Rowe had his pole in the water, as he probably did during his absence, the fishing had been good.

Early that year, the Mackubin, Goodrich partners realized that they would soon outgrow their quarters at 111 East Redwood Street, their home since 1917. In 1929 they bought a large white Georgian marble building just down the street at 222 East Redwood for $750,000 ($10.7 million in 2018 dollars). The partners planned extensive renovations and a move early in 1930.

A further sign of the firm's optimism, at what proved to be near the peak of the market, Mr. Legg bought a twenty-seven-room mansion with seven bathrooms on University Parkway. That summer, he took a deluxe ten-week European tour with his wife and daughter.

It can be argued that for the conservative investor in early 1928 the market remained reasonably priced. Earnings had continued to rise in the good business conditions of 1927 and dividends had followed suit. Ultimately, however, a major bull market usually needs a good dose of unreality – the belief that things are different now, that the rules of the past no longer apply, and that it is best to jump on the back of the sharply rising market rather than get left out.

The market started slowly in 1928. But the large gains in 1927 and the low valuations had drawn in more investors with increasing sums to invest. The stock market began to vault upward in great leaps. Following these jumps would be sharp corrections, but the sellers would prove to be wrong. The market would take off once again, with an even stronger spring upward.

A good example is the Radio Corporation of America (RCA), the AOL (a leader of the dot.com phenomenon in the late 1990s) of its day. After its stock reached $101 in 1927, it experienced a roller coaster of plunges and recoveries, until in 1928 it rose to $420, a 320-percent gain.

As the boom continued to develop, some of those executives from Rowe's DuPont days gained increasing public popularity and admiration for their stock market prowess. John Raskob from DuPont and William Durant, who had co-founded General Motors, began to move markets upward simply on their bullish pronouncements in the financial sections of newspapers.

In November 1928, Herbert Hoover, a well-respected businessman, builder of companies, and a Quaker, was elected president of the United States in a landslide, with more than 58 percent of the electorate voting in his favor.

Bull markets that continue over years require a large supply of easy money to keep moving upward. There have to be large banks and other lenders willing to support the brokerage firms and their clients by lending ever-increasing sums of cash as the stock market rises in value. The Fed has largely accommodated such explosions in lending to buy stocks and certainly did so with its monetary policies that began in 1927.

Easy money also directly supported the stock market itself. In the mid-1920s it was common for investors to put up only 20 percent of a stock purchase in cash. The brokerage firm would supply the financing on the remaining 80 percent. The interest on such loans then was only 5 percent. If an investor remained fully invested and fully leveraged in the stocks of the Dow Jones during 1928, the return for the entire year would have been more than 200 percent. Not bad for a year's work. Of course, there would have been a few nervous moments during the year, as the market fluctuated violently over several days. These fluctuations would have been amplified for the average investor because of his leverage.

With the loans from brokers and banks supporting the huge gains, the rise in the value of investors' collateral brought more capital into the market. Interest rates rose to 12 percent at the end of 1928. Bankers, however, still considered these loans to be perfectly safe.

Not only were loans being supplied to the brokerage firms by banks of all sizes, but money also began to pour in from overseas. Even well-run corporations that should have known better than to risk their shareholders' capital in the stock market began to borrow money and loan it to speculators at 12 percent and to invest in the stock market themselves. By early 1929, loans from corporations were equal to those from the banks and continued on to grow much larger.

With the stock market up some 10 percent in January and brokerage loans in step, 1929 got off to a strong start. As he was leaving office, President Calvin Coolidge said that business and the economy were "absolutely sound" and that stocks were "cheap at current prices." Naturally, the stock market rose sharply on this pronouncement. Catherine Overbeck, a Mackubin, Goodrich employee, wrote in her diary, "The firm grew by leaps and bounds."

But by the last week of March, the market seemed to hit a brick wall and fell sharply. On March 26, the first real wave of fear rippled through Wall Street. Eight million shares, more than double the trading on a normal day, changed hands. Panic took over as stocks dropped 20 or 30 points in a few seconds. To make matters worse, the ticker tape couldn't keep up, so no one knew how bad things were or how much money they had lost. With stocks so far down, margin calls went out at the end of the day, after the ticker finally caught up. Bank interest rates on such loans went up to an all-time high, as bankers perceived risks in the market for the first time.

Charles E. Mitchell, president of the National City Bank (now Citibank), stepped into the fray and announced that he would do what the Federal Reserve would not do – lend money so as to create loans to prevent liquidations – and he would borrow from the Federal Reserve to do it. This stopped the decline and the market took off for the sky again. As John Kenneth Galbraith wrote in *The Great Crash 1929,* "Never before or since have so many become so wondrously, so effortlessly, and so quickly rich."

To serve this huge demand for common stocks, investment trusts were formed – a vehicle that issued stock today to raise money to buy stocks of corporations over several years. In 1927, $400 million of the common stocks of these trusts were sold to the public ($5.72 billion in 2018 dollars), and in 1929, an amazing $3 billion ($42.9 billion in 2018 dollars). The trusts at that time were often valued in the market for more than twice as much as the total market value of their assets. Moreover, these trusts were highly leveraged, with bonds and preferred stock supporting the common stock. (Preferred stock is a class of stock that has a higher call on the corporate assets and dividends than the common stock. It also generally pays a dividend with the return greater than on the common shares. In these late 1920s trusts, the preferred stock was issued simply to increase the leverage for the common shareholder.) A typical trust in those days might have only 30 percent of its capital represented by common stocks.

Ultimately, a trust might also be held by a second trust with a similar leverage, producing a total leveraged gain on its common stock of 700 to 800 percent on a 50-percent gain in the market price of its assets. If the investor also borrowed heavily from his brokerage house or bank, the actual gain to him would be magnified even more. Fully leveraged, $100,000 invested in January 1929 could theoretically grow to more than $7 million by the end of June, if the trust assets kept up with the stock market and the investor was adventurous enough to leverage himself to the maximum!

As the market rose, creating many instant millionaires, the stock market bonanza became, for a small subset of society overall, increasingly part of the culture. The progress of the Dow Jones, as well as of individual stocks, was widely reported in the press and hourly on the radio. Typical were stories of nurses making $30,000 in a day by following tips from patients, or a broker's valet who quickly made $250,000. In August, brokerage offices connected by wireless radio were installed on transatlantic passenger ships so trading could continue uninterrupted on the high seas. For a young man in the middle of it, as Rowe was at Mackubin, Goodrich, it must have been exhilarating stuff – even though his chief responsibilities then were in the bond department.

Such a gigantic bubble couldn't continue to expand forever and it didn't. Historians mark September 3, 1929, as the date that the great bull market of the 1920s peaked at 381. Andrew Mellon, U.S. Secretary of the Treasury, said, "There is no cause for worry. The high tide of prosperity will continue." This might have been true in Mr. Mellon's eyes, but for Rowe and others in the market it certainly wasn't evident. The market continued to be extremely volatile with great swings in price on huge volume both up and down. Knowledgeable insiders continued to come out with optimistic statements. The same Charles E. Mitchell who had turned the market around from a severe slump in 1928 said on October 15, "The markets generally are now in a healthy condition." On October 22, following a sharp decline, he said, "The decline had gone on too far. [Prices] were now at a very fair level and buying could begin."

Under this veneer, the enthusiasm of the summer was turning into fear in the fall. The first really bad break hit Thursday, October 24, which came to be known as Black Thursday. Once more the ticker lagged far behind the trading in the morning, and panic began to set in. Large blocks of stocks sank into deep holes with no bidders. Toward noon, the market managed to come back, but soon the panic returned.

At noon, "a roar arose from the stock exchange floor that could be heard for blocks along Broad and Wall streets," according to a contemporary *Baltimore Sun* article. Many investors were being sold out by margin calls. Rumors began to take over, such as "stocks were selling for nothing" and a "suicide wave was in progress."

In the early afternoon of Black Thursday, a publicized meeting was convened of the chairmen of the four largest banks, National City Bank, Chase National Bank, Guaranty Trust Company of New York, and Bankers Trust, in the office of Thomas W. Lamont, the senior partner of J. P. Morgan and Company. Afterward, Lamont told reporters that there had been "a little distress selling on the stock exchange" because of "a technical condition of the market," and that the situation would "result in betterment."

As a representative of the group of bank chairmen, Richard Whitney, the vice president of the New York Stock Exchange, at 1:30 p.m. placed an order, later famous, for 10,000 shares of U.S. Steel at $205, the price of the last trade. Fear instantly vanished and greed again took over as the losses for the day were again mostly erased. The huge drop of the morning was reduced to a modest 6-point decline for the day. The real losers were those who were sold out on margin calls in the morning panic. Optimistic statements became the rule of the day from business as well as financial leaders. On Sunday, just before the new week opened, there were rumors of large buy orders piled up in brokerage offices. Anonymous sources quoted in the *Wall Street Journal* called the market an "amazing buy."

Then came Black Monday. On October 28, once again the ticker was hours late. Panic returned and fortunes were eliminated in a few minutes of trading, leaving only debts to brokerage firms that could not possibly be repaid. Matters became worse from there. The four bankers who had been represented by Thomas Lamont did not make another pronouncement and the market continued down all day.

Tuesday was even worse. A normal day's volume at that time would have been 3 or 4 million shares. This day, it was more than 16 million shares, with the ticker more than two and a half hours late at the close. The market had lost 33 points, or 12 percent of its value, in a single day. Lawyers, doctors, businessmen, and shoeshine boys came to watch the rapidly falling shares of their once-favored stocks.

There was chaos at brokerage firms, and Mackubin, Goodrich was no exception. "Lawyers, businessmen, and doctors jammed into Mackubin, Goodrich to watch frenzied board boys mark the quickly changing stock prices," the *Baltimore Sun* would recall. "The packed room was deathly silent as investors watched their wealth vanish.... When the selling stopped, the market had lost nearly $25 billion ($364 billion in 2018 dollars) in three days of trading, and some lost everything. 'They were in a state of shock. The mood was despair,' recalled Standish McCleary [retired senior vice president of Legg Mason Wood Walker, Inc.]. 'The immediate effect was devastating.'"

The stock market had had sharp breaks before: the panic of 1907, which was only stopped by the intervention of J.P. Morgan, and produced a decline of 50 percent from its peak in 1905; an effective free fall at the outbreak of the First World War, which was ended by closing the major stock markets of the world for four months; and the nearly 50- percent break in 1921. These drops, however, were over relatively quickly. This time, after a brief rally in 1930, the stock market would seem to decline forever. The market finally hit bottom in July 1932, with the Dow closing at 4. From September 3, 1929, to July 8, 1932, the decline of the Dow of 345 points was 89.4 percent. No one at the time, of course, had any idea that it was indeed the bottom.

The market's collapse, coupled with the tremendous loss of liquidity, accelerated what had been forecast by the economists to be only a modest inventory correction into the Great Depression. In July 1932 *Iron Age* magazine announced that steel production was down to 12 percent of capacity and pig iron output was the lowest since 1896. Trading on the stock market was only 720,000 shares – quite a change from the 10 million share days of 1929.

By 1933, the U.S. Gross National Product (GNP) was 33 percent less than in 1929. Twenty-five percent of the workforce was reportedly out of a job, although statistics were not precise in those days. It is estimated that perhaps 50 percent of the working population was either out of a job or was working only part time. Companies also sharply reduced pay levels to decrease costs and stay in business; as a result, not only were workers working fewer hours, but they were also being paid less per hour. On the other end of the income spectrum, the Crash directly affected the wealthiest Americans and thereby had a very significant indirect impact on the economy as a whole. In 1929, 5 percent of the population received 33 percent of all the income and accounted for more than 50 percent of all savings. The mood at the top quickly went from optimism and free spending in 1929 to pessimism and a propensity to save by 1932.

Corporations had invested heavily in the stock market near the top and now incurred huge losses. Holding companies collapsed under their heavy debt load. Foreign lending seized up and was replaced by an all-cash payment system for imports. The liquidity of most industrialized countries was under question.

This huge collapse in liquidity had an outsized impact on banks. Because many were not only highly leveraged themselves but also had foolishly invested their depositors' money in the stock market, the collapse of the banking system thus affected most Americans in real terms.

Before 1933, the national banking system was loosely regulated and many financial institutions operated outside of it. The Federal Reserve System exercised control over only the biggest banks. When a bank failed, the depositors lost everything. In the 1920s there were only a few bank failures, and of these most were in small rural areas. In 1931 a significant number of banks suddenly failed. Alarmingly, many of them were large and located in major metropolitan areas. This development turned the spotlight on the banking system.

When depositors heard a rumor that their bank might fail, they would rush to withdraw all of their funds. Even the soundest bank couldn't pay off all of their depositors at once. Thus began the chain reaction of failed banks, creating rumors that brought down even more of them. Not only did individual depositors lose their money, so did businesses, charities, and even local governments. GM's Durant would declare bankruptcy in 1936, with his only assets the clothes on his back.

Without savings and with much less income to make purchases, people and businesses began to resort to barter. IOUs and scrip served as a substitute for money. In February 1933, the governor of Michigan called the first statewide bank holiday to provide shaky institutions time to secure new finances. By the end of 1933, 5,500 banks were closed, at least temporarily.

Without the grease of financial liquidity, the wheels of industry began to slow down and grind to a halt. Even the charities and volunteer organizations providing soup kitchens ran out of cash. In Baltimore and other cities, citizens stood in orderly lines to go into the garbage dumps in search of food. The apple season that year was a large one and created many apple sellers on street corners. At five cents each, the activity generated an estimated income of only $500 per year, but people were desperate.

The national mood was grim, with the economy in total collapse as Hoover's term ended. On March 4, 1933, the eloquent young Franklin Delano Roosevelt made his entry onto the world stage with his inaugural speech, saying, "The only thing we have to fear is … fear itself." Thus began his hundred-day New Deal program. Instantly, the country and the stock market began to recover.

The first item on Roosevelt's list was a national bank holiday on March 6, included in the Emergency Banking Act, presented the day after he was elected. On the first day it convened, March 9, in four hours a frightened House of Representatives passed the bill. The Senate passed it just as quickly. All banks were included. Under the act, they would be inspected by the federal government and reopened when the institution was determined to be sound

Within two weeks, the banks holding 90 percent of U.S. assets were found to be sound and reopened. Money stuffed under mattresses and in wall safes flowed quickly back into the banks. The worst of the Depression panic was past, but the GNP would not recover to its pre-1929 crash level until 1941, twelve years later. The recovery was ultimately spurred on by the world's preparations for World War II. The Dow Jones Average would not surpass its 1929 high until November 24, 1954, more than twenty-five years later!

Rowe was an initial supporter of Roosevelt and his New Deal. It was obvious that the country needed a strong leader, and in future letters to clients he gave the president full credit for "saving capitalism." He originally thought that Roosevelt's intention was to "share, not give" the nation's resources to the underprivileged. As these programs shifted over time more to outright giving, FDR lost Rowe's support. He ultimately blamed FDR for creating a large population segment that was too dependent on government handouts.

Chapter Five

AFTER THE CRASH, 1930–1937

Emulating Mr. Legg's move to a bigger house in 1927 – although their timing was better and on a much more modest scale – in January 1930 Rowe and Eleanor upgraded from their small rental home and bought a stone and wood-framed 3,000-square-foot home on a nicely landscaped half-acre lot at 4309 Wendover Road, in the upper-middle-class neighborhood of Guilford in North Baltimore. The house was valued at $22,000 in the 1930 census ($323,000 in 2018 dollars). They probably got a very good deal, given the traumatic economic environment, and possibly were given some parental help. They would remain on Wendover Road for most of their married life.

Price home at 4309 Wendover Road. Photo online.

The relatively modest size of this house, compared to the mansions of many of his peers, speaks volumes of the man and the way he conducted his life and business. He had absorbed the lessons of the Quaker Way learned at Friends School and Swarthmore, letting results speak for him. He didn't need the pretense of a large house.

As the country plummeted into the Depression, Baltimore suffered along with it. Men would be up early looking for work, but by noon, unsuccessful in their search, they would join long bread lines to get hot soup and a piece of bread. Mackubin, Goodrich couldn't escape the devastation of the market. Rowe wrote in his journal on September 24, 1931, that he "had a talk with Mr. Legg and he advised me to liquidate my securities and take my licking. I could not write out a sell ticket on stocks after the decline they have had. My hand would become paralyzed." He went on in the same entry to say that if he followed Mr. Legg's advice, he "would have a loss of $11,000 and I would be years liquidating this loan, a few dollars at a time." The magnitude of this loss to him can be appreciated when it is remembered that his new house was valued at $22,000. The next day, he noted in his journal, with capital letters for emphasis, "When once again we are in good times with rising prices and the public is clamoring for profits, BE SURE to point out the horrors of a depression and BE SURE to state that the worst depressions come when least expected. If you are buying something which you cannot pay for in cash, you must be prepared to take losses."

Mackubin, Goodrich did have some major cash issues in 1930 following the market crash. Like the rest of the financial world, the partners had allowed the firm to become overextended during the bull market. They did proceed, regardless, to take possession of their beautiful building and moved their one hundred employees in on schedule. It had been expensively redecorated and outfitted with luxurious new offices. Shortly after the move, a partners' meeting was called to discuss the situation, during which it was decided that the only way Mackubin, Goodrich could be saved was for all of the partners, senior and junior, to liquidate their portfolios and put the resulting cash into the business. The gloomy conversations that took place over numerous dinner tables in Baltimore that night can be imagined. Everyone did chip in in the end, and the firm was saved. Fortunately for him, Rowe was not a partner.

The move by the partners to liquidate their stocks, although certainly painful at the time, ultimately proved to be a very good move. The market had a little bounce in 1930, during which the sales happened to take place. The market then began again to decline toward its bottom in 1932.

Such agreements by partners were commonplace in the 1930s and were the principal reason some firms survived and others didn't. The partners and their families usually converted these cash infusions into formal loans to their firms. Initially, they were regarded as only short-term loans, but as the long, slow recovery evolved, it became evident that they were going to be long-term, often over many decades. As late as the 1950s, there are stories of promising young employees turning down partnerships in brokerage firms because they could not afford, or did not wish to accept, the responsibilities of this "Depression debt."

As stock trading slowed down to hundreds of thousands of shares, the firm, now known as Mackubin, Legg & Co. (Clem Goodrich had died March 14, 1932), began to reemphasize fixed income securities. This involved bonds, but also mortgages. The 1933 difficulties in the mortgage market also caused three of the country's largest insurance companies to go bankrupt, which required them to get extensions from thousands of bondholders across the country. Because of the firm's experience with national, standardized mortgages, the U.S. government selected Mackubin, Legg and two other banking firms to contact these bondholders and arrange for a $100 million refunding. The mortgage market was rescued by this funding through the newly created Reconstruction Finance Corporation (RFC), backed by the U.S. government. The operation was directed personally by Mr. Legg and was the largest refunding operation up to that time, giving him and the firm considerable national recognition. It was also the first issue to be registered with the brand-new Securities and Exchange Commission (SEC). Although he doesn't mention it in his writings, it is possible that Rowe worked with Legg on some aspects of this transaction.

Rowe had been hired in 1925 to be a bond salesman. He had done a good job, procuring many new accounts. He soon began to proactively manage these accounts to improve their yields and their safety. After his experience at Jenkins, Whedbee & Poe, he was able to avoid the losses suffered by many of the new financial products created in the late 1920s.

In 1930, he was promoted by the partners to manager of the entire bond department. This was a major promotion and demonstrated the confidence that management had in his abilities. The department occupied the entire second floor of the firm's new offices. Bonds and other fixed income products were rapidly becoming their most important business.

As he gained more experience and confidence, he began to manage his clientele differently from the rest of the firm. As he had at Jenkins, Whedbee & Poe, he selected fixed income securities that, although good for the client, often carried only a small profit for the firm. Rather than describing just the good points about a security, he gave both sides of the transaction, spelling out the risks as well.

He began to gain the confidence of his clients. He found that they were in effect doing all of the sales work, bringing in their friends as new clients. As he recalled in his September 7, 1951, bulletin, "The Firm's Goal and How We Plan to Attain It," he typed the following quotation onto the front page of his work portfolio: "Profits in any business are not made on the first orders, but on the orders that follow, which come of their own accord and on which there is no selling expense." Although this method of handling his clients increased the firm's business and profits, Rowe was clearly marching to a different drummer. Most other members of the firm were more motivated by the quick commission, not the distant future or what might be the optimum investments for their clients. The concept of focusing on the client first possibly harked back to his days at DuPont. This fine company always took a long-term view of customer relations.

By late 1931, Rowe had become more interested in stocks and less in bonds, though they were still declining in value. To his journal – if not to Mr. Legg or his peers – Rowe began thinking of a future Mackubin, Goodrich that would be both an investment counsel firm, managing stocks and bonds for a fee, and a brokerage house. Profits would flow separately from both businesses. On October 22, 1931, despite the dire pessimism he found when he talked to financial industry leaders or read their advice in the *Wall Street Journal,* he wrote in his journal that he believed "we are faced with greater opportunities than ever before in the history of our nation." With the market moving down in wave after wave, the GDP declining, and earnings from corporations turning to deep losses, he was not saying to buy quite yet. But this comment revealed for the first known time in writing Rowe's uncanny ability to see into the future.

Those who knew Rowe well attributed this ability to his total focus on business, the stock market, and the underlying political, social, and economic trends, described in his 1937 pamphlet "Change: The Investor's Only Certainty." No one ever saw him with a book just for entertainment in his hand. He read only business reports, financial publications, and brokerage reports. When he wasn't involved with clients, preparing for client meetings, or running the department, he would be studying this material behind a closed door in his office. When he traveled, he took large briefcases with him and more would follow when those were finished. It is hard to imagine that anyone knew more than he did about matters that affected the stock market. If he were asked how he came up with his insightful recommendations concerning individual stocks or the stock market, he would grin and say "ESP," and then change the subject with a big wink. His son Tom would later say that there might be something to the "ESP" comment: "One night at dinner [my father] suddenly dropped his fork and said, 'Dick's been in an accident.' Ten minutes later, the phone rang and it was Dick saying that he had been in a bicycle accident. He was in the hospital with a chipped front tooth and seven stiches in his forehead." His father had a sixth sense, according to Tom: "He knew where things were going, whether it was the family, the country, or the world."

On September 28, 1933, the Dow Jones Average closed at 95, and Rowe wrote: "After carefully weighing the favorable and unfavorable factors, I believe it is time to accumulate stocks. I believe that the long-term cycle for the country and market is upward." This recommendation in 1933 was remarkably prescient. It wasn't the bottom of the market, but it was very close.

In 1934, in a decision led by Mr. Legg, the partners allowed Rowe to establish an Investment Management Department and to be its manager, which he had long lobbied for. He was thirty-six and finally in a position to create his dream. However, the path forward would prove to be more difficult than he anticipated.

The ground rules for the new department were clearly laid out by the firm. It would provide investment advisory services for a fee to clients with portfolios of $100,000 or more ($1.83 million in 2018 dollars). The primary targets would be charitable organizations, small banks, and insurance companies. At that time, there were only a few individuals with this much capital in Baltimore.

The team he hired for this department would stay with him for the next fifty years. Marie Walper came with him as his secretary and confidante. She had joined Mackubin, Goodrich & Co. a few years before he did and had begun to manage his office and business affairs. Isabella Craig, who had done statistical work for the economist Irving Fisher after graduation from Vassar, became the statistician. Walter Kidd had joined Mackubin, Legg immediately after Harvard Business School in 1933 and was appointed a senior security analyst. Charles (Charlie) W. Shaeffer joined in 1935, also from Harvard Business School, and became both a securities analyst and an assistant counselor.

According to "What Growth Stocks Have Done for Us," a bulletin that Rowe would issue in-house in January 1954, he had been thinking about "growth" stocks since 1921. In 1934 he started an experimental fund to prove that better results could be obtained by holding good "growth" stocks. His first mention of such a category of stocks was in a journal entry on October 8, 1935, in which he said that he was "hoping to be able to convince the firm that we should have two funds managed by the Investment Management Department ... one would have for its objective the building of capital through its commitment in the leading stocks, which have proven quality and prospects for continued growth." The second fund would be "more speculative and would be invested in the younger industries such as aviation, air conditioning and aluminum metals. Historic background for many such companies would be lacking, selection would be based on the belief in the strong outlook for the industry they were operating, and knowledge of the people managing the company." Rowe further wrote, "The realities are that most of the big fortunes of the country had resulted from investing in growing businesses and staying with them through thick and thin rather than switching from one security to another, a practice advanced by the brokers and followed by their clients."

This approach collided with the business experience and instincts of many of the partners at Mackubin, Legg. Like many brokers today, they felt that trading stocks was the way to create profits for the client, and the commissions from trading shares of stock for clients created profits for them and the firm. Mr. Legg, however, gave Rowe a great deal of support, listening in a fatherly way and at great length to his ideas and theories. He also supported him in debates inside the firm. But Rowe found himself a misfit, at increasing odds with the others. He did not believe in compromise when it came to his views of how to run an investment counsel business. While he had been willing to work in relative harmony within the firm as he expanded his responsibilities and his knowledge of the bond area, the investment management business was his baby and he protected it like a proud father. He had strong opinions and, occasionally, a sharp tongue. He noted in his journal that he was called "uncooperative, unpleasant, and unapproachable," and that he gave others the impression of feeling "superior." Even Mr. Legg told him that he was too "idealistic" and "too impatient." He almost fired Rowe when he blew up at a meeting of the executive committee and insulted some of its members. Rowe grumbled to his journal, "It seems I am guilty of many misdeeds and mannerisms."

Despite the market recovery from its 1932 low, by 1937 expectations still remained pessimistic, business was depressed, and the market appeared to be weakening. Worse for Rowe, his Investment Management Department was losing money and was not the great financial success that he had hoped. Because of this (and perhaps Rowe's personal "mannerisms") he was not being given the financial and personnel support he had requested for his new department. Rowe could be certain that the partners at Mackubin, Legg would soon consider the future of his department.

The following is a fictional account of what might have been said at a meeting that did indeed take place between Rowe and Mr. Legg: This is based on conversations with Truman T. Semans, long a financial leader in Baltimore, visits to Rowe's original home in Baltimore, review of photographs in the Legg Mason archives, and discussions with Bill Legg, Mr. Legg's grandson.

May 16, 1937. Rowe had turned thirty-nine two months before. The sun was beginning to feel warm in the Baltimore spring, even at 6:00 in the morning. Rowe was an early riser. Before he went to the office, he enjoyed tending to the rose bushes that had become a beloved hobby.

With the dew still on their leaves, they were just beginning to show some buds. It had been a little dry, so he made a note for Eleanor to turn on the sprinklers later.

He walked back to the house and collected his large leather briefcase with double straps, full of papers and magazines, as well as the notes he would send to his team from his evening reading. He felt good. There was an athletic spring to his step and he looked forward to his tennis match with his good friend Dinty Moore, who had been made the lacrosse coach at the U.S. Naval Academy the prior year.

As he slipped behind the wheel of his five-year-old gray Buick, Rowe's thoughts turned to his meeting with Mr. Legg, scheduled for that afternoon. It had not been easy running the Investment Management Department the last few years, and recently things had been getting worse. His stomach began to churn on the last cup of black coffee, as he thought about the criticisms from some of the firm's partners.

"Damn it," he thought. "I probably shouldn't have been so frank, but Joe Senner was really being a horse's ass! Why on earth would he force me to put shares of Baltimore Gas and Electric in Mrs. Ashton's account, with its slow growth and the increasing regulation by the heavy hand of a government run by Democrats?" He suspected that the reason might have been that the firm had a few too many shares of Baltimore Gas and Electric in its treasury, on which it had made a nice profit. Such a trade might be good for the firm, but, in his opinion, it wasn't a very profitable investment for Mrs. Ashton. But then how, he wondered, could he keep his group independent from the dictates of the firm, with the slow growth in his accounts and its nonexistent profits? He was so lost in thought that he uncharacteristically almost clipped the paperboy, who had veered over into his lane on his bicycle.

He had called a meeting for 8:30 a.m. of his small staff to review a few larger accounts and to get feedback from Walter Kidd on his visit to Glenn L. Martin, the local airplane manufacturer. Rowe was a believer in knowing the managers of the companies he invested in. This was difficult in the 1930s, when companies were still not very transparent and traveling was expensive. There was no excuse, in his mind, not to visit local firms like Martin or even Black & Decker, run by his cousin and doing well recently, despite some problems earlier in the Depression. He was a stickler for detail and demanded that both counselors and research analysts be current. Woe to the professional who had not read and absorbed the contents of the Wall Street Journal *before the first meeting of the day.*

Marie Walper handled the accounts and kept track of all of the trades and account performance. Isabella Craig had put together the up-to-date financial information on Martin. After a presentation by Walter and some discussion, it was decided to add Martin to several accounts at a few points under the market.

Rowe had a luncheon date at noon at the Merchants Club (now closed) with an old client, Loring A. Cover. Although his account was below the $100,000 cutoff, he was on the boards of several charities and had been exempted. As Rowe climbed the worn, white marble steps of the venerable old club, the noise of the usual Baltimore business lunch could be heard.

Inside, he shook hands with a number of business acquaintances and settled down at a small wooden table for two in the main dining room. Technically, business could not be carried on at the club, nor papers pulled out. A general conversation about stocks was perfectly fine, however, particularly if mixed in with upcoming events such as the Maryland Hunt Cup race and local business conditions. Loring, as usual, was amenable to the few changes Rowe suggested in his portfolio, although he did question the Martin decision, as he could not imagine the U.S. getting involved in another war with Germany. The current upset between Austria and Hitler seemed just some minor mistreatment of resident Germans by the Austrian government − certainly nothing worthy of another war.

When he returned to 222 East Redwood, Rowe returned a few calls and began to think again about his meeting with Mr. Legg. He knew it would probably not be an easy one. He was sure his request for a new counselor would be turned down again. A few minutes before the appointment, Rowe made his way up the steps to the executive floor. When he entered, he noticed a strange quieting of voices, but perhaps this was his imagination. Mr. Legg's secretary, Catherine Overbeck, looked up at him from her desk for a moment before ushering him into Mr. Legg's office.

Mr. Legg sat behind a large oak partner's desk. An ornate Persian carpet covered the floor. The walls were mahogany, with some pictures of Baltimore − horses ridden by red-jacketed hunters and one of a Chesapeake bugeye sailboat being unloaded of oysters at a Baltimore pier. A picture of Mr. Legg's wife and children sat prominently on his desk in a silver frame. The heavily draped windows were open to the warm after-noon air.

"Well, Rowe, what trouble have you been into today?" Mr. Legg boomed. He was a tall man, muscled and athletic. He was, as usual, elegantly attired in coat, vest, and tie, despite the temperature. His eyes were dark and piercing, and his mouth had just a touch of a smile as he stared across at Rowe. Rowe sat down in one of the two leather chairs in front of the desk.

"So far, it has been a good day, sir," he replied. "Haven't had a single argument."

"Well, that is a good day – although it's still early," Mr. Legg replied. "But we do have a problem, and I am afraid some of it might be due to a bit of a philosophical clash you've had with some of the senior partners. In fact, Rowe, to get right to it, at our partners' meeting last night, we decided to shut down your department. As you know it is not making money and the outlook for the market and the economy seems pretty grim. We're cutting back expenses where we can, and your department, unfortunately, is a big expense."

"Wow," thought Rowe. "I knew that there had been some friction, and profits haven't come as quickly as we had hoped, but I didn't think they would throw in the towel so fast." All he said to Mr. Legg was, "Yes, sir. I have to say, though I am very disappointed, I can understand your decision."

"Now Rowe," said Mr. Legg, "it doesn't mean that we want to lose your team. You have some very good folks in your department." He reached into his coat pocket and pulled out a handwritten note on yellow paper. "We are very impressed with the work that Walter has been doing in research. We would like to give him a promotion to be Head of Research and raise his salary to $3,500 per year. Charlie's got the making of a great stock salesman and we would like to offer him a base salary of $2,000, with the opportunity to earn more from commissions. Isabella can stay in statistics and, of course, Marie would stay as your secretary. You've done a good job with your accounts and we feel you can be a real asset to the firm by continuing to manage those accounts and bringing in others. My partners wanted to emphasize, however, that you would have to adapt to being more of a team player. We would offer you the same $12,000 per year that we're paying you now, plus the opportunity for commission *income. Of course, we won't be charging your clients a management fee any longer.*

"Thank you for your offers, sir," said Rowe. "I don't know how the team will respond. It will probably take a few days to sort out."

"Take your time, son," replied Mr. Legg. "I know it is a bit of a shock and you had your heart set on making this thing work. It's just the bad economy. We have had to mind the store a little tighter with some of the debt the partners have taken on. And Rowe, I'd like you to know that I still believe in your idea of an investment management department and your concept of holding stocks for longer-term gain. We just can't afford to keep pushing against the wind now, but I fully expect that when things get better, we can restart the department with you as the head."

"I understand," said Rowe, as he rose from the chair and turned toward the door. The office was a blur of light and color as he walked to the stairs. He had been working on his first important paper on how he would manage money, which he hoped to publish, titled, "Change: The Investor's Only Certainty."

"How appropriate," he thought.

On May 18, 1937, Rowe resigned from Mackubin, Legg & Co., where he had spent twelve important years. That evening he wrote in his diary, "Why did I resign? There must be 100 contributing causes, but the main reason is the final realization that ML [Mr. Legg] and Company's goal and mine do not parallel. I am convinced beyond a shadow of a doubt that ML and Company are, first, dealers and brokers. While Mr. Legg would like his firm to be recognized for its research and counsel, no member of the firm has sufficient understanding of the problems, nor is the firm willing to make the necessary financial sacrifices or to contribute sufficient time, to do a first-class job. Furthermore, I can see no prospect of ever being a dominant factor in directing the affairs of the firm and even if it were possible, I would not want to be a partner – because of the tight business they do, the people who now comprise the partnership, and their descendants. I like a good fight, but I don't like domestic conflict whether it's at home or at the office. In short, I am a misfit and the sooner I change the better for all concerned."

Fate had also handed Rowe an essential element at this important moment in his business career. His father-in-law, William Gherky, had died January 17, 1937, of a heart attack and left each of his three daughters $130,000 ($2.22 million in 2018 dollars). As manager of Gherky's account, Rowe was well aware of the size of the estate. Here, suddenly, were the funds that could support the startup of his own company. His wife's inheritance would allow him to go without a salary during the firm's early years, as well as funding most of its early losses.

Part Two

HIS OWN BOSS

Chapter Six

BIRTH OF T. ROWE PRICE AND ASSOCIATES, 1937

From here on in this narrative, Rowe will be called "Mr. Price." After he started his own firm, T. Rowe Price and Associates, he was called Mr. Price by all but his close old friends. It's how those of us in the younger generation addressed him.

T. ROWE PRICE, JR.

ANNOUNCES HIS RESIGNATION AS

DIRECTOR OF THE INVESTMENT MANAGEMENT

DEPARTMENT OF

MACKUBIN, LEGG & COMPANY

TO CONTINUE HIS ACTIVITIES IN

INVESTMENT RESEARCH AND MANAGEMENT

UNDER HIS OWN NAME

WITH OFFICES AT 1522 AND 1523 BALTIMORE TRUST BLD

BALTIMORE, MARYLAND

PLAZA 1992

Announcement of the formation of T. Rowe Price, Inc.

After resigning from Mackubin, Legg & Co., and consulting a number of executives both on and off Wall Street, Mr. Price decided to start his own business from scratch rather than work for a more established firm. He believed that his investment philosophy would produce superior results and that working for someone else would only be frustrating in the end. Most importantly, he felt that only by doing the things that he personally believed in could he be happy. He was strongly supported in this by Eleanor. He began to look for an office for his new firm. There was no lack of opportunities in 1937. He ended his search by leasing half of the twenty-ninth floor in the Baltimore Trust Company Building at 10 Light Street, only a block from his old office. The building had been finished in December 1929, a little over a month after the crash. The Baltimore Trust Company was the largest banking institution south of Philadelphia, and the building was designed to match its reputation. At thirty-four stories, it was the tallest building in Baltimore. The main floor of its huge public banking room on the ground level was laid out in mosaic tile, with large murals on the walls by prominent local artists,

10 Light Street. Photo by the author.

depicting scenes from Baltimore history. Its exterior was classic Art Deco, similar to the Chrysler building in New York, with gargoyles peering down at Light Street. The roof was copper, which had quickly turned a beautiful green, interlaced with thick beams plated with pure gold.

The bank began to have financial difficulties early in the Depression and never reopened after the 1933 bank holiday. Its failure resulted in a bankruptcy totaling a figure in excess of $20 million (approximately $374 million in 2018 dollars) in losses.

The shareholders of banks that went bankrupt in the 1930s not only lost their entire equity investment in the bank, but they could also be assessed for as much as the par value of their stock to repay the debts of the bank – par value being the price below which a corporation would not issue shares, as stated in their prospectus. This price was deemed by the court to be $5 per share in the case of Baltimore Trust Company.

At that time, a bank's officers and directors were normally held accountable for a bankruptcy. In the case of Baltimore Trust Company, the court held the directors to be personally liable for their grossly negligent acts, in that they failed to exercise proper supervision. The directors were some of the leading businessmen of the city, according to the *Baltimore Sun*. Yet they were all sued. In total, another $250,000 ($4.7 million in 2018 dollars) was eventually extracted from the directors – a stark contrast to the lack of a similar fallout after the financial crisis in 2007–2008. According to the Center for Public Integrity: "In the seven years since the financial crisis, none of the top executives at the giant Wall Street banks that fueled and profited from the housing bubble have been personally held to account" (Alison Fitzgerald, May, 22, 2015).

The bank vacated 10 Light Street in 1935. Shortly thereafter, Maryland's Public Works Administration moved in, but the rest of the building remained empty. The only tenants that were expanding in those days were either government agencies or those directly connected with local, state, or federal government. As a result, when Mr. Price signed the lease in mid-1937, he had plenty of potential space for expansion. Although he no doubt hoped that some of his accounts would continue to employ him at his new firm, this was not a certainty, given the economic environment. He was not closely tied to the Baltimore social elite, which was an important source of potential new clients.

The building was in an ideal location, close to the Baltimore financial establishment, but not directly in it, as befitted his concept for the new firm. The structure was elegant and thus served to impress potential new clients. Mr. Price's office, which had been designed for the president of Baltimore Trust Company, had beautifully crafted woodwork, including many broad wooden mahogany shelves, a big desk, heavy, carved chairs, and a comfortable leather sofa. The views were impressive, facing east over the city and the financial district to the outer harbor. To the south, he looked toward the bustling inner Baltimore Harbor. The other, much smaller corner office also faced the outer harbor and would soon be occupied by Charles Shaeffer. The rest of the staff was in the open area in between, except for Marie Walper, who had her own small office next to Mr. Price.

Ms. Marie Walper. TRP archives.

His official separation from Mackubin, Legg did not take place until June 30, but Marie followed him to their new quarters before his resignation in early June. She was the first employee, although she initially didn't receive any salary. She well understood his frustrations at Mackubin, Legg, as well as his ambitions for the new firm. It was a real vote of confidence in Mr. Price that she would leave the relative safety of her old job, at the age of thirty-three, to join his new firm in the midst of the Depression, especially as she knew that the new firm would operate based on a concept that had only lost money at Mackubin, Legg. Her spouse offered her some security, as he had a good job as a salesman at the H. J. Heinz Company. This extra income would come in handy in the future. When the firm's income failed to cover expenses in its early years, she would not only be able to forgo her own salary, but to loan the firm a little money. She would voluntarily do so on several occasions, to cover items such as modest Christmas bonuses, for which Mr. Price would later give her full credit in recounting the early history of the firm. In his journal, he mentioned that she once offered to lend her Christmas Savings Club money.

On the morning of July 1, 1937, Mr. Price would have punched the button beside the ornate brass elevator door for the express to floor twenty-nine. The firm was born with an official announcement in the *Baltimore Sun*. There was a great deal to do immediately after Mr. Price and Marie took over their new office. First came the legal structure of the new firm, for which Mr. Price chose a sole proprietorship. He wanted to be clearly the boss from the outset. In the most diplomatic but positive manner, he and Marie had to quickly notify Mr. Price's clients of his change in status before it became known through Baltimore's efficient rumor mill. Finally, they had to move twelve years of his personal files and papers from one office to another. (Mr. Price was a strong believer in extensive records, charts, bulletins, and correspondence.)

A month later, Isabella Craig also made a break from Mackubin, Legg. She became the head, and only member, of the T. Rowe Price Statistical Department, where she tracked the financial data of the firm's investments. She lived at home with her parents and was thus better able to handle the financial risks of the early years of the firm. Walter H. Kidd and Charles "Charlie" Shaeffer, the two other official founders, did not arrive until January 3, 1938. Peter Shaeffer, Charlie's son, recalled that their delay in joining was entirely due to money and not a lack of confidence in the new company. Mr. Price could not afford to pay them through the organizational phase of the business, before there was any income coming in. Charlie and Walter had no other source of income, and Charlie had recently married his childhood sweetheart, Ruth Smyser. It must have been a particularly difficult decision also for them to leave a relatively secure nest and fly over to the thin, shaking bough on which Mr. Price's new firm perched.

Isabella Craig. TRP archives.

It is also possible that the six-month delay in employing Walter and Charlie could have been due to external events. When Mr. Price opened his door for business on July 19, 1937, the Dow Jones Industrial Average stood at 170. On August 14, it rose to 190 and then proceeded to plummet, in the sharpest bear market since 1929. It appeared to bottom in November and, by year-end, it was holding its ground at 120. The market ultimately bottomed on March 31, 1938, at 99. This sharp decline possibly gave Mr. Price some brief second thoughts about his timing in starting a new business.

The two men who joined the new firm in January would prove to be nearly as essential to its success as Mr. Price himself. It's worth going into some detail about each of them – their background, education, and skills.

Charlie Shaeffer was born in Bridgeton, Pennsylvania, outside of York, in 1910. His father started out as a tobacco farmer and at one point had his own cigar company as well, but he lost everything in the crash and the Depression. Charlie enrolled at Penn State on a scholarship that included working three separate jobs simultaneously. He also supplemented his income by playing bridge for money. He won his varsity letter on the tennis team, and was president of his senior class and of his fraternity, Alpha Sigma Phi. After graduating in 1933 with a degree in commerce and finance, he got a scholarship to the Harvard Business School from an anonymous member of the Harvard Club of Maryland. Following his first year at Harvard, he needed a job and Mr. Price was looking for an analyst for the summer at Mackubin, Legg. In 1934, there were very few such jobs. The unemployment rate was at an all-time high of more than 25 percent, not including those on part-time work or forced to work on reduced salaries. The two men hit it off. Like any good aspiring salesman, Charlie could sell himself well in an interview. He was hired by Mr. Price to work in the research department at Mackubin, Legg on a study of the tobacco industry, a subject with which he was very familiar. When he graduated with an MBA from Harvard in 1935, he was offered a job as a full-time analyst at Mackubin, Legg. He ultimately found himself working closely with Mr. Price as he began to bring in clients to the Investment Management Department. Charlie soon moved out of research to become an investment counselor, working directly for Mr. Price.

Charlie Shaeffer. Property of Pete Shaeffer.

In most ways Charlie and Mr. Price were opposites, and the differences were why they made a good team. Charlie was outgoing and informal. He was very good with people and made friends easily. Mr. Price was much more reserved and prickly. Charlie was intuitive; Mr. Price was analytical. It was very natural for Charlie to become involved in new sales while Mr. Price focused on investment strategy and investing.

In an interview conducted for the firm's fiftieth anniversary, Charlie said that he was attracted to the investment counseling business because he saw how his family's life was totally upended by the poor investment decisions made by his father in 1929. "To me," he said, "it seemed that there should be some way to invest money in securities more intelligently and with greater prudence, which would reduce the magnitude of investment losses by the investment public in a poor economy, and afford the possibility of producing a good return over the longer term."

Walter H. Kidd, the third founder, was born in 1907 on a farm near Columbus, Ohio, where his father raised dairy cattle and had commercial orchards. His first jobs were farm chores, including feeding the chickens and acting as a midwife for the cows. He attended local schools and then Ohio State University, majoring in architectural engineering, and graduating in 1929. He worked for two years at the Mount Vernon Bridge Company in Ohio designing bridges, until it was clear the bridge business was closing down in the Depression. He needed a new career

Walter Kidd. TRP archives.

and fast. A friend suggested Harvard Business School. The last bridges were being designed at Mount Vernon just as Walter entered the gates to Harvard Yard.

When Walter graduated, the economy was worse than it had been when he entered. He received no job offers. He was, however, interviewed by Joe Bent, then the head of equity research at Mackubin, Legg, who, due to a mix-up, had arrived at Harvard to do recruiting interviews after the class had graduated. Walter was one of the few still on campus. He didn't hear back from Joe, but wrote him a thank-you letter and took a short consulting job offered by a professor at the business school. The letter seemed to trigger Joe's memory and he offered Walter a job at Mackubin, Legg as a securities analyst.

Unlike Charlie, Walter was quiet and introverted. He had little social life outside of occasional dinners with the Prices and the Shaeffers. He was, however, smart, hardworking, and detail-oriented. He developed into a first-class financial analyst. He did not marry, so he had considerably more free time than Mr. Price or Charlie. In addition to being an analyst, he assumed the roles of acting administrative director, chief financial officer, and in-house counsel, as well as the young firm's only research analyst. He kept the company's books, filled out the various forms and filings associated with the business, took care of those internal matters for which a lawyer was not required, and performed the research on most of the companies in client portfolios. He was a valuable, busy, but uncomplaining member of the team.

Walter was also the secret soul of the company. Growing up in the heart of the Midwest on a farm, he had developed a strong sense of right and wrong. In his mind, there were no gray areas and no cutting of any corners. Although Mr. Price always operated to the highest business and personal ethical standards, there were moments he might weaken, such as when faced, for example, with endless government red tape or a quicker way to get a complex job done by cutting a few perfectly legal corners. At such times, there would erupt from a corner of the boardroom table, "Just a damn minute!" and a forceful Walter Kidd, his face flushing red, would face down the boss. With Walter, there was only one way to do business – the right way – even if it took longer and was more expensive.

Walter, in the opinion of the author, who worked under him for his first several years at the firm, was one of the best true analysts in the business at that time. He could very accurately ferret out the pluses and minuses of a corporation as an investment. He generally left the exact timing of an investment to Mr. Price's finely tuned sixth sense. They made a very good team. He had left Mackubin, Legg because he shared Mr. Price's belief in a long-term, research-driven investment approach. He had recognized that when Mr. Price left, the firm would move to a more common, trading-oriented investment format where real long-term research was not so important.

The economy in the 1930s would continue to follow the stock market closely. Industrial production fell almost 30 percent from mid-1937 throughout most of 1938. Unemployment jumped from 14 percent in 1937, a recovery low, back to its 1933 Depression high of 25 percent, in what would be called the "Roosevelt Recession." With an eye toward the 1940 presidential election, Roosevelt reversed his move toward financial conservatism, and once more increased government spending. The economy recovered, and the stock market obediently followed, rising through much of 1938. It would not decline again until the end of 1939, when World War II got underway in earnest in Europe.

Mr. Price knew that a new investment counseling organization had to clearly show above-average performance if it was going to be successful. To demonstrate this, he had established three "model accounts," as he called them, prior to starting T. Rowe Price. The performance of these portfolios would be the company's major sales tool at its inception.

The first model portfolio was started many years before in 1926, just after Mr. Price and Eleanor were married. It was called the Diversified Investment Portfolio, and was Mr. Gherky's personal account. It consisted of growth stocks, corporate and tax-free bonds for income, and short-term government securities for safety of principal. Its objective was growth of both principal and income. It represented the account of the typical wealthy businessman – which would be the firm's primary marketing target in those early years.

The second model account was the Price Inflation Fund, begun in 1934 to test Mr. Price's Growth Stock Theory. Its goal was growth of capital and, secondarily, growth of income. Later, the name was changed to the Growth Stock Fund and, after 1937, consisted primarily of Eleanor's inheritance from her father.

The third portfolio was the William D. Gherky Trust Fund, originated in 1937. Following Mr. Gherky's death, the Philadelphia's Girard Trust

Company was the trustee, but it was managed by Mr. Price, and consisted of growth stocks and tax-free funds. It was structured as a "balanced" portfolio (roughly 50 percent stocks and 50 percent bonds).

Over the years, Mr. Price would start a number of such model portfolios to test different investment strategies. In several cases, much later, they became the basis of new mutual funds. Each of these model portfolios was carefully tracked and updated on a daily basis by the firm's statisticians. The three original model portfolios were also audited by outside firms on an annual basis.

With these model accounts Mr. Price could, therefore, at the outset of the firm, present a longer-term record of performance, whether the new client's goal was growth of capital and income as befitted a wealthy executive, a more aggressive portfolio of all growth stocks geared for a younger person, or a more conservative trust account, where income and preservation of capital were both important. In coming years, he would often refer to the performance of these model portfolios in his bulletins to clients and newspaper and magazine articles. They were, thus, vital marketing tools.

In addition to these track records, the new firm had one other initial asset. Some of Mr. Price's old clients did indeed come to the new firm and entrusted it with at least a portion of their assets. As the performance of these portfolios continued to be strong under the management of the new firm, these clients added more capital over the years. In the same pattern that he had developed at Mackubin, Legg, they became some of his best salesmen, recommending him to their friends.

In years to come, Mr. Price would often remind younger counselors that, by providing superior performance to their clients and excellent account service, they were creating their own future potential income stream. Service to the customer was the single most important concept that was drilled into every new employee: "If you treat the customer right, he will reward you longer term." He frankly told new counselors that should they ever decide to leave T. Rowe Price for any reason, a significant number of his or her clients would follow, lending him or her credibility and instant cash flow. Mr. Price's other important keys to his success were a reputation for integrity, professionalism, and innovative, strategic thinking.

The original stated goals for the firm appear modest in retrospect, but they seemed very optimistic at the time. These were to ultimately attain

399 accounts, generate $310,000 in fees, and manage the business with a staff of 28. Such a firm would be profitable, produce reasonable salaries, and Mr. Price could easily manage it. Running a large organization or generating a large stream of income was never important to Mr. Price. His ultimate goal was simply to produce the best investment record in the country. He was very competitive. He liked to win. In later years, many of his young associates would feel that he was even competing with them! There were few words of encouragement or congratulations for a good job, only suggestions that they could have done better if they had but followed his ideas more closely. He was indeed a tough boss. Fortunately, Walter or Charlie was there for a pat on the back and the mention of a job well done.

Chapter Seven

"CHANGE: THE INVESTOR'S ONLY CERTAINTY"

M r. Price's first article, "Change: The Investor's Only Certainty," was written when he was still at Mackubin, Legg & Co. It was deemed "too liberal," as he recorded in his journal, so the firm would not allow it to be published on their letterhead. This was another clear indication of the philosophical disagreement building between Mr. Price and many of the partners. The article was finally set into a pamphlet and privately published after he had launched his own firm. Having left Mackubin, Legg, he was free to have the work recognized as completely his own. It is indeed a remarkably perceptive and important discussion of the major long-term trends at work in the world, and how they impact the investor. Most of its basic concepts are as true today as they were then.

When I asked Mr. Price much later how he managed to develop such an enduring long-range forecast, he used a favorite water metaphor. To paraphrase his response:

It was easy. All you had to do was find a comfortable tree stump beside a creek that eventually flowed into the ocean. You might sit on the stump and observe the creek. You at first would notice the strong current that was flowing down the creek towards the ocean, as it had for thousands of years. If you sat long enough, you would observe that there was a tide at work that changed direction on a regular basis. Sometimes it enforced the current when it flowed with it; at other times, it would significantly slow the current down. Finally, when the wind came up, you might note that waves were created on the surface of the creek. They could be large or small, depending on the force of the wind, but these waves would suddenly appear and just as quickly disappear. Sometimes they would run generally with the current and sometimes against. The timing of these waves was unpredictable, as was their direction. Sitting longer on the stump by the creek, you could begin to contemplate how the natural rhythm of this little scene might pertain to life and investing.

The following are some of Rowe's views and opinions as expressed in a booklet published in 1937: "Change: The Investor's Only Certainty." They are as true today as when he wrote them in the 1930s:

When the Czar of Russia was murdered, when Hitler became dictator of Germany, when Franklin D. Roosevelt was elected President of the United States, it was front-page news. People realized that important changes had taken place. Few people, however, recognized that these historic events were but outer evidences of political, social, and economic forces, which had been working for a long time. These forces are constantly at work, have a direct bearing on business trends and consequently influence property values and security prices.

SOCIAL: The gradual evolution of civilization, reaching vital importance in time of great depressions, are given too little consideration by businessmen and investors.

POLITICAL: A greater influence on intermediate trends in business than on the long term or major trends, and frequently over-emphasized by business interests.

ECONOMIC: The most important of the three in its influence upon security prices.

While there is a distinct relationship between these forces, each influencing the other, the economic trend has a greater influence upon politics (both national and international) than politics has upon economics.

SOCIAL TREND: The social trend over the centuries is reflected in the rise of the masses to power and influence. It is necessary to recognize that for centuries there has been a gradual liberation of the common people from slavery, both social and economic, through the slow process of civilization and education. This social movement, for obvious reasons, takes different forms in different countries. The timing and velocity of the movements vary as do climatic conditions and racial characteristics. The thought that must be kept constantly in mind, if perspective is to be maintained, is that the common people are having and will continue to have a more important part in making the laws that govern social and political life and will continue to acquire a larger share of economic wealth and power in the future.

POLITICAL TREND: The political trend is influenced by both the economic and social trends. Too frequently, we place undue emphasis on the importance of politics as a factor, making for prosperity or depression. The rise in social consciousness of the masses of common people gives expression through political action. The overthrow of monarchies and decline in power and influence of royalty are evidence of this trend.

It is often stated that democracies are on the way out; that the trend is towards Fascism, Bolshevism, or other forms of dictatorship. This is merely an intermediate reaction in a major political trend from the rule of kings to the rule of the masses. The overthrow of royalty in Russia and Germany, for example, was too abrupt. The common people had insufficient education and experience in self-government to cope with the economic crises following the World War. Stalin and Hitler were in power because they are supported by public opinion. When the masses want a change of government, these leaders must change or be overthrown. Russian and German politics are different because their social and economic backgrounds are different, but both nations are headed towards governments that give the common people a larger share of economic wealth and power.

ECONOMIC TREND: In order to get a clear perspective of the economic trend, consider that people are divided into two groups – the "Haves" and the "Have Nots". The "Haves" are those who have economic wealth and political power and are usually spoken of as the conservatives. The "Have Nots" are those who are constantly fighting to acquire economic and political power, and are often termed liberals, progressives, or radicals. This contest is continuous all over the world. If we think in terms of nations, we group Germany, Italy, and Japan as "Have Nots," scheming, plotting and fighting if necessary to gain a larger share of power from those nations which may be regarded as the "Haves," and are represented by Great Britain, France, the United States, and Russia. The natural tendency is for those nations with a common objective to ally themselves against their common enemy. The nations which are in power are constantly trying to keep their adversaries at odds, as they fear a united front on the part of the "Have Nots," particularly when they represent aggressive peoples.

It is simpler to give the proper weight to current events as they take place if we recognize these underlying trends in international politics. We should recognize that the nations grouped as "Have Nots" are going to acquire a larger share of the wealth and natural resources by one means or another. Italy's first step was a conquest of Ethiopia and Japan's was a conquest of Manchuria. Germany will acquire territory preferably through peaceful means, but unless the "Haves" make concessions, it will be through military force. There may be some doubt as to the timing, but little doubt as to the final outcome.

Regardless of one's nationalistic or political prejudices, a better distribution of the world's natural resources is constructive if accomplished without war and it is a step toward increased trade and world prosperity. Unbalanced purchasing power and the mal-distribution of wealth restrict trade.

So far, this represents a sketchy outline of the social and political trends as they apply to the world in general. If we consider our own country, we find that a similar social and political revolution has been taking place here, although very dissimilar in the external aspects. Our revolution is against what is called "privilege." As in other parts of the world, the economic and social status of our people is the motivating force behind politics. The "New Deal" is the result of this movement and not the cause. It is an attempt to correct maldistribution of economic wealth and political power that have been abused.

In the United States, a democratic nation, there has never been a political dictator, but during the past hundred years of rapid growth in industrial wealth, economic rulers or financial dictators came into power, with the result that too large a share of the nation's wealth was controlled by too few men. The recent Depression was the culmination of several generations of economic oppression. We did not experience a bloody revolution like Russia or Spain, but the "New Deal" is a social and economic revolution. The term "Economic Royalists" is unpopular, nevertheless it is very expressive of the situation which existed in the past decade.

We are now in the process of a great *change* in the kind of *capitalism* rather than in the *overthrow* of *capitalism*. The movement has been hastened by the [First] World War, which brought millions of people from all over the world together in a common cause. It has been hastened by inventions, which have made most of the people in the world neighbors. Rapid communications and transportations have increased the velocity of this change. A correct appraisal of these Social, Political, and Economic changes is essential to the successful management of invested capital."

TRENDS AT WORK IN THE 1930s: "Basic New Deal Concepts"

Greater centralization of power in the Federal Government to impose a broad program of national economic planning. Regardless of one's personal opinion about the increased power of the federal government and of the difficulties which will be encountered in the attainment of this end, this is a natural trend in the social evolution, hastened by rapid communication and transportation. States' rights and private ownership will gradually be subordinated over the years to federal control, both political and economic …

Redistribution of wealth. Redistribution of wealth is going on all over the world, as it has done ever since the world began. Wealth breeds indolence and selfishness, and the possessors adopt conservative or defensive tactics. Gradually the more virile or aggressive peoples revolt and fight to obtain or regain a larger share. In this country, the redistribution is being conducted under the leadership of the Federal Government. We call it the "New Deal." It is actually a "Re-Deal" of wealth. This process seems to be a necessary one, although the method is most objectionable to the "Haves." ... The Government, by increasing taxes on the wealthy, is taking away from the "Haves" and giving it to the "Have Nots" in one form or another – relief, bonuses, public works projects, agricultural payments, etc. At the same time, the dollar has been devalued and prices are being inflated with the result that the creditor is having his principal depreciated in purchasing power value. It is a long, complicated process, but in simple language it is an attempt to redistribute wealth by lawful means, taking it from the "Haves" and giving it to the "Have Nots." Ultimately, it will lead to more even distribution of wealth and increased trade until finally too large a share will again gravitate into the possession of a few, and the whole process will start all over again. The only difference is that the game will be played with a different set of rules by a different set of people. The basic fundamentals will be the same and they can all be traced to the weaknesses and strength in the character and habits of human beings.

More equalization of earning power. While many important financial powers will dispute this, one of the causes of the Depression was the concentration of too much wealth in the hands of a few who could not spend it all and thereby create demand for sufficient goods to keep the factory wheels turning.

Smooth out business cycles. It may appear that the Government is being successful in this undertaking, but the success will only be temporary. The most that can be done is to defer the sharp upturns and downturns in the business cycles or lengthen the time preceding a boom or collapse. Artificiality is not lasting. Nature eventually wins and nature requires resting periods as well as growing periods. You may take a stimulant and conceal your fatigue temporarily, but eventually collapse, rest and recovery follow whether plant life, animal life, human beings, or business, which is conducted by human beings and influenced by nature. It is absurd to think business cycles can be smoothed out, unless you think man can permanently overcome the laws of nature.

Regulation by taxation. Which is just another way of redistributing the wealth – taking it from the "Haves" and giving it to the "Have Nots."

FORECASTS BASED ON CURRENT TRENDS

Wealth will be subjected to increased taxation, corporations of great size and influence will be special targets, and their profits will be restricted by various means.

Labor will receive a larger percentage of corporate income in the future than in the past.

The greatest opportunity for profitable investment will be in new and rapidly growing industries employing relatively few people and less subject to government interference.

Foreign trade is very likely to be very slow in recovering to pre-Depression levels.

Inflation will cause the dollar's purchasing power to decline during the years ahead, resulting in the rise of the cost of living to a higher level than existed during the post World War era."

Back to the stump with Mr. Price:

If you decided to cool off from the heat of the setting sun with a swim in the chilly waters of the creek, you would soon discover that when you swam with the current (which represented the long-term social trends based on human nature) you would drift easily and comfortably, pushed by the current. If the tide was flowing in strongly against the current, your progress would be slow and you might have to readjust by paddling a bit to reach the other shore. Such are the changing political trends.

The wind might have come up a bit more than you realized. This could also make your return passage a bit more difficult. Occasionally, the wind might change direction, helping rather than hindering you along your way. This is similar to the ever-changing economy.

At the end of the day, the creek would have taught you some important lessons about nature and investing.

We will come back to thinking about the future in Chapter 16 and try to guess how Mr. Price might perceive the world today, how he might modify his 1937 advice to long-term investors in the twenty-first century, and what he might anticipate for the next five years or so.

Mr. Price updated this original bulletin in 1963. There were, however, only modest changes, considering the amount of water that had flowed down the creek in the intervening years, the huge storms with high winds that had pummeled its shoreline, and the occasional trees that had fallen, temporarily blocking its course.

1. He added to the long-term social trends a movement toward internationalism and away from the isolation that existed prior to World War II, due to increasingly high-speed transportation between nations and the ability to instantly beam pictures and information from one end of the earth to the other. The Internet is a recent further extension of this trend.

2. He predicted that the growth of pension and retirement funds would tend to push up the premium of stocks that best qualify for these funds, such as the larger, premier growth stocks.

3. Because of the increasing power of the Federal Reserve and Congress in regulating all aspects of banking, he saw that banking was no longer under the control of private interests and was not a fertile field for investing.

4. He felt that the socialization of industry was increasing. More businesses were being run for the benefit of the masses, not the stockholders. Examples that he listed were utilities, transportation, communications, and health care.

5. Although inflation remained a major economic "current" for Mr. Price throughout his entire investing career, it became his major focus in 1963, as inflation rose due to accelerating government spending on both the Vietnam War and, later, President Lyndon Johnson's social programs. This will be a focus in our later discussion of long-term trends today.

Chapter Eight

THE FIRM'S ADOLESCENCE AND WORLD WAR II, 1938–1942

Despite the founders' initial optimism, business was disappointingly slow in the beginning. The large fluctuations of the stock market in 1938 didn't help and the economy remained weak. Still, by the end of the year, the new firm had accumulated $2.3 million in assets under management, which was entirely made up of Mr. Price's old clients. Most of these accounts were accepted at low, beginning fees. At that time, Mr. Price said, a $6,000 account and/or a $250 annual fee were gratefully accepted. In fact, the firm would frequently take on a new account and manage it for free in order to demonstrate to a reluctant potential client that the value they added more than justified the fee. Revenues for 1938 were only $6,090, Walter would recall in an interview, which took place as part of a series of interviews conducted for the firm's fiftieth anniversary. Fortunately, these fees were paid in at the inception of the management contract for work to be performed during following twelve months. But this income, and any further new accounts, had to cover the rent, a small amount of advertising, general office expenses, and salaries for the whole year.

Living expenses were low. As Walter said in the same interview, Mr. Price had been making $12,000 at Mackubin, Legg, which was considered a generous executive compensation, but that first year he did not pay himself a salary. Walter was paid $3,400, a little less than the $3,600 Mr. Price had promised him when he joined at the beginning of the year. Charlie, who by then was an expectant father, was paid his full $2,400 salary.

Early TRP accounting book. TRP archives.

On February 17, 1938, Mr. Price wrote "State Capitalism," one of his more prescient client advisories. He regularly wrote such reports, had them typed, printed on the firm's pale-yellow paper, using an Addressograph-Multigraph machine, and sent out to clients and important prospects – as he had "The Investor's Only Certainty." He defined state capitalism as the government control of capital, as opposed to private capitalism, which had been the norm before the New Deal. Under state capitalism, he explained, the federal government raised capital through taxation and the sale of government bonds backed by the credit of the U.S. Treasury Department. In 1938, 20 agencies were authorized to raise their own funds outside of the control of Congress. Half were backed by the full faith and credit of the U.S. Treasury. The government was also actively engaged in furnishing capital for farming, banking, railroads, utilities, insurance, home building, and more. With these financial entanglements by the government came increased government regulations and control. Nineteen thirty-eight marked the end of the New Deal, as far as legislation was concerned, but the seeds it sowed continued to grow in future decades.

The second step of state capitalism, as Mr. Price would describe in more detail in the November 1981 issue of *Forbes*, is the regulation of wages, profitability, prices, and working conditions for various industries through state public utility commissions and federal agencies, such as the Environmental Protection Agency, the Public Utility Commission, and the Federal Communications Commission. The final move to true socialism, according to Mr. Price, comes when the government actually takes over complete control of the means of production, which has only occurred, so far, on a localized scale in the U.S., in projects such as the Tennessee Valley Authority created in the 1930s.

In order to make ends meet that first year – as the sole owner of the business, he had to cover all the expenses – Mr. Price had to borrow from his life insurance policy. Toward the end of 1938, he approached Walter and suggested that they change to a partnership, wherein he, Mr. Price, would be the managing partner. Neither he nor Walter would take any salary out of the partnership, but they would both work for "time credits." A time credit had a value equivalent to the individual's salary. When the partnership started to make money, these credits would be repaid. At the end of 1938, Rowe had accumulated his full $12,000 of salary in credits and Walter had $3,600, having put the $3,400 he had already received in cash back into the business. Charlie needed the money, so he did not take any time credits in the first year. He would eventually join the partnership in 1940, but by that time both he and Walter had teaching jobs and could better afford drawing time credits instead of a salary. Charlie, with more expenses, taught two courses, one at the College for Teachers at Johns Hopkins (later McCoy College and now known as the Johns Hopkins School of Education) and the other at the Baltimore College of Commerce. Walter taught at the College for Teachers.

Even with these arrangements, cash remained tight. Mr. Price wrote in his journal on May 15, 1939: "We don't have enough money to pay the rent and the advertisement that appeared in the *Sun* paper last week. It is not a very comfortable feeling to have paid out all you have borrowed and still have insufficient capital to pay salaries and bills each month."

He had high hopes that a series of five articles publicly describing the Growth Stock Philosophy for the first time, which he had been asked to write for *Barron's,* would generate some sales. He had them reprinted, and they became important new sales material sent out to various prospects. A small amount of business did indeed begin to trickle in from these mailings, some initially and more later.

From Mr. Price's 1939 series of articles on Growth Stocks in *Barron's.*

Mr. Price continued to insist that he, Walter, or Charlie had to meet the management before the firm invested in a new company. According to Walter, Mr. Price wore two hats at these meetings: One was to perform the necessary research, because of his strong belief in the importance of management; the other was to be aware that he might find a future client or two from these visits. When the firm was contacted by an executive from the Sperry Corporation, after he had read one of Mr. Price's articles in *Barron's,* Mr. Price accompanied Walter on the research trip. As Walter mentioned in the same series of interviews for the firm's fiftieth anniversary, the firm's clients already had an investment in the stock of Sperry, which was growing rapidly just prior to World War II, based on a gyroscope-controlled autopilot system. The executive, his family, and the Sperry Corporation pension fund all eventually became clients of Mr. Price.

New business generated a nice pickup in sales in 1939, with cash revenues rising some 66 percent to $10,538. This, however, was still a long way from break-even. Mr. Price continued to take no salary.

When Hitler invaded Poland on September 1, 1939, what would develop into World War II began. England and France declared war on Germany within two days. Mr. Price wrote a memo two weeks later entitled, "This Is No Time to Be Panicky." He had been surprised when the market went up strongly on the war news, and the public began buying steel, nickel, and aircraft stocks that Mr. Price called "The War Babies." Investors were, at the same time, selling companies that Mr. Price believed were excellent long-term growth stocks. He wisely suggested in this memo to sell the War Babies into the rally and thus build up a cash reserve for buying growth stocks later. The market declined from the peak of this rally on an irregular course, reflecting the events of the war, and would hit a low on April 28, 1942.

Mr. Price followed this investment advisory with another in October: "Why We Advocate Greater Liquidity at the Present Time." Like other forecasts he made at times of enormous uncertainty, these proved to be remarkably accurate. Rumors were the rule of the day and hard facts very difficult to ascertain. Censorship of the news was being imposed, not only in Europe, but also beginning in the U.S. Newscasts and newsreels were cranking out propaganda rather than accurate facts. The economic indexes were greatly distorted by the war effort.

Mr. Price's forecasts from the memo:

1. The United States is unlikely to engage in the European War for at least one year because we are totally unprepared in a military sense, and the majority of our people favor neutrality. [The Neutrality Act of 1939 would be passed by Congress in November.]
2. Rearmament in this country will continue until we are prepared, whether war is long or short.
3. Profits to shareholders will be limited, regardless of a war-induced prosperity, because, in most instances, increased labor costs and taxes will soak up a large share of the resulting earnings.

4. Great Britain and France are decadent nations and their leaders are less confident of victory than propaganda would have us believe.
5. War will quicken the trend to state capitalism.

Hitler and his then-ally, Russia, quickly divided up Poland, after which the war paused for months. The British media took to calling the conflict the "Phony War." On April 9, 1940, the German army invaded Norway and captured Denmark. On May 10, German forces swept through Belgium, Luxembourg, and the Netherlands and attacked the French army at the north end of the Maginot Line. France was conquered in six weeks and German forces entered Paris on June 14, 1940.

Reflecting this disastrous turn, the Dow Jones Industrial Average fell to 114 in May 1940, a drop of 23 percent. On May 15, 1940, Mr. Price distributed his investment bulletin "War on Capitalism and the Investor's Battle for Survival." He wrote, "Hitler is waging a war in Europe to overthrow capitalism following the New Deal that has been striving successfully to redistribute wealth in this country." He insisted that the investor must "FIGHT TO SURVIVE!" He must have both a strong offense and a strong defense. "The investor," he continued, "should mount a strong defense, [which] consists of building a well-balanced list of common stocks, which represent a share in the best brains and natural resources of this country. Investors should hold these stocks and with funds from short-term government bonds, be in a position to buy securities at depressed prices."

It was excellent advice for those trying times and well to remember in a future major crisis.

With Europe largely conquered in two months, Hitler turned his attention to England. That campaign began by air and British cities began to be bombed daily. Despite extreme attrition of pilots and airplanes, the Royal Air Force ultimately won what Churchill called the Battle of Britain, handing Hitler his first defeat. After this significant German setback, as Mr. Price had predicted, the American people did wake up. Congress allowed the sending of crucial aid to England under the lend-lease program that was passed in early 1941.

Unfortunately for investors, Congress also passed the first of several excess profit tax bills. The purpose of such legislation was both to limit the profits a company might receive from the war, such profits being considered unpatriotic, and to raise needed cash for the country's war efforts. A base period was selected before the war effort began. Any profits earned above this base level were taxed at a high rate. This had a particularly onerous impact on growth stocks. In normal times, such companies are by definition growing more rapidly than other companies. Monsanto Chemical Company, then an excellent growth company, would have had its 1939 earnings reduced an estimated 22 percent and probably would have suffered a similar decline in its stock if the excess profits tax had been in effect for the whole year, according to Isabella Craig's in-house analysis.

The concept of an excess profits tax goes back to World War I. Enacted in 1917, by 1918 the tax ranged all the way up to 80 percent. It was repealed in 1921, despite powerful attempts to make it permanent. During World War II, four such bills were passed, with the excess profits tax becoming a major issue affecting the performance of growth stocks. In the 1940 bill, the tax ranged from 25 to 50 percent; the final such bill, in 1943, carried taxes up to 95 percent. Fortunately, growth stocks were only affected for a limited time, as the excess profits tax was repealed in 1945, just before the war ended. Mr. Price carefully tracked the impact of these taxes for all of the companies owned by his clients, with constant communications on this subject.

After Germany conquered Yugoslavia and Greece in April 1941, Mr. Price issued an investment bulletin on May 22 titled, "Why Buy Stocks Now?" This was probably the last thing any investor was then considering. The market had been going down for four years, reflecting Hitler's takeover of country after country. Very few investors had any profits left in their portfolios. Mr. Price pointed out that under the surface, however, things weren't so bad. Earnings and dividends both were near ten-year highs. Dividends paid by the stocks in his income and capital growth portfolio (his father-in-law's account) were yielding eight percent on initial cost, while bonds (most investors' choice then) were only yielding a little more than three percent.

Investing during a war was indeed a tricky process. Not only was there the possibility of ultimate defeat at the hands of the enemy, but also the government had assumed almost total control of the economy: essentially, the government decided which companies would do well and which would not. The free economy ceased to function as "State Capitalism" took over.

On June 22, Hitler launched a massive invasion of the Soviet Union, a disastrous move that would ultimately cost Germany the war. Japanese aircraft attacked Pearl Harbor on December 7, 1941. Congress declared war on Japan on December 8, with one dissenting vote.

The Japanese attack had severe ramifications for the young firm. Walter applied to the Army Air Corps soon after Pearl Harbor and was accepted as a lieutenant. Expecting that he would quickly be inducted, he gave up his apartment and did not sign up for the firm's 1942 partnership. But the Army was not as efficient as Walter. At the end of March, he had no job and no place to stay. For a while, he tried sleeping on Mr. Price's office couch. Ruth Shaeffer finally took pity on him, and Walter moved into the Shaeffers' tiny white house on Joppa Road, with the baby sleeping in the bathtub. Pete, their eldest child, said the experience was like "having an elephant in the closet," with "Uncle" Walter in close proximity. On May 1, 1942, Walter was able to report for duty and was assigned to Wright-Patterson Field in Ohio, to ensure that aircraft engines were available when the planes on the production lines were ready for them.

Charlie had a bad back and was married with two children, so he was exempt. Mr. Price was married with children and too old at almost 44. Isabella Craig felt it wasn't patriotic to work with an investment management firm during the war, and she got a job with aircraft manufacturer Glenn L. Martin in their statistical department. As a result, for the duration there was no official research department at T. Rowe Price.

On December 3, 1941, Mr. Price wrote in his journal that the firm only had $11.07 in the bank and that Marie had not been paid during November. When they went out to lunch for their partners' meeting that week, the bill was $3.00. Mr. Price and Charlie, after finding a few coins in their suit pockets, each managed to come up with their $1.00 share, but Charlie had to lend Walter the money. Later that month, Marie had to lend the firm her Christmas savings to pay their bills at the end of the month.

The firm went into hibernation for most of the war. Mr. Price and Charlie did a bit of prospecting and ran a few small ads, but not too much happened. There was even some talk about closing up shop, but everyone had committed too much time and energy for that.

The one good thing about losing staff was that expenses dropped. In 1942, Mr. Price was finally able to pay himself $2,700 in salary as the market began its climb up from its depths. Revenue for the firm rose to $19,000 for the year. It was able to get a few new accounts as the war wore on. Particularly important was Mr. Price's meeting and ultimate friendship with J. Jefferson (Jeff) Miller, II, the executive vice president of the Hecht Company department store chain, which was domiciled in Baltimore. Jeff Miller became a client, followed over the next few years by the Hecht Company, as well as other members of the Hecht family. By the end of the war, these accounts had added significantly to assets under management.

On January 6, 1942, Mr. Price wrote another *Barron's* article, "Growth Stocks in War Time Markets," an update to his series in the late 1930s. He pointed out the superior long-term growth of his 1939 list of growth stocks from 1929 to the present, but even he had to admit that growth stocks had not distinguished themselves in the recent war years. They had been penalized by the excess profit tax and an economy that rewarded companies heavily involved in the war effort. In later years, Mr. Price would stress that growth stocks could only be expected to perform over a longer time period of approximately seven to ten years, which would include a business cycle. He did concede in the article that some "decadent" (meaning old, declining, and being replaced by other newer industries and technologies) industries like railroads and steel might actually be a good investment in the present environment. For one of the few times in the history of the firm he conceded that these companies might actually outperform his favorite growth stocks, at least over the short term. These industries were flourishing in the war effort, with their earnings rising rapidly. Growth stocks were not only handicapped by the excess profits tax but, in many cases, actually suffered from the war effort, if they were involved in such areas as consumer products. Mr. Price was always a realist. He once again recalled the mantra in his first publication, "Change: The Investor's Only Certainty."

However, he seems to have quickly changed his mind a few days later. In "The Investor Faces War, Peace, and Inflation" an investment advisory that he mailed to clients, he clearly stated that he did not advocate actually investing in any of these "over-the-hill-but-temporarily-rejuvenated-companies," even though they might be performing better for the moment.

He did express concern about postwar inflation. In a theme that he was to develop much more fully in the late 1960s, he suggested modest investments in real property and natural resource companies, as a hedge against inflation and as a supplement to growth stocks. Mr. Price also pointed out in this 1942 investment advisory that the worst holdings in an inflationary environment are bonds, bank deposits, cash, and life insurance. Such "paper dollars" will not protect an investor's purchasing power when the dollar falls. He further pointed out that although growth stocks were declining in value, they were doing much better than inflation or the market indexes. Ever the consummate advocate, he mentioned how well their dividend income was growing.

The long wartime bear market bottomed out on April 28, 1942, ending the day at 93. The stock market would rise from that level for more than 25 years without a major decline. Mr. Price sensed this and began to turn his attention to the likely economic environment after the war and what industries and companies would be the best investments at that time. In June 1942, he produced "Looking Toward a Post-War Economy," another of his remarkably prescient advisories. At the time, the U.S. and its allies appeared to many to be losing the war on both the European and the Pacific fronts. Japan, like Germany in the late 1930s, was marching from victory to victory throughout the Pacific. Although the Battle of Midway, fought that same month, would mark a fundamental change in the war against the Japanese, most Americans were thinking more about building a bomb shelter than investing in the stock market.

In this advisory, he listed a number of new "currents" that would be pushing the economy in the postwar world and in which he would begin to invest:

1. *Scientific.* Communications and travel will shrink the globe. New chemical products will enhance the economy.
2. *Internationalism will replace Isolationism.* The United States will have to accept leadership in world affairs.
3. *Socialization.* The new world order will be more democratic and less imperialistic, both politically and economically.

These forecasts turned out to be remarkably accurate. His few clients at that time benefited substantially, as did his family accounts. By the end of June 1942, the market was at 103. In less than three years, by June 3, 1946, it would more than double to 211. Once again, Mr. Price had hit *the* time to buy stocks.

Chapter Nine

THE GROWTH STOCK PHILOSOPHY

Mr. Price was well known in investment circles for the development of the "Growth Stock Philosophy of Investing." By rigorously following this deceptively simple philosophy, he established one of the best investment records in the financial industry during his investment career. The Growth Stock Theory remained fundamentally unchanged during his forty-five-year career as an investment manager, although he did modify the wording slightly and added some additional sentences over the years. His final version would appear in a brochure published by the firm in April 1973: "A Successful Investment Philosophy based on The Growth Stock Theory of Investment." (Mr. Price often used Growth Stock Philosophy and Growth Stock Theory together. Theory meant the facts behind the overall philosophy.) "A growth stock," the brochure read, "is defined as a share in a business enterprise which has demonstrated long-term growth of earnings, reaching a new high level per share at the peak of each succeeding business cycle, and which gives indications of reaching new high earnings at the peaks of future business cycles. Earnings growth per share should be at a faster rate than the rise in the cost of living, to offset the expected erosion in the purchasing power of the dollar. The goal is a portfolio of companies that will double earnings over a 10-year period. It is believed that dividends and market value would do the same."

His Model Inflation Portfolio began in 1934, while he was with Mackubin, Legg. It consisted entirely of growth stocks. The first time, as far as is known, that Mr. Price used the term "growth stock" was

October 8, 1935, in his journal, in describing his attempt to persuade the partners at Mackubin, Legg to establish the mutual fund to be run by his investment management department. Its objective was the building of capital in stocks, which would "be of premium quality and have prospects for growth." He later changed the portfolio's name to the Model Growth Stock Portfolio. He first fully defined his "Growth Stock Theory of Investment" to the public in the series of the five articles published in *Barron's* in 1939, setting out a complete program for managing the financial assets of individuals and institutions. As he later often repeated to new clients and new counselors, "Most people would not consider building a house without hiring an architect to carefully design it before beginning construction," he wrote, "yet these same people might well spend the equivalent amount on a portfolio of stocks and bonds with no plan at all. As a result of this lack of planning, most security portfolios are unbalanced and contain numerous securities which are not suitable to the particular individual or his goals."

The cornerstone to his approach to creating a portfolio was "building that portion of the portfolio dedicated to common stocks with 'growth stocks." The second article in the *Barron's* series defined growth stocks as "shares in business enterprises which have demonstrated favorable under-lying long-term growth in earnings and which, after careful research study, give indications of continued secular growth in the future."

Every word in this first definition had a particular meaning. The investment was not in paper stocks, but in shares of a business. The business had a "favorable growth in earnings," as it was growing faster than the economy as a whole. It promised "continued secular growth" over the long term, not just a brief acceleration in growth from a new product or a boost from momentarily favorable business conditions. "Careful research" was required to ensure that growth would continue "into the future." The Growth Stock Theory of Investment emphasized careful research, not just the hope or belief that this superior growth would go on for years.

When the Growth Stock Theory was first expressed, it was considered to be quite radical. The focus of investors at that time was on the preservation of capital and current yield. It's hard to blame them after the sharp recession in the late 1930s, which had been preceded by the long dark days of the Great Depression. Very few investors were anticipating much appreciation of their remaining capital in 1939.

The basic rationale for the Growth Stock Theory goes back to Mr. Price's early days working as a chemist for DuPont, where he began to compare DuPont to his first employer, the Fort Pitt Stamping & Enameling Company, and how the two companies rewarded their investors and employees. In a tough competitive market with no special advantages, other than its location near its suppliers and customers in Pittsburgh, Fort Pitt Stamping & Enameling had been an education in what not to do. It might very well have provided a modest return to its investors if it had not been for the 1919 nationwide steel industry strike, which put it into bankruptcy, but any gains would have been small and relatively short-term. Its weak balance sheet and limited profitability made it vulnerable to even small changes in its marketplace. In addition, its manufacturing technology was not unique and its plant was old. The best option for its investors would have been to sell out to a competitor.

When Mr. Price arrived at DuPont in 1920, the company had been in business for more than 100 years. It was growing rapidly into new markets, with up-to-date, efficient manufacturing plants. Having long since diversified out of its original business of gunpowder and explosives, its major businesses then was chemicals and chemical products, which were increasingly technology-driven. As the leading innovator in the chemical industry, DuPont backed up its position with large investments in research and development. Its fiscally conservative management was generating enough cash to pay for its rapid growth, as well as providing steadily increasing dividends to its shareholders.

"The real fortunes in this country," Mr. Price would point out in "What is a Share in a Business Worth?" a speech given on October 25, 1947, "have been made by the people who put their capital into a business that had a future, worked hard, invested more capital, and stayed with their investment throughout the years – depression and boom alike. Such names as Ford, Du Pont, Rockefeller, Duke, Carnegie, Woolworth and many others that are well-known to all. These names are legend. Fortunes are still being made in this way," he continued, "and you and I can participate in their continued growth as their shares are available in the market."

In a speech given in January 1954, titled "What Growth Stocks Have Done for U.S." about his early experiences at DuPont, he recounted how he was "impressed with the fact that the able and farsighted management encouraged its employees to become shareholders, and paid bonuses to key personnel in the form of DuPont stock. During the years that followed my entrance into the investment business in 1921," he continued, "I observed that DuPont's stock, which always seemed too high to buy when compared to most other stocks, grew and grew and grew in market value. Another observation which made a lasting impression was the fact that those employee shareholders who tried to make a greater profit in the stock of their own company, by selling when they thought it was too high and then trying to buy it back at lower prices, did not do as well as those who held their shares throughout the market cycle."

In 1965, Mr. Price published a list of seven growth stocks that he had bought and held since the 1930s and 1940s. All had remained growth stocks over this entire time period, and all proved to be outstanding investments: DuPont, Black & Decker, 3M, Scott Paper, Merck & Co., IBM, and Pfizer. Their average appreciation had been thirty-six times. He understood that no one could be 100 percent right in picking growth companies, but he believed that results would be "spectacular" if you were just 75 percent correct. According to the records of his model accounts, his own performance in selecting growth stocks was better than 80 percent over his lifetime of investing. He both bought and sold stocks gradually over years, at prices based on what he felt the shares were worth. Selling a company completely was done only after he became convinced that it was no longer a growth stock. His expected holding period for any investment was measured in decades. By gradually buying and selling at calculated prices, the exact timing of purchases and sales was not an issue.

One of the most important concepts underlying the Growth Stock Theory of Investment is the study and understanding of life cycles, both the life cycles of industries and of individual companies. When he was first developing the Growth Stock Theory, Mr. Price also called it "The Life Cycle Theory of Investing" as he outlined in his *Barron's* article of May 15, 1939. He noted that companies go through a life cycle similar to the human life cycle. Both have three important phases: growth, maturity, and what he termed "decadence." In the May 22, 1939, *Barron's* article, he states there is a well-understood risk of a decline in health when one reaches maturity, and much more toward the end of life. Insurance companies understand this and demand a higher premium to insure the life of a person fifty years old than they do for one who is twenty-five, and an even higher fee at seventy-five.

In much the same way, Mr. Price noted in the 1939 *Barron's* series that common sense indicates that investment in a business offers more gain and less risk while the earnings are growing strongly than when they reach maturity and decline. Often, however, the decline can be masked by a rising business cycle and be hard to detect.

"It is easy to grow in a fertile field," he wrote in the June 5, 1939, *Barron's*, "whether a seed of corn or a company. Just as weeds will impede the growth of the corn, so will competition impede a company." A fertile field is free of intense competition and such impediments as government interference. "No matter how good the farmer and how hard he works," he said, "his output and his profits are limited if the soil is thin and rocky."

It was important to continually monitor the fertility of the entire field and not just the results of an individual company. An early warning sign can be a decline in growth of an industry's dollar volume, particularly if unit sales are still rising. This would indicate that the price per unit was falling and a sign of lower profitability for the companies participating in the industry.

Because of his emphasis on management, Mr. Price continued throughout the time that he ran T. Rowe Price and Associates to require that all companies in which the firm invested be physically visited at least once by a firm analyst before making an investment, and on at least an annual basis thereafter. This practice is generally maintained to this day at the company. During this visit, the analyst should meet several members of management, including, if possible, the chief executive officer, in order to discuss the company's outlook and to assess the management team.

Assessing management is not easy. It takes a lot of experience and exposure to many different management styles and practitioners. A stock analyst needs a good ear. How are the analyst's questions answered? With perception and understanding, or is it a canned response? How thoughtfully does the CEO present the company's projected growth in terms of product life cycles, financials, people, and material resources? If this is not a first visit, how had management met its prior forecasts in terms of product introduction and projected unit and dollar sales? What is the competition doing that might threaten the company's position and what is management doing in response?

Growth companies can arise in new dynamic industries, in an old company with a major new vigorously growing product, or through a change in management. A growth company can also be a specialty company, outside of any single industry, like 3M, which produces a great variety of unique innovative products for many markets.

The second important financial criterion for judging whether a company is a good investment, after growth of sales, is its return on invested capital. DuPont was the pioneer in developing this concept, and it was a major factor in its success. Most companies in the 1930s – and even today – measure profitability by their profit margin, or how much money they make, after all expenses are deducted, on each dollar of sales. This is a good way to compare companies in the same industry, but it can't determine how much a company is really earning, how fast it can grow, or how long it can stay in business.

For example, when shopping for a savings account, the most important factor is the annual return, assuming equal financial strength of the institution. A 4-percent savings rate would be better than 3 percent, all things being equal. In a similar vein, managers at DuPont were required for many years to undertake only those projects that would earn 20 percent or better on the estimated required capital. This limited the company's focus to the few projects that could meet this high hurdle rate, and it adequately allowed for the inherent risks of any new project that could involve many millions of dollars of up-front capital and marketing costs.

Another reason for the 20-percent return was subtler. If DuPont earned a 20-percent return on its invested capital after taxes, it could grow its plant and equipment at a 20-percent rate, which, in turn, would support a 20-percent growth in sales. Even after paying out a comfortable dividend, DuPont could easily sustain a 15-percent rate of sales growth without borrowing any money. This is twice the minimum return that Mr. Price hoped for a portfolio of growth stocks. Many fast-growing, otherwise successful companies have spun into bankruptcy because they did not pay attention to this important metric. They hit their sales targets but ended up drowning in a sea of debt because of an inadequate return on capital.

Finally, the focus on a 20-percent return kept DuPont continually looking for profitable new products and businesses that would continue its rapid growth in sales and earnings into the future. From the firm's research and development, old, maturing businesses and products were constantly being replaced with exciting new emerging stars. DuPont at

122 years old in 1920 would have felt much more dynamic to the young chemist than the eight-year-old Fort Pitt.

Other characteristics of typical growth companies were outlined by Mr. Price in a speech on Growth Stocks given at John Hopkins University in November 1954:

> "Intelligent research: Intelligent research which develops new products or new markets for existing products or both is essential if a company is to forge ahead in a rapidly changing world. It is easier for a company to realize high profits on new products than on old ones which have attracted competition.
>
> Strong finances: Strong finances enable management to take advantage of opportunities to expand when business is good and avoid bankruptcy or financial stringency during bad times.
>
> Favorable profit margins: Profit margins before taxes must be reasonable, the percentage varying with the industry. A profit margin of 6 percent is satisfactory for a company which retails consumers' goods such as food, clothing, and low-priced sundries, having a rapid turnover. On the other hand, a 10 percent–15 percent profit margin is necessary for the company which sells high-priced products and has a low turnover.
>
> Favorable management-employee relationships: Employees should be well paid, but the total payroll should be relatively low and easily adjusted to changes in business volume."

As he emphasized, it is difficult in actual practice to determine just when a company goes from its growth phase to maturity and then into decline. The best time to sell is usually just before this final slowdown begins. The problem is that temporary slowdowns can occur because of the natural decline in a business cycle, product transitions, material shortages, or a number of other temporary factors that can hide what is really going on. In his May 15, 1939, *Barron's* article, Mr. Price used the railroad industry as an example of a business that was reaching maturity. Before the First World War it had been growing strongly. Ton miles, defined as a ton of freight carried one mile, almost doubled in the decade prior to the war, but due to competition from trucks and pipelines, they slowed after the war and dropped dramatically during the Depression. Profits dropped even more precipitously.

A more recent example of a maturing industry is the personal computer market. As described by Statista, both units and dollar sales grew vigorously through the 1980s and into the 1990s, doubling every five years. Even in the Great Recession of 2008, units grew more than 30 percent between 2011 and 2016. Worldwide PC shipments began to decline in 2012. This decline in unit shipments continued into the first quarter of 2018 with a 1.4 percent drop, according to Gartner.

This doesn't mean that all companies in the industry stopped growing or become unprofitable. Some switched into another business or had a special niche that remained uncompetitive. Apple introduced the iPhone in 2007, which turned into a huge business. The company also enjoyed a group of loyal followers for its computers with its own special software, allowing it to maintain prices. Its sales and earnings continued to grow. As Fortune reported in April 2013, "Apple sells only 5% of the market but takes home 45% of the profit." Clearly that profit came out of the hide of the other 95 percent of the PC companies.

HP maintained a growing, very profitable printing ink business throughout, which hid the early problems of the PC business. Dell had a unique, low-cost marketing model that kept it profitable while others of the 95 percent (above) went into the red. It also moved into the rapidly growing field of low-cost servers, which gave its earnings a short-term boost after 1998. By 2002, however, it was desperately trying to diversify out of the PC business. Its profit margins began to weaken in 2004 and the stock entered a long nosedive in 2005. It ultimately went private in 2013 at about a third of its 1995 price.

In the meantime, Gateway, IBM, Act, Packard Bell, and others either died or merged. It was a mature business and not the fertile field that characterized growth stock investment.

One of Mr. Price's favorite expressions in the late'60s was the old saying, "A bird in the hand is worth two in the bush," as described in his August 9, 1978, bulletin, "Investing for Future Growth of Income and Market Value." In his analogy, income is similar to the bird in hand. It is dollars that can be spent. Capital appreciation is like the two birds still in the bush. You don't have it until you sell the stock. He felt that too many members of the firm were buying stocks for their appreciation and forgetting about the importance of dividends in a portfolio.

Growth stocks usually pay small dividends because of the many opportunities to invest shareholder capital. Rapid growth in earnings, however, does provide a rapid growth of dividends, even from a smaller base. A classic growth stock, with a 2-percent yield at purchase, growing 10 percent, would produce a 4-percent annual yield on the original invested capital in a little more than seven years. At the end of fifteen years, this would rise to a 10-percent annual return on the original capital. Mr. Price's Model Growth Portfolio showed an increase in dividend income of 222 percent from its inception in 1934 through 1950, earning in that year a 20-percent dividend return on the original cost of the portfolio. It is still not well understood by the investing public that a low-dividend-paying, fast-growing stock can pay out far more dividends over time than a bond or a high-yielding but mature company. "In order to rationally buy or sell a growth stock," he wrote, "it is necessary to 'determine what a share in a business is worth.' There is usually quite a bit of difference between what a stock sells for in the market and what that share is worth as a business. There is no magic mathematical formula for determining this price. To a great extent, it rests on experience."

He did, however, develop a few guidelines related to stock value, based on his many years in the investment business. He believed that stock valuations were directly related to interest rates on bank deposits, U.S. government bonds, and corporate bonds. A 5-percent government intermediate bond yield would produce a reasonable stock valuation of ten times earnings, twelve months ahead, for the average company in the Standard & Poor's Industrial Index. If interest rates dropped to 3 percent, the average stock should be valued at twelve times earnings, twelve months away. The lower the bond yield, the more investors will pay for the same growth of earnings of a company.

If the company was a growth stock, he believed it was worth twenty to twenty-five times earnings, twelve months in the future, if interest rates were 3 to 5 percent. He believed that a growth stock is basically worth twice what the average company stock is worth. This will be discussed more in Chapter 16.

Stocks continually move irrationally higher or lower than what they are determined to be worth, and can be over- or undervalued for long periods of time. Mr. Price always advised patience, buying or selling over time at what is believed to be reasonable prices, always being alert to pounce and buy more if the opportunity presents itself. News events can often provide excellent buying opportunities.

Once a position is established, if a stock then moves to a significant premium over what it is deemed to be worth, he suggested that the stock be sold until the total cost of the stock position, plus capital gains taxes, is realized. The profit, he believed, should be reinvested in long-term government bonds, or good-quality corporate bonds for safety and income. The profit represented by the shares left in the portfolio should be allowed to continue to grow in value until the company matures and is no longer considered to be a growth company. These shares effectively have no cost.

This simple but very important rule in managing assets has led to astonishing results. In a private paper titled "Performance: T. Rowe Price Growth Stock Fund versus Model Portfolios," dated April 15, 1969, Mr. Price pointed to gains in a number of the companies in his model portfolio: by 1968 more than 10,000 percent for 3M, which was first bought in 1939; nearly 12,000 percent for Merck, first bought in 1941; more than 5,000 percent for IBM, bought in 1949; almost 7,000 percent for Avon, bought in 1955; and Xerox almost 4,000 percent, bought in 1960. Of course, many other companies did not fare as well, but like a well-pruned garden, by letting the strong companies continue to grow and cutting back on the weak, the strong companies can come to dominate over time.

A carefully planned investment program, tailor-made for each investor, was an important part of the Growth Stock Philosophy. As Mr. Price would often remind clients: "Everyone wanted to maximize his capital growth while ensuring the safety of his principal, and realizing a high stream of income." In many of his in-house client advisories, he would go on to say that as this is obviously not possible, each portfolio should contain a portion of short-term government bonds, which provide the ultimate protection of principal. There would also be a part of the portfolio in tax-free bonds or corporate bonds to supplement income. Such bonds will vary in price due to fluctuations in interest rates. The remainder would be typically in 30 to 40 growth stocks, to give adequate diversification.

He further suggested that an individual's portfolio should reflect current and future cash needs, as well as maintaining some liquidity for emergencies. A younger person might design a portfolio tilted toward rapid growth of principal, with cash requirements adequately met by a rising salary. Marriage, children, college education, and retirement all create changes in the mix of stocks and bonds, with more liquidity required with age and approaching retirement.

Many modern market theorists believe that fluctuations in a company's stock price are a measure of its risk. The more a stock fluctuates in price, the riskier it is. In Mr. Price's view, risk is only financial, reflecting the likelihood that a company might go bankrupt. To him, Fort Pitt was clearly very risky and DuPont was not. To the modern theorist the reverse would be true. Because Fort Pitt had little or no market or trading, it had very little volatility, therefore it was not considered "risky." DuPont had an active public market, which could be volatile on occasion. Contrary to common sense, DuPont would be considered by this school of investment to be much riskier.

To determine the true risk of a company, Mr. Price believed in carefully analyzing the balance sheet, its return on capital, and the quality of its management. The fluctuations of the stock price of a growth company simply provided welcome investment opportunities. If sales by speculators forced the price well below what he perceived to be its fair value, it could be profitably bought at bargain prices. When it was pushed well above this value, it should be trimmed to recover his cost. If Mr. Price were alive today, he might find the current market, dominated by short-term traders, to be a good environment for making money, using the longer-term Growth Stock Philosophy. The focus on the near term by most investors can create large swings in stock prices. For example, if one quarter's earnings fall far short of most analysts' expectations, a stock might fall well below what it's worth, looking out five or ten years, thus providing a profitable buying opportunity for long-term investors.

From its beginning in 1934 to the end of 1972, assuming the reinvestment of all dividends, Mr. Price reported that his model portfolio of growth stocks rose more than 2,600 percent in value. The Dow Jones Industrial Average was up 600 percent over the same time frame. Dividends for the portfolio rose 600 percent. The Cost of Living Index (CPI) only rose 205 percent. This was an outstanding record during a particularly challenging time in the stock market, featuring the Depression, World War II, and the postwar economic transition, as U.S. industry changed from producing weapons to consumer products.

As we shall see, in the decades following World War II, Mr. Price's Growth Stock Philosophy would become world-famous for its superior stock market performance.

■ Chapter Ten ■

POSTWAR ERA, 1945–1950

On April 30, 1945, Hitler fatally shot himself in the head with his Walther pistol in his bunker beneath the streets of Berlin. Soon thereafter the Germans surrendered and the war in Europe was over. On May 8, President Truman and the Allies declared V-E Day (Victory in Europe). The first atomic bomb was dropped on Hiroshima on August 6 and the second on Nagasaki on August 9, the same day the Russians invaded Manchuria. Japanese Emperor Hirohito took over control of the country from the military and announced Japan's surrender by radio on August 14, to "save mankind." The following day, V-J Day, Truman addressed the nation about the Allied victory, and the official surrender was signed on September 2.

Mr. Price had drafted an investment bulletin to clients prior to these major events and then attached an addendum outlining their possible impact. He began this attachment with his usual understatement by noting, "Important events have taken place since the last bulletin on February 1945."

From an investment perspective, this quick end to the war would both reduce the U.S. gross domestic product (GDP) as production tapered off for war materials, and create economic dislocation as factories switched from war to peace production. This could cause a business slump when the war was finally over. During the war, the government controlled the economy, distorting prices with controls, allocations, and taxes. During peacetime, the consumer once more would become the most important factor in the economy, and the free market would set prices and determine demand in its usual inscrutable manner. In between these two economic states was what he called the "reconversion," during which strong cross currents could create severe fluctuations in the stock market and the economy

He well remembered what happened after World War 1. As has been presented before, a small recession began in March 1919, which was partly attributed to the large number of soldiers returning home, all looking for jobs at the same time. They were strongly resisted by the unions, which resulted in disruptive strikes. In 1920, a conservative government was elected into office. President Harding encouraged the Fed to raise interest rates sharply and rein in the money supply to bring down the high existing rate of inflation. High excess profit taxes on corporate earnings, levied during wartime, were left in effect. These moves caused the economy to rapidly contract into the recession of 1920.

Having been laid off from DuPont during this recession, Mr. Price was painfully aware of the impact of this "reconversion." He believed that there was a high probability this might well happen again after the even larger World War II. He was not alone. Many economists also realized that such transitions can be rocky, and some companies, like Montgomery Ward, held off planned postwar expansions because of economic concerns. As a result, it ultimately fell far behind its major competitor, Sears, Roebuck.

Overall, after-tax corporate earnings had declined for the entire duration of the war, due to the excess profit taxes, price controls, and material shortages. Corporate earnings indeed fell sharply in 1946, as Mr. Price had predicted, due to the costs of transition from war to peace. The GDP dropped significantly in 1946, making it the worst one-year recession in American history.

Yet the stock market did not fall as he expected. The Dow Jones rose, following the end of the war, to a peak in May 1946. In June, Mr. Price published a bulletin, "Opportunity Versus Accomplishment," in which he made one of his few professional apologies: "It is always easy to see in retrospect how one could have done a better job. We know now that if we had been less cautious, higher profits would have resulted."

He should have waited to put this bulletin out. Only three months later the market did finally break, dropping more than 20 percent from its high. This decline gave him the opportunity to savor a bit of vindication, and to recommend that clients fully invest their reserves in selected growth companies.

With perfect hindsight, Mr. Price should have followed his own oft-quoted advice and not tried to guess the short-term swings in the economy or the stock market. Yet he was human, and he was immersed in the sharp short-term fluctuations of a drastically changing postwar economy. If asked what his greatest failing was during his career as an investor, he might well have said, "selling too soon." He might have added, although modesty might have prevented it, that because of his uncanny insight into the market and the economy, he saw much further into the future than most investors. It was this foresight that made him usually early in both selling and buying.

What truly separated Mr. Price from other investment managers, and created his remarkable long-term investment performance, was his systematic research to find the very best growth stocks and then staying with them. The excellent growth of sales and earnings of these companies was translated into a rising stock price that outperformed the growth of the market averages over long periods of time, as mentioned in the last chapter. The DuPont employees who did the best in building retirement portfolios, he recalled in a memo, "What Growth Stocks have Taught Us," written January 1954, were not "the employee-shareholders who tried to make greater profits in the stock of their own company by selling when they thought it was too high and then trying to buy it back at lower prices … [but] those who held their stock throughout the market cycle."

Despite the fact that World War II was much more traumatic for the U.S. than World War I, the difficult economic transition following the first war was not repeated after the second for a number of reasons. The country had been attacked and the future had looked very bleak in the war's early years. Even with these challenges, the U.S. helped win World War II by pulling together as a country and utilizing its huge production capacity. This created a feeling of great optimism in the country about its ability and future that was not true following World War I.

The federal government under President Truman was much more oriented towards the health of the economy than that of President Harding had been. There was no attempt to immediately balance the budget with taxes and high interest rates. The excess profit tax was eliminated, even before the war was over. The Fed was quite accommodative. Price controls were eliminated. When the Consumer Price Index increased sharply, price controls were reinstated by Congress, but the bill was ultimately vetoed by Truman. Most importantly, there was a huge underlying suppressed demand from consumers following the long Depression and lengthy war. This forced savings over many years, and the liberal credit advanced by the Fed, fueled a boom in consumer products.

This is not to say that some of the same problems following World War I did not reappear. More than 20 million soldiers, and those employed to build military equipment, found themselves without jobs between August 1945 and July 1947 (Walter Kidd temporarily among them). Military spending also dropped like a rock from a peak of $100 billion in 1944 (45 percent of GDP) to $24 billion (nine percent of GDP) in 1946.

The unemployed were scooped up by optimistic companies looking forward to a bright postwar economy. By the end of 1946, the unemployment rate was about 4 percent. This was actually on the low side for a noninflationary business expansion.

The free market made amazing progress in the postwar period, surprising Mr. Price as well as most economists. Auto manufacturers, for example, quickly switched from making tanks and planes back to producing automobiles in the same plants. They produced 1946 and 1947 cars by using the dies and parts that they had kept in storage from 1941. Declining government spending, while it did affect some defense equipment suppliers, freed up resources to supply the postwar boom in consumer goods. Led by consumer spending, the U.S. GDP began a strong twenty-year postwar advance.

Mr. Price had stated in "Forecast for February 1945 and Beyond" (February, 1945) that the United States could no longer afford to be isolationist. "The long-term trend in world affairs is towards internationalization," he stated. "Modern communication and air transportation have forced the people of all nations to be neighbors and, as such, to have a community conscience in social, political, and economic affairs. Isolationism as a national policy is unrealistic. "The other countries are watching the United States," he continued, "and until they are assured that the [U.S.] government is ready to underwrite a recovery and commit the United States to world leadership, they are not likely to pursue an international policy." He went on to forecast that during the early years of reconversion, the United States would have to furnish capital to other nations to allow them to buy from us.

As if following Mr. Price's suggestion, in 1948 President Truman signed the Marshall Plan, an initiative to aid Europe's recovery from the ravages of World War II and named after Secretary of State George C. Marshall, former U.S. Army Chief of Staff. In total, the United States gave away $12 billion between 1948 and 1952. This was a significant amount when compared to the U.S. GDP of only $158 billion in 1948. At a commencement speech at Harvard on June 5, 1947, Marshall said,

"It is logical that the United States should do whatever it is able to do to assist in the return of normal economic health in the world, without which there can be no political stability and no assured peace." Mr. Price would have agreed wholeheartedly.

The Marshall Plan did indeed act as a catalyst for Europe's recovery. The plan also added to the U.S. economy, as it was the only major industrial nation to survive the war with its production facilities intact, and thus had the ability to produce the products and natural resources needed under the Marshall Plan. Marshall also realized that Germany, as the historic flywheel of Europe's economy, needed to be funded despite widespread political reservations. By 1948, Germany had received very little aid and its people were starving. Some powerful voices, such as Henry Morgenthau, the Secretary of the Treasury under Roosevelt, advocated reducing it to a pastoral state. Reason, however, prevailed, and Germany was added as a recipient of aid from the Marshall Plan.

The plan also helped to invigorate Europe by reducing artificial trade barriers and beginning the cooperation that ultimately became the European Union. With all of these major positive economic and political forces at work, it was a very good time to be an investor in the stock market. Despite the firm almost closing down at the outset of the war, T. Rowe Price and Associates had actually not done badly. Thanks to the rising market and some new accounts, revenues had risen from $16,449 in 1941 to $48,000 by 1945, according to Walter's interview for the firm's fiftieth anniversary.

Mr. Price and Eleanor must also have been swept up in the enthusiasm. In December 1945, they moved to a 4,000-square-foot home, just a few blocks up the street, at 219 Wendover Road. This house was handsomer and had a bigger yard, providing plenty of room for the children to play, for Rowe to grow his precious roses, and for Eleanor to have her own garden.

A new postwar addition to T. Rowe Price and Associates was John Ramsay, Jr., who joined before the end of 1945. He was honorably discharged soon after the surrender of Japan, having served in U.S. Naval Intelligence aboard several aircraft carriers in the Pacific. Prior to the war, he had worked at a few small, quality Baltimore brokerage firms and was just what Mr. Price was seeking. None of the founders had any particular contacts in the clubby upper reaches of Baltimore society. John was a ranking member of that group, serving on many prestigious Baltimore boards of directors. His father, John Ramsay, Sr., had been president of the National Mechanics' Bank for many years and became vice president and chairman of the board following its merger with the Merchants' National Bank. John had gone to the private Gilman School. At Princeton, he played football and roomed with several men from Baltimore who later became prominent businessmen in the city. He was outgoing and an active member of the Baltimore Bachelors' Cotillion, which held an annual dance for the city's socially prominent debutantes. Although older than Walter and Charlie, he fit in well with the three founders and significantly helped build the firm's image and prestige locally. At his own insistence, he worked for a salary, which was directly based on the business that he brought in. He helped in the recruiting of several fine young employees from the Baltimore community, who rose to important positions within the firm.

John B. Ramsay joined the firm as a vice president in 1945. TRP archives.

Walter returned early in 1946 from the Air Force at Wright-Patterson, where he had been for the entire four years of his war service. The final member of the senior professional staff to join the firm a few months later that year was Loring Cover. He came in as both a research analyst and a counselor, with responsibility for several accounts that he brought with him. Loring had also graduated from Princeton and had worked at Bendix in Baltimore during the war. Like John, his initial salary was based on the fee income that he brought with him.

In March 1946, the three founding partners entered into a new partnership. With Walter having been absent from the firm during the war, there was quite a bit of jockeying back and forth concerning the respective percentage interests in the partnership, as Walter described in an interview for the firm's fiftieth anniversary. Charlie and Mr. Price had kept the business going while Walter was off at war. The initial offer Walter said was a low 5 percent stake in the partnership, and one could imagine his heated reply! But, in the end, Mr. Price and Charlie recognized Walter's tremendous value to the firm. He continued to be most of the research department, with some help from Loring. He also again headed both the firm's finance and administrative departments, which Marie happily surrendered. In effect, he was again wearing three hats. Walter was also a known quantity to both men, having worked closely with them for more than seven years before his departure. They ultimately settled for an 80/10/10 split.

The firm incorporated on January 2, 1947. Based on the minutes of the first board meeting, directors included the three founders and Eleanor. The first board meeting was held at the firm's offices on Light Street. When things were especially bleak, Eleanor had loaned the firm $10,000, which was still outstanding. With husband and wife holding 50 percent of the votes, it was likely Mr. Price would not be outvoted. It was clear that he intended to continue to be the boss. Charlie received 999 shares of stock in the new corporation, while Walter got 900 shares. The negotiations for percent ownership in the new company must have been ongoing until the last minute. Mr. Price was granted an annual salary of $12,000. Both Walter and Charlie received $6,000. John and Loring were made vice presidents and received salaries of $3,600, plus an additional amount equal to 50 percent of the fees generated by their clients. Charlie and Walter were also made vice presidents.

Three other employees received shares of stock, including Marie and Isabella. Dorothy Krug, an assistant counselor working for Charlie, also became a shareholder. She had joined in 1943 when Isabella left to help the war effort at Glenn L. Martin. Mr. Price felt strongly that a company's management team should each have a meaningful amount of stock so that their goals were the same as those of the shareholders. In the same way, as described in "The T. Rowe Price Story" published for employees in December 1974, he felt that it was important for "the people who provide the service in a service business, such as T. Rowe Price and Associates, which is dependent upon the knowledge, judgment, and integrity of the people who provide the service, that ownership be provided" to them. After the firm incorporated in 1947, stock was regularly given out as a year-end bonus. As shareholders, these employees became true members of the team with a vested interest in the firm's profits and growth.

In Mr. Price's words, "The key to business success is a reputation for integrity, professionalism, and innovative thinking." Building a firm of the highest character was a core belief. Employees would be hired based on "integrity, honesty and loyalty." "The success of a firm such as ours," he said, "is dependent on its personnel. The most important asset we can have is goodwill, which is so difficult to build up and so easy to lose. Personality, tact, and a desire to help and please clients are essential.... Each member of the staff is expected to play his particular part well, but to be ambitious to win through teamwork rather than through personal selfish gains at the expense of his associates.... Members of this team must possess a sincere desire to produce good results and obtain the public's goodwill." He only promised an average salary, with a bonus at the end of the year for a job well done. An individual's income would grow over time as the firm grew. This would be augmented by the growth in value of their shares.

His focus on the clients' well-being, as well as good communication and excellent long-term performance, slowly began to be noticed by potential clients in the postwar years. Even today, if a knowledgeable investor were asked what one word defines T. Rowe Price, the answer would probably be "integrity."

In 1949, the firm crossed a major hurdle. It became profitable for the first time in its history, earning $1,000 that calendar year, despite paying all expenses plus full salaries. The profit was generated with little help from the stock market, which had been virtually flat for the prior four years. This is a major event for any small company – the ultimate difference between success and failure. With a profit, a company can continue to exist and grow. With continued losses, its future is uncertain.

Mr. Price had bought a small farm in Baltimore County in July 1941. When asked about this purchase after the war, he said that because of his fear of inflation, he had decided to put some of his assets into land. The real reason, according to Charlie, in recounting a story about the farm to me when I worked at T. Rowe Price, was that Mr. Price became concerned that the Axis powers might win, in what was then rapidly developing into a world war. This seemed a distinct possibility to many after the fall of France and much of Europe in 1940. "Mr. Price figured if we lost the war," Charlie said, "there would be no need for investment counsel. He could just disappear with his family into the countryside and live off the land." With Charlie as a partner, who had grown up on a farm, and his family adding to the work force, they "could establish a little business by growing vegetables, maybe milk some cows, and raise a steer or two."

The farm was on 77 wooded acres, 20 miles north of the city. A stream flowed through the property. Mr. Price stored a two-man crosscut saw in a small shed. According to Pete Schaeffer, Charlie's oldest child, during the war Charlie and Mr. Price would often take advantage of a slow Wednesday or Friday afternoon and drive out to the farm. They would typically stop off for sandwiches on the way at Peerce's Plantation, a historic old restaurant. Their "mission was to deliberate business matters," Charlie recalled, "saw some locust fence posts" and enjoy the outing. Charlie said that they didn't actually saw many fence posts because Mr. Price never got the hang of the crosscut saw. They did apparently resolve a number of issues about the firm, however. According to Charlie, Walter came out once, but he got his car stuck in the mud and never returned.

Mr. Price at his farm on his "customized" stump; photo probably taken by Charlie Shaeffer. TRP archives.

Those occasional afternoon meetings served as a catalyst for regular annual planning meetings. The first was held in late 1958, when the firm was still very small, at Eagles Mere in the Pennsylvania mountains, where Mr. Price rented a house in the summer. Not much, apparently, was accomplished, other than enjoying the beautiful views and a good supper. These meetings later became more formalized in the mid-1960s, with agendas and assigned topics. As the firm became more profitable, they were held at places like Bedford Springs, the Seaview Country Club on the New Jersey Shore, and the Homestead in Hot Springs, Virginia. All of the professional staff was invited, and at each event a significant number of the young professionals would discuss and defend projects and their ideas about the future direction of the firm. There was much interaction between the seniors and the juniors, between youth and experience. The seniors were Mr. Price, Charlie, Walter, John, and, later, Edward Kirkbride (Kirk) Miller, all of whom sat back, listened to the presentations, and handed out advice. The juniors were everyone else and they organized the events, set up the discussions, and did all the work that facilitated the meeting. Supplementing the business side of the meetings were lively games of tennis and golf, with individuals carefully matched with others from different departments. Everyone had a roommate, with great creativity being exercised in putting different personalities together.

Planning meeting at Seaview Country Club, early 1960s. TRP archives.

In the evenings after supper, there were often intense games of ping-pong. Mr. Price was generally very reserved at large events, but even he let his hair down and enjoyed a good laugh or two late in the evening. He always enjoyed the company and intellectual stimulation of the young.

Robert E. Hall, the firm's oil analyst at the time and later chairman of the investment committee of the New Era Fund and then president and chairman of the Growth Stock Fund, tells the story of he and several other juniors being invited one night for dinner to the Prices' home on Wendover Road. After dinner, he and the other men joined Mr. Price in his study while Eleanor took the wives into the sitting room. Mr. Price closed the door and turned to the others. "Boys," he said, "I'd like to give you three pieces of advice: Marry smart women and, after tonight, I know you've done that; stay involved with the young, as long as they'll put up with you; and save something for the health care staff." The more Bob thought about it, the more profound this advice became.

John Ramsay, after a heated game of ping-pong, would often lead in a nice baritone a number of songs from the 1920s and his days at Princeton. Several of us would join in on the newer Princeton songs that we all remembered, but John would continue on to songs from his generation in an unabashed solo to much applause at the end. All of the best ideas came in these after-dinner sessions, when the songs had sufficiently relaxed inhibitions, so that even the most junior members felt free to contribute their thoughts. As the firm grew, these meetings became increasingly important in promoting teamwork and communication between ever-larger groups of people. They also allowed even the newest employees to mix freely with Mr. Price and other senior members of the firm. They learned about the firm's character and beliefs and heard stories about the history of the firm and the people and events that had made it a success. The camaraderie was very good for morale, gave everyone a sense of participation in the business of the firm, and a voice, even if a small one, in its direction.

In keeping with its policy of treating both men and women equally for doing a comparable job, all professionals were invited to these off-site events. Mr. Price was an early proponent of equality in the workplace. The firm remains committed today to rewarding based on the individual performance of the associate – regardless of gender – offers competitive compensation to attract top talent, and actively promotes a diverse and inclusive workplace that welcomes and values all.

■ Part Three ■

THE SAGE OF BALTIMORE

Chapter Eleven

NEW OPPORTUNITIES: MUTUAL FUNDS, PENSION PLANS, AND THE LAUNCH OF THE GROWTH STOCK FUND, 1950–1960

Almost by accident – or perhaps the reward of a divine providence for a lot of hard work and an enormous amount of patience – the firm became involved in two large growth markets in the early 1950s: mutual funds and pension plans. They were to become the major driving forces of its business in the future.

The timing was perfect. The Growth Stock Fund's stellar performance was the best advertising the company could have. Certainly Mr. Price had known about the mutual fund business, and had suggested it fifteen years before at Mackubin, Legg. But even he could not have imagined the powerful political and economic forces that would propel these two industries over the next fifty years, with his firm on the crest of the wave.

To be properly executed at that time, a business like T. Rowe Price and Associates was a high-overhead operation. A research department had to be in place, with at least five or six analysts to actively cover some two hundred corporations. A strong administrative staff was required to run the back office, keep up with government paperwork, perform the accounting, and keep track of client and fund portfolios. A well-trained and experienced assistant counselor staff was needed to provide strong support to the counselor teams in dealing with clients. Several senior counselors had to be in place to make investment decisions and directly interact with important clients.

The research department provided the basic product of dynamic, well-managed growth companies, and then tracked them closely, making appropriate buy and sell suggestions. The counselors adjusted these suggested investments to appropriately match the portfolio needs and requirements of individual clients, adding or subtracting positions from their portfolios as needed. With the costs of building this necessary overhead, profits had been minimal. This was about to change.

There were no individual "stars," such as those who still exist at many other similar financial institutions. Everyone worked together as part of the team. Similarly, there were no major differences in compensation among different categories of employees, although exemplary performance did bring a somewhat higher bonus and an increased opportunity to buy shares of company stock over time. Seniority was rewarded with an increased salary, as analysts and counselors became more valuable through experience and as the size of the portfolios they oversaw increased. Different job categories, of course, carried different remuneration. All members of the staff were encouraged and were given the opportunity to move upward, depending on interest and ability. Counselors were generally paid better than research analysts or administrators because, as Walter always pointed out to the prospective new analyst, "salesmen are generally the highest-compensated employees in any company."

Prior to 1950, remembering the destruction of retirement funds in the Depression, many corporations bought annuities from insurance companies for their workers' pensions. This was conservative and safe because the ultimate payout to employees was guaranteed by the insurance company. A smaller number of pension plans turned their money over to banks or trusts to invest in government and high-quality corporate bonds for safety and large high-dividend-paying corporations. The big banks and trusts had a virtual monopoly on this market.

In 1950, these pension plans managed by the banks and trusts totaled $6.5 billion in assets at book value, or an estimated $8.1 billion at market. In those days, it was considered unwise to count on unrealized capital gains, as these could vanish quickly. Accountants preferred to use book value, or cost, instead of market value.

Very few companies invested their pension plans in common stock in 1950. That year, however, General Motors' president, Charles E. Wilson, spearheaded an abrupt change in these practices. He proposed that pension plans invest a significant percentage of their assets in common stocks. Based on the excellent long-term return of common stocks in the ebullient postwar economy, he felt that companies could adequately fund these plans with less money, and employees could be granted better retirement benefits. Wilson's idea was that the General Motors fund would invest in the broader American economy. This concept was revolutionary at the time, and was only slowly adopted, first by corporate pension plans and, much later, by public employee plans.

According to Peter Drucker, a prominent management consultant and author of *The Pension Fund Revolution*, this new policy turned out very well for the workers overall, but it initially created a gap between the older and the younger workers. The former, who would receive their payoff in the near future, wanted their funds left in more secure investments, such as bonds or annuities, which would not fluctuate very much. Younger workers were willing to bet on the appreciation of stocks to create a greater retirement benefit in the more distant future. Fortunately, both the economy and the stock market grew for more than twenty years without a serious downturn, so both groups did well in stocks in the end.

To the dismay of labor union executives, this program did make workers less militant, according to Drucker, "by making visible the worker's stake in the company profits and the fact that the company's success in the stock market enhanced their retirement benefits." As the stock market rose in the long bull market, more corporations began to follow the example of General Motors, cutting back on insured plans and establishing pension plans with a higher percentage invested in stocks. The pension business quickly became a fertile field for financial advisors such as T. Rowe Price Associates. Over the next ten years pension assets rose more than five times to $33 billion.

By 1980, three years before Mr. Price's death, the reserve value of pension assets was more than half a trillion dollars and equities were more than one-half the assets. Total pension assets had grown an amazing 15 percent compounded since he led the company into the market with its first corporate pension plan.

Thomas L. Perkins, a well-connected corporate attorney in New York and chairman of the trustees of the Duke Endowment, board chairman

of the Duke Power Company, and a director and member of the executive committee of Morgan Guaranty Trust Company and J. P. Morgan &
Co., Inc., heard about Mr. Price and became impressed by his investment
record. As a director and a member of its finance committee, Perkins
introduced Mr. Price to American Cyanamid, a large producer of chemicals, plastics, and pharmaceuticals. Cyanamid had begun to look for
new investment management for their pension fund, which was totally
insured at that time. Following General Motors' lead, the board had
made the decision to move substantially into equities. The company
hired T. Rowe Price and Associates in October 1951 as its sole manager,
and became the firm's first major corporate pension fund account.

By year-end, the Cyanamid fund totaled $22.6 million, with 1.5
percent already invested in equities. Mr. Price took full advantage of
what he believed to be a reasonably priced equity market to continue
to significantly build up stocks. The portfolio totaled $40 million by the
end of December 1954, with the growth based on both appreciation
and cash contributions. It had taken the firm fifteen years to build assets
under management to $40 million, managing only individual accounts,
and only five years later they had quadrupled that amount.

Perkins's father, Judge William R. Perkins, had been James Buchanan
Duke's attorney and the executor of his will. Duke had accumulated
one of the largest fortunes in the United States, largely from tobacco
and hydroelectric power. Upon Duke's death, Judge Perkins became the
trustee for the estate. His son, the attorney Thomas Perkins, inherited
this position, which included being chairman of the board of trustees
of the Duke Endowment and the Duke University Endowment, as well
as chairman of the board of Duke Power. Both of these latter accounts
would come to the firm in the early 1960s, following the excellent performance of the Cyanamid pension fund. Soon thereafter, Doris Duke,
Duke's only child and, at that time, reportedly the richest woman in
the world, would also become a client. The timely arrival of these major
accounts, when both the stock market was rising and growth stocks were
outperforming the market, provided a major springboard for the firm to
expand outside of Baltimore.

The idea to create the Growth Stock Fund, which propelled T. Rowe
Price and Associates into the business of managing mutual funds, might
have occurred something like the following fictional account. The

author and Bob Hall visited both Peerce's Restaurant and Mr. Price's farm and sat by his creek on a fall day similar to the one described below:

On a beautiful late October day in 1949 Charlie walked over to Marie Walper, sitting guard outside of Mr. Price's office.

"Is he in?" he asked. "Yes," she replied. "He got in around six this morning. He's trying to write a new investment bulletin for clients."

Charlie tapped lightly on the large oak door. "Come on in," a voice replied from inside. Charlie opened the door and peeked into the dimly lit office. "Hey, Rowe [as an old friend and senior associate, Charlie was able to use the familiar term]. It's Wednesday," he said. "How about attacking a few fence posts up at the farm?"

"Sounds good," Mr. Price said. "Probably just what I need, to get some of the old brain cells circulating" They were soon in Mr. Price's new light blue Buick (his old one had fallen apart at the end of the war), driving north on Charles Street toward Baltimore County. "Should we stop at Peerce's for some supplies?" Price asked.

An hour or so later, after leaving the city's crowded streets and traveling through the late fall vistas of Baltimore County, they pulled into the gravel driveway of Peerce's restaurant. Mr. Price settled into one of the outdoor chairs at a table overlooking the Loch Raven Reservoir. The leaves had already begun to turn red and yellow, filtering the view across the water, and there was a pleasant freshness to the air as the sun warmed the dew still on the grass. Charlie bustled back from Peerce's interior with two large, rare roast beef sandwiches, with mustard, freshly picked tomatoes, and lettuce on rye.

Charlie suggested, "We have to remember to pay our bill to Mr. Lake [the owner], Rowe. It's awfully nice of him to give us the run of the kitchen. I got a twenty-dollar check cashed in our lobby, so we're loaded."

"It is nice to have the money to pay him," said Mr. Price. "Remember that time that Walter didn't have the money for his lunch? We had to pool all of our cash to pay for it, and we just barely made the $3.00 bill?"

"Charlie," Rowe continued, more seriously, "I can't tell you how pleased I was to make money last year, while paying everybody full compensation. Now I know that we are okay and that we can make it all the way."

After Peerce's, they headed further into the county, where the roads got narrower and the potholes more numerous. Road crews had not filled in all of the holes created during the long war. Mr. Price groaned as his new car bounced through some of the worst of the holes. They turned off Carroll Manor Road into a little clearing and walked down the path into the woods. They could smell the old leaves and the wet earth. They soon came upon a weather-beaten old shed where Charlie extracted a well-oiled two-man saw

Somewhat reluctantly, Mr. Price picked up a handle of the saw. "Rowe," said Charlie, "I know you are the genius in the financial world, but don't forget that I'm an old farm boy. I know it might be tough for you, but please try to follow my lead this time on the saw."

"All right," said Mr. Price with a grin. "I will give you a little time in the driver's seat."

Soon, they had seven new locust fence posts sawed and stacked near the shed. They settled on two stumps that had been cut expressly to fit their respective backsides. Mr. Price asked, "What do you think of Walter's idea about starting an investment unit trust fund to handle our clients' kids?"

Charlie replied, "I know that before Walter brings up a project, he has well researched it from top to bottom, but it sounds a little complicated with the government looking over our shoulder, and it's a little out of our skill set."

First offering of the Growth Stock Fund. TRP archives.

"You're right, Charlie," said Mr. Price. "It would be a bit of a different business, with all of the new rules and regulations from the SEC, but we really have to do something. Since the Uniform Gifts to Minors Act, I am getting pressure from the clients to handle their kid's money. Jeff Miller just called me this morning about managing the $500 he gave his son last Christmas for his college fund. We would lose money on each one of those small accounts if we handled them the normal way. We really have to put something in place. Besides, I don't know if you remember, but I suggested setting up a fund at Legg years ago. Of course, old man Legg and the other partners shot me down."

"I do remember, Rowe," said Charlie. "Maybe we should give Walter the go-ahead. We can always change our mind if he turns up something negative."

"Done," said Mr. Price.

And so, the new T. Rowe Price Growth Stock Fund was born. Walter quickly began to work on the complicated forms. He filled out all of the paperwork and dealt directly with the SEC himself. Mr. Price would quickly grow irritated at the bureaucratic tangles, but Walter steamrolled through all the issues in his methodical manner, making sure every detail was in place before he went to the next one, determined to save the firm the exorbitant legal fees normally charged in setting up a mutual fund that they couldn't afford. He personally studied all of the legal rules and regulations. The total startup cost to launch the Growth Stock Fund was only $6,000.

The fund was launched and its first board meeting was held on April 13, 1950, according to the "lost" journal. All members of the board had to own shares for the public prospectus. By the end of the next day – after soliciting all the clients for which such an investment would have been appropriate – the fund had 21 subscribers. With his small legal budget, Walter had, unfortunately, missed the rule that only 25 people can be solicited at the inception of a fund. The firm had solicited more than the limit. Fortunately, Walter and Mr. Price had paid the normal courtesy call on the chairman of the SEC when they were first registering the fund. The meeting had seemed to go well, and they were able to arrange another. After he had heard all the circumstances, the chairman allowed the fund to be registered on schedule.

From its inception, the Growth Stock Fund was managed by an investment committee: Mr. Price was the first chairman; Charlie, Walter, and John Ramsay were the other three original members. Typically, the committee met Friday afternoons, often over lunch in a private room at the downtown Merchants Club. At this meeting, companies were discussed and decisions made to buy or sell. These orders were collected, usually on a yellow tablet, by a committee member or, later, by Austin George, the firm's head trader. The orders were placed with several local brokerage firms that afternoon. It was rare for the committee to vary this pattern or to meet more than once a week.

The Growth Stock Theory of Investing is long term by nature. Well-selected growth companies have a long growth cycle. They have resided in Mr. Price's model portfolios for more than thirty years, as Merck, 3M, IBM, and Abbott Laboratories did in the Growth Stock Fund. There was no need to continually monitor the stocks in the portfolio, trying to outguess the stock market by trading them. When a particular stock weakened below what the committee felt to be its fair value, buy orders were placed at specific prices. Similarly, when a stock rose substantially above its value (see Chapter 9 for a discussion of how this is determined), sales were made at preset levels. The Growth Stock Fund then consistently maintained a low turnover rate (the dollar value of the stocks in a portfolio that are either bought or sold within a calendar year, divided by the average portfolio value during the year). Many mutual funds have turnover rates exceeding 100 percent. This means that within a one-year period or less, the entire portfolio of the fund is either bought or sold and replaced by new companies! To be successful, the manager of such a fund has to be right in his timing of both buying and selling of individual stocks, as well as guessing the direction of the stock market. This kind of market timing is extremely difficult to consistently do well in a competitive world.

Mr. Price claimed to have given up any attempt at guessing the direction of the stock market when, as a young man, he lost a great deal of money on his investments early in the Depression. He said that he had never known anyone who could successfully trade stocks over an extended time, although many schemes have been tried over the years. Rapid trading also tends to generate high transaction costs, as well as short- and long-term taxable gains, which do not show up when measuring fund performance, but can significantly impact a client's financial assets. Although he always counseled against guessing short-term swings in the market, Mr. Price would very occasionally violate his own rule in managing his own account. As he wrote in his journal, the results of such short-term trading only proved the wisdom of his own advice.

The mutual fund industry, like corporate pension funds, also represented a fertile field and, long-term, a very large business opportunity. According to the annual Investment Company Fact books, over the twenty years between the introduction of the Growth Stock Fund in 1950 and 1970, the year before Mr. Price would officially retire from the firm, the total mutual fund industry would grow nearly twenty times from just $2.5 billion to $47.5 billion. In 1983, the year he died, equity mutual funds would total $293 billion for a compound growth rate of 16 percent between 1950 and 1983, a slightly higher rate than the pension business.

Fixed income funds would grow to an amazing $216 billion, far outpacing the growth of equity funds and the overall mutual fund market from 1970 to 1983 and confirming Mr. Price's suggestion to Charlie to establish a fixed income department. By then, as indicated in the 1986 prospectus, the firm would be well represented in fixed income mutual funds, as well as equity.

At the outset, T. Rowe Price charged no sales fees because the Growth Stock Fund was conceived as a service for existing clients. The firm employed no mutual fund salesmen. For this reason, the T. Rowe Price funds were called no-load funds. Sales charges for so-called load mutual funds, which do employ salesmen, could be more than 5 percent. This amount was usually taken out upfront, significantly reducing the amount of the actual investment by the client in the fund.

Both pension and mutual funds grow from appreciation of the portfolio and cash flow. Cash flow occurs in a mutual fund because of new sales from new and existing clients and the dividends and capital gains paid to the shareholder, which are usually automatically reinvested. Today, mutual funds are also an important part of the myriad of individual retirement plans for individuals. Individual retirement accounts are replacing large pension funds as the primary retirement vehicle for corporate employees

Pension funds are either defined benefit or defined contribution. In a defined benefit plan, the benefits to be received at retirement are defined at the outset. The company or government entity invests an amount of capital that it calculates will be adequate to meet these obligations, assuming that the assets in the pension plan appreciate at a predetermined rate. Unfortunately, in many cases today this rate is considerably higher than what has actually been realized by the fund over the past decade. Many plans, particularly at the state and local level, are underwater and are unlikely to have the assets to meet their obligations. If the pension does not achieve its projected return and can't pay its obligation, the plan becomes insolvent, and so can the entity guaranteeing it, as the city of Detroit discovered in July of 2013. If a private pension plan and the corporation guaranteeing it go into bankruptcy, it becomes the responsibility of the Pension Benefit Guarantee Corporation, a federal agency providing specific employee benefits, which are usually lower than those written into most pension plans.

Because of the risk of not hitting investment goals, and the large resulting financial obligations, most corporations have moved to defined contribution plans, in which the corporation or government body contributes a "defined" dollar sum each year and employees usually also contribute. There is no obligation to pay out any specific sum at retirement. This is called the "democratization" of pension plans, wherein the employees take on the actual responsibility of providing for their own retirement, with some help from their employer. In such pension plans, the employee is usually offered the option of investing in several mutual funds. Accounting for thousands of individual employee accounts, each with different objectives and investments, became a major issue. Only the larger fund management companies, with expensive, sophisticated technology, are able to supply all these services in-house. Some local governments are beginning to follow the trend to democratization, but lag far behind private funds. The traditional IRA was established in 1974 and the 401(k) was established by the Revenue Act of 1978. The resulting shift to individual employee retirement accounts (IRAs) has been a major driving force behind mutual fund sales in recent years. The firm's sudden bonanza after 1950 from the growth of mutual funds and pension funds was not part of Mr. Price's initial plans for the firm, and in some ways he did not welcome the accelerated growth. It is very difficult to maintain quality of service and stock market performance when new accounts begin to grow exponentially and the money floods in.

Again, Mr. Price took the longer-term view. He wrote the following on September 2, 1951, in a bulletin to everyone in the firm:

"Our objective is a medium-sized investment counsel firm with a reputation for the highest character and the soundest investment philosophy. Quality not quantity is our goal in the selection of both the associates and clients. Profitable operations are essential if the firm is to survive and grow, but profits must follow a job well-done, the results of the goodwill of the investing public."

It is hard not to admire such goals, and all those who knew Mr. Price understood that these words were from his heart.

Walter Kidd said that Mr. Price thought like a college professor: "To be successful, he believed he must publish or perish." Such a belief goes back to the beginning of the firm, when Mr. Price began to communicate regularly with his clients through carefully written investment bulletins, a practice he would maintain until right before his death. It was common knowledge in the firm that Mr. Price wanted to be recognized beyond Baltimore. He wanted to be on the national stage. The series of articles that *Barron's* invited him to do as a follow up to his 1930s articles on growth stocks fit right into these plans. The first article, "Picking Growth Stocks for the 1950s," appeared February 6, 1950. He again outlined his definition of a growth company – with no changes, despite the tumultuous intervening eleven years. He reviewed the lists of the growth companies that he had published in 1939. Of the forty-three "premier" growth companies, only one had failed to attain a new high in earnings in the postwar recovery and, among a second list of twenty-four less-proven growth stocks, three had failed to achieve this goal. Only 6 percent of the 1939 companies in his model "growth" portfolio had failed to measure up as growth companies over the intervening time period. Earnings for this list had grown 365 percent, versus only 129 percent for the companies listed in the Dow Jones Industrial Average. This was considerably better than his promise to clients in 1939 that he expected to be right 75 percent of the time. In this postwar article, he stated that he anticipated that his batting average would come closer to his prior 75-percent goal in the next decade. As usual, Mr. Price believed in under- rather than overpromising performance.

His emphasis going forward would not change greatly from 1939, he said, although there would be some subtle shifts. He would emphasize international business more in his selection of U.S. stocks, as American business became much more global. As socialism and the welfare state, put in place in the 1930s, continued to grow, he anticipated that the dollar would continue to decrease in its buying power and inflation would be a force to be reckoned with. He therefore chose growth companies that would have the power to increase prices. Research and development had made tremendous strides during the war, and would also be more emphasized in his stock selection in the postwar period.

In his next *Barron's* article, February 20, 1950, with the same title, he made the first revision of his original definition of a growth stock. Due to his increasing concern about inflation, he changed the rate of growth of earnings of a growth stock, saying that it must not only "reach a new high in earnings from one business cycle to the next," but it must also demonstrate a growth in earnings "faster than the rise in the cost of living."

At the end of 1951 Mr. Price was in a good mood. He wrote in his journal on December 31:

> This has been the most successful year in my business career from every angle. Including dividends, it looks like my pretax income exceeded $23,000, nearly double what I made in 1949. I am taking a bold step in expanding our office facilities by moving Charlie and his team to the 27th floor, increasing the number of associates, and I hope to give salary increases next year in excess of what has been done in the past, so that our older associates' compensation will not be so close to what we have to pay for a new person.

The early 1950s, however, would prove more difficult for the firm than he expected. The excess profits tax was passed again during the Korean War and, once more, had an impact on growth stock reported earnings, as it had in World War I and II. Moreover, stocks generally did not rise with the good business conditions and increasing earnings, but tended to lag, due to the Korean War. As their annual reports revealed, and would prove to be true when Mr. Price introduced each of his first three new equity funds, the new funds he launched during his career all initially lagged behind the market, as outlined in their annual reports. In frustration, he reportedly wrote in his journal, and told some of the members of the advisory committee, "If the fund ever reached $10 million [in assets], I would close it." By this, Mr. Price meant that he would turn the Growth Stock Fund into a closed end fund – closed to new shareholders. As such, it would be organized as a publicly traded investment company under SEC jurisdiction. It would continue to be managed by the firm, and it would be listed and traded on a stock exchange. Mr. Price, however, would give up his dream of building a major mutual fund featuring Growth Stocks. Fortunately, the market turned upward and his threat was never acted upon.

The acquisition of the pension account of American Cyanamid as a client created the need to hire a senior counselor. Kirk Miller joined in 1952 to fill this role. Kirk was the last so-called "senior" to be hired, although he was only thirty-four. Born in Baltimore, he graduated from MIT in 1941. He was an officer in the Navy during World War II, supervising shipbuilding. In 1950, he was awarded a degree from the Harvard Business School.

Kirk Miller (left) and John Hannon. TRP archives.

Each of the senior members of the firm was identified with a company that became a premier growth stock for many years and an important profit contributor for the firm's clients. For Mr. Price, DuPont and Merck were such companies. Charlie became a proponent of IBM in the late 1940s, after a one-hour appointment with the president and CEO, Thomas Watson, turned into a full-day visit and a long-term personal relationship. Walter Kidd fell in love with 3M in the late 1930s, after a chance visit with William L. McKnight, the president. Walter said it was the only company that he recommended before returning to Baltimore.

For Kirk, it was Avon Products, which he learned about from a client who had been an officer of the Baltimore Press, which had just merged with International Paper. The client mentioned to Kirk that Avon was rapidly increasing their use of paper cartons and "he should take a look." After doing a bit of an analysis, with Walter looking over his shoulder, Kirk bought it for client accounts in 1955, not long after he was hired. In the December 31, 1960, report of the Growth Stock Fund, Avon was carried at a value of $1.2 million and a cost of only $118,000. It continued strongly upward, rising ten times over the next twelve years.

Kirk's primary job was working with Mr. Price on American Cyanamid, the Duke accounts, and as a counselor on a few smaller accounts. He was a good counterpoint for Mr. Price. In addition to being bright, unassuming, and a very good tennis player (still Mr. Price's favorite game) he, most importantly, brought an intense interest in the newer, exciting areas of investment. Like Charlie Shaeffer, he never competed with Mr. Price, but supplemented him.

The History of T. Rowe Price Associates, Inc., indicates that by the end of 1954, assets under management at the firm were $152 million, of which $4 million was in the Growth Stock Fund. It was in 1955 that the firm delivered Mr. Price's original goals. According to "The T. Rowe Price Story," written in December 1974, the professional staff numbered 28, there were 399 accounts, and the firm was generating $310,000 in annual fees. The market was moving up strongly, and growth stocks, including the Growth Stock Fund, were once again leading the way. The firm was beginning to get a national reputation for performance, with Mr. Price's articles in *Barron's* and the quotes of the Growth Stock Fund's net asset value per share printed daily in papers around the country, broadcasting its strong performance.

In 1956, the firm began to hire the next generation of management, bringing in Donald E. Bowman as a counselor. An economist and a graduate of the University of Wisconsin, Don had also served a term of active duty with the Navy and had continued to serve as a naval reserve officer on weekends. He took his service as a naval officer seriously, tended to be more formal in his relations within the firm, and did not socialize easily. He worked very well with Charlie, however, and would eventually become the firm's third president, following Mr. Price and Charlie, and serving for four years.

The most significant new hire at that time was John Hannon in 1958. John came from Cedartown, a small community in Georgia, had graduated magna cum laude from Washington and Lee University, but did not go to business school. More of an artist than an analyst, he operated on an intuitive basis, rather than analyzing numbers. He was fascinated by smaller, rapidly growing companies that were changing the way things were done with new products and new technology. In the process, such companies were growing very quickly. He fell in love with two of them – the Haloid Photographic Company (which became Haloid Xerox in 1958, then Xerox Corporation in 1961) and Polaroid Corporation, whose film technology was just coming of age. By December 31, 1960, the Growth Stock Fund had more than $3 million invested in Haloid Xerox, which had quadrupled over cost. Happy clients made millions more. Polaroid quickly came thereafter, with much the same results. John was also a good writer. As the firm began to get larger, the written reports of analysts became more important than oral communications.

According to "The History of T. Rowe Price Associates, Inc.," in 1965 T. Rowe Price and Associates' total assets under management crossed the $1 billion mark. That year, the Growth Stock Fund stood at $197 million in assets, and total revenues were $1.9 million, according to the "Report to the Advisory Committee of the Growth Stock Fund," August 5, 1966. In 1966 the total staff numbered eighty-nine employees, based on the Employee Directory.

People around the country and the world now listened to – and followed – the "sage of Baltimore," as Mr. Price was described by *Forbes* in 1977.

▪ Chapter Twelve ▪

TRANSITIONS, 1960–1968

The driving forces behind Mr. Price's next investment emphasis on small growth stocks would be the accelerating growth of government spending for defense research and development, particularly for manned space exploration. Just as the strong growth in the consumer-led economy of the 1950s drove many of the large growth companies in the Growth Stock Fund, defense spending and the new space program would propel the stocks of these small technology companies.

The year 1960 was a good one for Mr. Price, the firm, and much of the country. The earliest members of the Baby Boom generation were no longer babies. They were beginning to enter their teenage years with all of its questions and questioning, seeking answers from an older generation that had survived the Depression and a world war.

In the last years of his term in office, President Eisenhower had begun to seem to some a bit grandfatherly. The communist threat was very real. To a great extent, the Cold War had become a war of technologies. In 1945 America was the only owner of an atomic bomb. Just as the Russians caught up with an atomic bomb of their own, the U.S. exploded the hydrogen bomb on November 1, 1952, vaporizing a portion of the Enewetak Atoll. This new weapon had a force of more than 10 megatons, almost 500 times more powerful than the atomic bomb dropped on Nagasaki. By the 1970s, the U.S. would know how to miniaturize these huge bombs so that they could be placed on the nose of an intercontinental missile. The Russians would continue to match U.S. developments in the science of mass destruction throughout these 10 years, lagging only a few years behind.

In 1957, the Russians leapfrogged ahead of the U.S. in a different sphere of this technology competition by launching Sputnik. A 23-inch polished sphere that rotated around the world in an elliptical orbit, it broadcast ominous radio pulses, which sounded like loud clicks to the global audience that listened on radios, eyes turned skyward.

All of a sudden, America was no longer the technology leader of the world. Its Cold War archenemy had beat it to the next scientific level. The military potential could be easily imagined as Sputnik clicked its way overhead. Historically, the advantage in battle had always gone to the army higher up on the hill. Not only did the first two U.S. launches in response fail completely, but on November 21, 1960, after John F. Kennedy's election as president, the National Aeronautics and Space Administration (NASA), established in 1958, attempted to celebrate the new young, forward-looking administration by launching a satellite before a large crowd of reporters. It ended up sitting awkwardly on its launch pad after its launch rocket had fizzed out all of its fuel. To add to the picture, its rescue parachute had deployed ingloriously around its lifeless form. On April 12, 1961, only a few months after Kennedy and his family had moved into the White House, the president watched as Russia launched the first manned spaceship into orbit.

A month later, America seemed to catch up by sending astronaut Alan Shepard into space in the *Freedom 7* capsule. It was nowhere near as big or as complex as the Russian rocket, but America felt like it was back into the new space race, with their new president at the controls. The technology race of the 1950s was back in full force, as both nations pointed toward the moon, with Kennedy's 1961 challenge to have the U.S. be the first to the moon.

The production of consumer goods still dominated the economy in 1962, but continued spending on defense and the rapid escalation of outlays for space assured that there would be a strong scientific overlay to the economy in coming decades. The nation's GDP had risen 51 percent in the 1950s and, due to increased government spending, would rise slightly faster in the 1960s at 56 percent.

The publicity for T. Rowe Price and Associates was in effect taken over by the reporters at many financial newspapers and magazines, who were impressed by the firm's performance. In contrast to its relative lack of publicity in the 1950s, the firm and the T. Rowe Price Growth Stock Fund got full credit in the press for outperforming all other U.S. equity mutual funds, according to Wiesenberger, with an objective of capital growth and, secondarily, income for its first ten years, as discussed earlier.

There was no need for Mr. Price to write in *Barron's* about the performance of his model accounts; favorable performance was more believable when publicized by others. It is one thing to have an excellent record of performance based on a family account, even though it was externally audited. It is quite another when this record is printed daily and discussed in the financial pages. Although the Growth Stock Fund began as a way to economically manage the accounts of the children of the firm's clients, its real value became obvious as the publicity surrounding its extraordinary record began to bring in large new investment counsel clients, as well as shareholders.

By early 1961, at the age of 62, Mr. Price had achieved his life's ambition. After twenty-four years of financial struggle and occasional disappointments, he was now recognized as the country's best investor. Winning such respect was very important for him. Whereas few knew his name when he first published his articles on the Growth Stock Theory in *Barron's* in 1939, in 1961 every serious investor knew it.

But he was still a relatively young man with other investment theories to put to work. His thoughts began to turn to his next project. The firm was beginning to get too large, and at heart he was a loner. Walter Kidd recalled, "Mr. Price hosted parties basically to satisfy his wife, Eleanor, and he only gave the minimum number that was socially acceptable." He was never one for much small talk and certainly did not suffer fools kindly. We at the firm noticed that the social interaction that he seemed to enjoy the most was the stimulation of investment ideas, particularly when it was from the junior members of the firm.

Despite being an old-style gentleman to the core, almost always dressed in a coat and tie, and with a generally smiling exterior, he was known to let a careless waiter know just where he had erred in thirty seconds or less. He gave his best to his work and expected others, in any job, to do the same. The same could occasionally happen to an associate who had spoken badly out of turn. As Walter Kidd said, "We were all just a little bit afraid of him."

In 1960, Mr. Price formed the Rowe Price Management Company. His initial plan was that this would be a small mutual fund management company designed for his retirement. Managing individual accounts for clients had lost much of its allure. There was too much client interaction involved, with a lot of stress when the market took one of its periodic nosedives. He also grew increasingly uncomfortable as the firm's rapid growth began to cause him to lose control of the company. He intended to pack his own files for Rowe Price Management into several big leather expandable briefcases and take them with him wherever he went. His office would become the Hillsboro Club in Florida for six months in the winter, Eagles Mere in the mountains of Pennsylvania in the summer, and, perhaps, a cruise ship or his garden at other times. For research at Rowe Price Management, he initially expected to use input from analysts on Wall Street, who would be rewarded by commission dollars resulting from stock trades. He also planned to continue to get reports and information from the firm's research analysts, with access to specific analysts as needed.

In 1960, Mr. Price officially started the New Horizons Fund, the first fund launched by his new company. The New Horizons Fund would follow the Growth Stock Theory of Investing, but it would target smaller companies. Size in the investment world is most often described either in terms of sales or the "total market capitalization," determined by multiplying all of the shares outstanding by the current market price. Smaller companies are typically in the early growth phase of their life cycle, which means they are often growing faster. It is far easier to add $2 million in sales with a new product for a 20-percent gain when a company's total sales are only $10 million, than to add $10 million for the same percentage growth when sales are $50 million. In addition, just as the risk of death for humans is greatest at the beginning and at the end of life, so it is with corporations. At that time, before the emergence of the venture capital industry, small companies, early in their life cycles, were often run by managements that were untrained and untried, with little access to capital. Their balance sheets were often quite weak.

Based largely on the Growth Stock Fund's well-advertised perfor-mance, money began to pour into the new fund. By year's end, its asset value was more than $6 million. It became rapidly apparent that the New Horizons Fund was not going to remain the small fund that Mr. Price could bundle up and take with him. Nor, he found, could he depend on Wall Street for the quality research in these small companies that he required. Small capitalizations meant fewer dollars of trading volume, with lower commissions, and far fewer interested Wall Street analysts.

I joined the firm in October 1960 as a 27-year-old technology analyst. Although I was born in Baltimore, I had grown up in eastern Tennessee and had graduated with a degree from Princeton in electrical engineering in 1956. I had worked in a number of engineering positions at Westinghouse, ultimately as manager of the manufacturing engineering laboratory at the Air Arm Division at the Friendship National Airport (now known as the Baltimore/Washington International Thurgood Marshall Airport). Westinghouse produced advanced airborne avionics. I became a night student, working on a certificate in business management at Johns Hopkins. (The university's part-time and night programs were then offered by what was known at the time as McCoy College.) I took a course in corporate finance taught by Walter Kidd.

Similar to Mr. Price's experience during his days at DuPont, I had begun to believe that investing in companies was a far more interesting subject than electrical engineering or manufacturing. This was despite the fact that both my father and grandfather had successful careers in manufacturing proprietary products and did not think highly of the financial field as an occupation. Walter Kidd and I had long conversations about the investing business after class. His low-key sales pitch ultimately developed an interest in me to leave Westinghouse and work for T. Rowe Price and Associates. Walter, conservative by nature, waited until after he had graded my final exam to make an offer. Like Mr. Price, I learned that following your passion created the most satisfying work experiences. Fun and the job become combined, but you have to jump when the opportunity presents itself. I never looked back.

Late in 1961, I introduced Curran (Cub) W. Harvey, Jr., to Mr. Price, with the idea of Cub becoming Rowe Price Management's first full-time analyst. Cub, born in Baltimore, was then 32, and had earned an engineering degree from Yale. Most of his work experience had been in sales and sales administration at small technology companies. Cub said that during the first part of his employment interview, Mr. Price was a bit stiff and distant. Maybe he was thinking about the New Horizon Fund's poor performance over the past year. Finally, there was a long pause in the somewhat banal conversation about Cub's past responsibilities and ambitions for the future. Cub decided to take the bull by the horns and asked, "Tell me, Mr. Price, what do YOU do?" According to Cub, that stopped him cold. Mr. Price looked at Cub, got a small grin on his face, and they had a fine, open discussion, after which Cub was hired.

John Hannon and a few other T. Rowe Price and Associates analysts were in regular attendance at the investment committee meetings of the New Horizons Fund, along with Cub and Mr. Price. I was honored to be invited to join the committee later in 1961, and ultimately became a vice president of Rowe Price Management. Cub soon became the fund's administrator, as well as its principal analyst; he would later become president. When Mr. Price left for the Hillsboro Club that winter, the fund stayed in Baltimore, although the briefcases flowed back and forth, keeping the express mail service busy.

Today, the national computer exchange known as Nasdaq, maintained by the National Association of Securities Dealers, offers price quotes by market makers trading thousands of stocks. Most trades are now done directly, computer-to-computer, without human intervention. In 1960, trading in small companies was much more difficult than in the stocks of large corporations, which were often listed on stock exchanges. The prime source of trading information for small companies was the so-called "pink sheets" – a listing of market makers on pink-colored paper, and their respective offers to buy and sell specific stocks was available only to registered brokers, but not to their clients. Small investors could buy and sell, through brokers, small quantities of shares fairly easily with this system, but large institutional investors could not. Transactions involving a large number of shares that weren't done carefully could easily greatly distort these thin markets. To perform the larger trades required an individual who knew his or her way around these markets.

Good research was even more critical in such a world. If a major problem developed in a small company, with such thin trading, it was difficult to extricate oneself without large losses. This type of investing, however, fit well with Mr. Price's long-term approach of buying slowly at carefully predetermined prices and taking profits in the same manner – very gradually. The success of T. Rowe Price and Associates in the early 1960s was not limited to the Growth Stock Fund and New Horizons. The firm's counseling accounts also performed very well. Soon, managers of some of the largest pension funds in the country were making their way to Baltimore.

Hiring the next generation of professionals at T. Rowe Price and Associates began in earnest with six key hires in counseling and research, made in the first three years of the decade. In order to better serve other new and existing accounts based in New York, in 1962 the firm established an office in Rockefeller Center in the heart of Manhattan. This marked the beginning of the transition of the firm from a local Baltimore company to one with a national and, ultimately, an international footprint.

The firm was also running out of space at 10 Light Street. In 1937, it had begun operations on part of one floor. By 1962, it was occupying three full floors, with additional space on two others. It was getting difficult to operate efficiently with all the necessary "vertical communication," as everyone began to spend an inordinate amount of time on the elevators. In 1963, the firm moved to One Charles Center, where all the employees once more fit on one floor, at least initially. Mr. Price had to give up his large office, the view of Baltimore's historic Harbor District, and the working fireplace for comfort on cold winter days. It had been his office for twenty-six years.

One Charles Center's architecture was the opposite of 10 Light Street. A twenty-three-story aluminum and glass building designed by Ludwig Mies van der Rohe, it was constructed in 1962, and was the first postwar modern office tower in Baltimore. At the center of the city's nationally acclaimed urban renewal program, the project was spearheaded by Mr. Price's long-time friend Jeff Miller – also a member of the Growth Stock Fund board and the Greater Baltimore Committee.

One Charles Center, T. Rowe Price's second headquarters. Author's photo.

The stock markets continued irregularly upward. In December 1961, the New York Stock Exchange hit a new all-time high of 735. Business was good and Mr. Price remained positive about the economy, but conscious that stocks were selling at very high prices relative to earnings. As prices rose, dividends for growth stocks dropped far under long-term bonds, which had been a historic measure of overvaluation. In May 1962, this overvaluation was sharply corrected with a stock market decline of nearly 50 percent.

Such a drop may not look like much on a chart, particularly on the typical logarithmic charts, which tend to minimize swings in the market. It was, however, the sharpest decline since the war, and many younger, inexperienced associates, I among them, were caught off-guard by its severity. It was made worse by the leverage of borrowed money, which many of us employed to leverage our gains. Banks, still remembering the Great Depression, were unforgiving when there was not a healthy cushion between the money the bank was owed and the underlying collateral. Many investors lost much of their capital when their collateral was liquidated near the bottom of the market by their bankers.

Like Mr. Price in 1939, I also nearly lost my house in the bear market. I had collateralized my loan to purchase a new home with stocks instead of paying for an expensive mortgage. Fortunately, I was saved by another bank who saw some possible future in me as a customer and realized that my home, although illiquid, actually also offered good collateral. A valuable learning experience. Even though the decline was over quickly, Mr. Price was seen roaming the halls daily, pausing outside my office and those of other recent hires for a few nervous moments, as if he were having buyer's remorse.

When Russian Premier Nikita Khrushchev felt threatened by ballistic missiles recently placed by the United States in Turkey and Italy, on his doorstep, he began to secretly ship medium- and intermediate-range ballistic missiles to Cuba, which could deliver an atomic warhead anywhere on the East Coast of the United States without warning because of their proximity. When the missiles were detected on October 16, 1962, Kennedy ordered a blockade on October 22 and, in an accompanying speech to the nation, he said that the nation's policy would be "to regard any nuclear missile launched from Cuba against any nation in the Western Hemisphere as an attack on the United States, requiring a full retaliatory response upon the Soviet Union." The U.S. Armed Forces (with the exception of United States Army

Europe [USAREUR]) were ordered to DEFCON 3. On October 24, Strategic Air Command (SAC) was ordered to DEFCON 2, just short of nuclear strike. "I thought it was the last Saturday I would ever see," recalled U.S. Secretary of Defense Robert McNamara, as quoted by Martin Walker in *The Cold War*. A similar sense of doom was felt by other key players on both sides. When Khrushchev backed down at the last minute and the missiles on both sides were taken off ready, the market moved up strongly on heavy volume, ending the bear market.

Shortly after what would come to be known as the Cuban Missile Crisis, Mr. Price turned 65 and began to experience health issues. As the firm continued to grow larger, he also began to have disagreements with his associates. He wanted the firm to continue to operate in the same way it had when it was much smaller, although he knew, according to his comments to his journal, that it was impossible for him "to continue working 60–65 weeks." He was suspicious of many of the changes in the investment process that were being implemented by others. He knew, as well, that he no longer had the energy to run the whole firm. The time was approaching when he would have to yield some of his authority.

In fact, this was already happening. As it grew larger, the firm on its own began to evolve into a committee form of management, just as it had always managed its accounts. Walter moved into an overall administrative role, passing along his position of research head to younger associates. By mid-1963 there were more than 150 professionals and Mr. Price found, to his dismay, that he didn't know the names of many of his own employees.

He decided that the time had come to take a second step, following the establishment of Rowe Price Management. At the March 29, 1963, board meeting of T. Rowe Price and Associates, Mr. Price stepped down as president of the firm to focus all of his attention on Rowe Price Management. Charlie Shaeffer took his place. He was the obvious choice given his tenure, stock ownership, and success in client management. His outgoing personality and the ease with which he delegated made him easy to work for in a larger company. Walter was not interested in running the firm, and Kirk had no desire to get involved in administration, being much more interested in the investment side of the business.

A major reason for the timing of the management change was Mr. Price's continued frustration with the New Horizons Fund. He felt that he had to devote all of his time to managing it. Although the stock market as a whole was rising, New Horizons was not. Within T. Rowe

Price and Associates it became known as the "New Horizontal Fund." Though the Growth Stock Fund had also gotten off to a slow start, with little or no advance in its first three years, New Horizons was moving even slower. During 1962 the Dow Jones declined 1 percent, but, as noted in its 1962 annual report, the New Horizons fund dropped 29 percent. In mid-1962, Mr. Price wrote over a thousand words in his journal, recording his impassioned efforts to keep an important client from dropping not only his position in the New Horizons Fund, but in the counsel service as well. The client ultimately reconsidered and kept the firm as his investment counselor, as well as his position in the fund, but it was a close call.

By early 1964, with no progress in the fund's performance, Mr. Price was becoming truly concerned. In his March 31 journal entry, he wrote: "The New Horizons Fund is my greatest disappointment. It seems that everything is working against us. Not only are science and automatic merchandising stocks still in bear markets, but we are stuck with a number of special situations that continue to decline in price.... The research department is uninspiring. I lack confidence in most of the men. But I am unable to determine, now, how much of this pessimism and adverse criticism of associates is due to old age and frustration, and how much is justified. One thing I am sure of – there is too much work to do!" In another notation, he wrote in his journal – as he had earlier, with regard to the Growth Stock Fund – that if its performance did not improve, he would close it at $100 million and create a closed-end fund.

Vindication finally came in 1965. New Horizons caught up in a hurry, exploding 44 percent for the year compared to a 10-percent increase in the Dow Jones. The fund had suddenly become an outstanding performer. Many of the young technology stocks became extraordinarily successful. Some retailing and service companies did even better. The fund acquired a position in Wal-Mart, Inc., when it went public, at an effective cost, after all subsequent stock splits to date, of 8.6 cents per share. After only two years, this holding had risen more than 12 times. It continued to climb many more times in the following decades. Ultimately, T. Rowe Price Associates became one of the largest holders of Walmart, outside of the Walton family. Early investments in Optical Scanning Corporation, Millipore Corporation, H&R Block, Inc., and Eckerd Corporation also helped build the fund's outstanding performance. Large growth stocks were doing well, and once more money began to flood into the firm. In 1965, total assets under management climbed over $1 billion, including Rowe Price Management.

The market for emerging growth stocks ultimately became so heated that on October 17, 1967, the New Horizons Fund suspended sales and remained closed to new investors for nearly three years. Management simply could not find suitable stocks to invest in at reasonable prices. Closing the fund was an unprecedented move in the mutual fund industry at that time. The fees that a mutual fund company receives are based on assets under management. Closing the fund to new sales slows the increase of income to the fund manager. This move, however, simply echoed Mr. Price's belief that if you remained focused on what is best for your client, you will ultimately be rewarded.

The economy continued to do well, as it recovered into the 1960s. President Kennedy in action was more conservative than in his words. He even proposed a tax cut, which would have dropped the top income tax rates from 91 to 65 percent. Many felt that he was beginning to improve America's image in the world. It could have indeed developed into the golden era that some had begun to forecast, with rising income for all, amid a stretching out the boom of the 1950s.

All of this ended with Kennedy's assassination in Dallas. His successor, Lyndon B. Johnson, swung hard to the left with his Great Society programs. This included a sharp boost in government spending for a variety of social causes, including education, welfare, old age, housing, and urban renewal. Mr. Price called it "a continuation of the New Deal." Johnson also accelerated the NASA space program, further increasing spending on this already large government program.

After Johnson was elected president in 1964, he moved two destroyers into Vietnam's Gulf of Tonkin. The USS Maddox was attacked by three small torpedo-equipped North Vietnamese patrol boats. It was undamaged but sank one of the North Vietnamese boats; a second controversial attack was reported August 4. These two attacks taken together, however, led to Congress to pass the Bay of Tonkin Resolution, which effectively allowed President Johnson to use military force in Southeast Asia without a formal declaration of war. U.S. military expenditures accelerated over the next three years to $210 billion ($1.57 trillion in 2018 dollars). Propelled by huge spending for both butter and guns, the budget deficit rose to $25 billion ($181 billion in 2018 dollars) in fiscal 1968, the highest peacetime deficit in the country's history at that time.

Chapter Thirteen

THE UNITED STATES ENTERS A NEW ERA, 1965–1971

Given the unpopular, increasingly expensive, out-of-control war in Vietnam, the huge costs of the Great Society program, and the large ensuing budget deficits, Mr. Price's sensitive antennae were up. His concerns began to increase about the country's future and the outlook for the stock market. He believed that economic history continually repeated itself because it was driven by human nature. As he had written in the 1937 pamphlet "Change: The Investor's Only Certainty": "The basic social, economic, and political currents flow as long as human beings remain in control."

The huge postwar economic boom following the war was similar, Mr. Price believed, to what occurred in the 1920s, following World War I. This current boom also had to end. By 1966, the nation's huge pile of gold, which had reached record levels in 1947, had virtually disappeared. Mr. Price wrote in a memo, "Change – The Investor's Only Certainty in 1966" (June 10, 1966), that "gold reserves were at the lowest levels since prior to World War II."

The 1929 stock market crash had turned into a depression, many believed, because of the leverage from the huge stock market-related debt taken on by Wall Street, corporations, individuals, and the banks themselves. But, "in the mid-1960s," Mr. Price wrote privately, "it was the consumers, supported by the banks and other financial institutions, that had engorged, not on stocks, but on houses and automobiles, under the easy lending conditions following World War II." The consumer was saturated with goods, loaded with debt, and could not afford to buy much more.

Europe's economic growth was also slowing, Mr. Price pointed out. The long postwar economic expansion of the entire industrialized world was clearly getting overextended. It had been an amazing run – the longest in the history of the United States – while maintaining a very low rate of inflation. Per capita income, after adjusting for inflation, had gone up a remarkable 60 percent between 1946 and 1966. This was capitalism at its finest, showing what it could do with very little government intervention in the corporate world.

As he explained in a memo to clients, "Areas of Concern, 1/27/60," other changes in the mid-1960s were subtler. "The United States had financed the reconstruction of the capital nations of the world, friends and enemies alike," he wrote. "We have transmitted to them our 'know-how' and our ability to build modern plants for mass production at the greatest efficiency. United States corporations have spent billions of dollars to build plants in the principal nations around the world. We are facing now opposition from those we have helped."

He began to worry about inflation, due to the large government deficits and an end to the long business expansion. In an important statement of a changed investment strategy, "The Long Look Ahead," February 1964, he wrote: "I am convinced that more inflation, either before or after a business depression, is inevitable ... more emphasis should be placed on natural resource companies, such as oils, metals, and timber than has been placed on these companies during the past ten years, when inflation was not an issue." In "Areas of Concern," February 1965, he stated, "No nation, including the United States, is rich enough to support all of the Have Nots of the world, or strong enough militarily to protect all of the non-Communist people against Communism.... President Johnson's Great Society will lead us further down the path to socialism. This means more of a welfare state, more regulation of industry, more government management of money, and a further depreciation of the purchasing power of the dollar."

Mr. Price was a conservative by almost any standard – hostile to the New Deal, hostile to government regulation, and a strong supporter of American might and leadership. Yet he was also a pragmatist who denounced what he saw as wrong-headed policies by America's hardliners from both parties.

Mr. Price blamed the country's failures of leadership on the failure of the free world's "dollar diplomacy." As he said in "The Long Look Ahead" (February 1964), "You cannot buy friends for keeps, whether you are an individual or a nation. You must have understanding and mutual respect for the other fellow's point of view, whether a person or a nation." He was also very concerned about the increasing U.S. involvement in Vietnam because of the potential drain of manpower and resources, as well as its absolute cost. This was at a time when few people even knew much about that conflict. Mr. Price felt that a bear market of indeterminate magnitude and duration was about to occur and would very possibly be "of greater severity than any since the end of World War II."

As a result of his concerns about the country, the economy, and the stock market, he decided to drastically alter his own accounts in preparation for the rough seas he saw ahead. His largest single asset was the shares that he and his family owned in the firm. These shares were illiquid, and earnings of T. Rowe Price and Associates could suffer significantly in the environment that he foresaw. In what must have been a very difficult decision, in 1965 he offered to sell all of his shares in the company to the other founders and employees of the firm. One suspects that this decision could also have had something to do with his increasing inability to control the firm, with its larger size and complexity. Mr. Price had demonstrated, when he departed from Legg, that he had no desire to be part of an organization that he didn't control. His health also continued to worsen.

Charlie and Mr. Price began a dialogue on the sale of his stock and particularly a fair price. These shares, of course, represented the controlling interest of the firm. Charlie was dragging his feet a bit, however, because he had no idea where the firm was going to get the money that he knew might be required to buy out Mr. Price. Finally, Mr. Price arranged a lunch at the Merchants Club with Charlie and a prominent Baltimore attorney with a number of wealthy clients who could be interested in buying an interest in T. Rowe Price. Toward the end of lunch, Mr. Price asked the attorney if he was interested in buying his share of the company. Charlie recognized this as a transparent ploy to get the ball rolling, but it also evidenced to him that Mr. Price was getting increasingly serious about cutting a deal. Following lunch, Charlie went directly to the First National Bank of Baltimore. By late that afternoon he had sketched out a deal. The price, however, remained an issue when he discovered that Mr. Price was demanding a value well in excess of what a majority of the employees thought the firm was worth. The amount was, also, more than they could afford to pay, even with financing from First National.

The critical turning point came April 12, 1965, when Mr. Price was rushed to the hospital with a blocked small intestine, complicated by an ulcer. For five days, he lay in intensive care, fed only through intravenous tubes. It was two months before he was allowed to come back to the office. This near-death experience convinced Mr. Price that he should sell his shares in the firm – even at a lower price than he had been hoping for. As he noted in his journal, "I am convinced my illness was due partly to my state of mind. As I had been worrying for many, many, many months about my inability to reach an agreement on the purchase of my stock."

He wasted little time after his health returned. On June 28, 1965, he signed an agreement with Charlie, Walter, Kirk, and several other senior associates who were large shareholders. Unfortunately, this sale did not go through. Jack Dreyfus, the founder of the Dreyfus Fund, which was the largest public mutual fund at the time, coincidently filed a registration statement to sell his controlling interest of the management company of the Dreyfus Fund on October 5, 1965. In studying this transaction, the SEC discovered that a significant change in ownership of a mutual fund management company had not been included in the Investment Company Act of 1940, yet there were obvious serious implications of such a sale for millions of fund shareholders. The SEC did not allow any sales of controlling interests of other management companies while they studied the Dreyfus issue. This clearly included the sale of Mr. Price's stock. As a representative from the SEC told Charlie, T. Rowe Price and Associates was "like a bird caught in a badminton game."

Mr. Price began to feel better. The market had improved some. The Growth Stock Fund performance was improved; shareholders were beginning to return. The firm's client performance was also much better. When the one-year term of his original deal with T. Rowe Price and Associates ran out and with the SEC's freeze on the sale of controlling interests of mutual fund management companies still in effect, Mr. Price decided to ask for a higher price for his stock. This change in the terms of the deal did not go over well with Charlie or most of the T. Rowe Price employees who would be the buyers. They thought that, as the saying goes, "a deal was a deal."

John Hannon had a different view. Highly regarded for his excellent calls on Xerox and Polaroid, which had made a great deal of money for the firm's clients, as well as his courage to take controversial stands at difficult times, he made a brilliant and impassioned case for the purchase of Mr. Price's shares. Even at the newly elevated price, Hannon argued that it was still a good deal if one took a longer-term view.

Check for Mr. Price's controlling interest in T Rowe Price & Associates.

After much grumbling and argument, a new deal was finally signed June 28, 1966. The firm paid Mr. Price $792,000 for his shares, Eleanor received $50,000, possibly related to her original $50,000 note, and the Price children another $50,000, for a total of $892,000 for the controlling shares of T. Rowe Price and Associates. This included the counsel business and the Growth Stock Fund. As it turned out, John was absolutely right. It was a great deal for the firm and for the associates who participated. Almost on cue, the bull market fully blossomed the next year. The money began to roll into the Growth Stock Fund and clients were knocking at the door. The New Horizons Fund continued its excellent performance, as noted in its annual report. Mr. Price went from feeling that he had gotten a very good deal to thinking that he had sold the company way too cheaply. It must have been difficult to remind himself, as he was always a competitor, that making money had never been his objective in starting the firm. As he is quoted in *The History of T. Rowe Price and Associates, Inc.*, "It is better to be too early than too late."

Immediately following the sale of his stock, the name of the firm changed from T. Rowe Price and Associates to just T. Rowe Price

Associates. Mr. Price resigned in 1966 as chairman of the board, and Charlie, already president, became chairman as well. Mr. Price also gave up most of his clients. He did keep the controlling shares and his titles as chairman and president of the Rowe Price Management Company. He also continued as the president of the New Horizons fund, Rowe Price Management's only client at that time. The Growth Stock Theory of Investing had been proven yet again to be a winning strategy, although this very success would become a problem.

Once an investment concept of his had been proven to the world to be successful, the challenge altered for Mr. Price. There was no one left to compete with. He began to seriously develop yet another new strategy, a significant modification of the Growth Stock Theory. It was an investment concept that would prove to suit the new, highly inflationary environment that he saw coming.

Shortly after his agreement to sell his interest in the company had been signed, he wrote "Change – The Investor's Only Certainty in 1966." This was his first update to the paper written just before he started the firm in 1937. In this version he wrote, "Our national leadership has deteriorated, our dollar diplomacy has failed, and our brand of democracy is not being accepted by the underprivileged of the world. Not only has the metallic backing of our currency been discontinued, and our currency today is only redeemable in paper, but also our silver coins are no longer silver. Our currency has been printed at an accelerated pace and our gold supply continues to diminish."

To his few remaining clients he wrote a memo in March 1966 titled "My Program for Preparedness Has Been Completed," informing them that he had trimmed those stocks in his own accounts that he considered overpriced or not suited for the world that he saw developing over the next decade. The proceeds from sales of these stocks had been invested in dollar obligations to provide for:

1. Greater safety of principle.
2. Higher spendable income.
3. Reserves for state taxes.
4. Reserves for future purchases of common stocks.
5. Reserves for unpredicted expenses.
6. Reserves for expenditures for PURE PLEASURE AND EXTRAVAGANCE!

He also outlined several areas for the investment of new funds that would be appropriate for the challenging times that he saw ahead.

1. Business Services.
2. Science and Technology
3. Natural resources: land, gold, silver, timber, oil, and gas.

These three categories consisted of large and small growth stocks, many of which were already approved for the New Horizons and the Growth Stock Fund. The last category was new. Companies in this category weren't growth stocks, but he expected them to do exceptionally well in an inflationary environment.

This sudden shift in his investment strategy was more evidence of Mr. Price's true genius. Well ahead of other investors, he had the ability to recognize a major change in the world's social, political, and economic conditions. This ability wasn't magic, but based on long experience and careful study of important trends, as spelled out throughout this book. An important ingredient was his basic understanding of human nature. "Growing up on a farm," as he said to us, "had helped a lot."

His new focus on natural resource stocks was due to the historic emphasis investors had long placed on tangible assets, and the rejection of paper currencies in a highly inflationary environment. The earnings and value of such companies increased rapidly in an accelerating inflation, as did profits. They were able to sell the materials they produced at ever-increasing prices. These resources had been acquired at low prices over a long period of time, whereas their prices went up rapidly as the overall price structure rose with inflation.

In 1966, the firm's research analysts covered only growth stocks. A new team would be required to analyze this third, natural resource category. For this job Mr. Price hired Howard (Pete) P. Colhoun, a thirty-one-year-old engineer. Since graduating from Princeton and Harvard Business School, Pete had been with the management consulting firm Arthur D. Little, Inc., as a consultant involved in a variety of different industries. Mr. Price immediately put him to work looking at the nuclear power industry. Pete became the first member of this new "inflation" team working directly for Mr. Price at Rowe Price Management.

Just as Mr. Price had developed the Growth Stock Philosophy first within his own model accounts, he set up a new model account with the proceeds from the sale of his stock in the firm to invest in the above categories. Because of his concern that there might be a significant decline in the market before the rise in inflation, he kept 50 percent of this model portfolio in short-term government bonds and treasuries.

After testing this concept for two years, he decided to create a new mutual fund named the New Era Fund. Interestingly, less then a year before the fund was launched, an article called, "Despite Our Current 'Inflation Psychology,' a Serious Inflation Is Not in the Cards," appeared in the February 2, 1968, issue of the *New York Times*. Mr. Price was well ahead of the economists and market forecasters, as usual. The experts mentioned in the article had no idea what was coming.

He had wanted to call it the Inflation Fund, but the SEC did not allow that. He also wanted to buy raw land and actual commodities, such as copper, gold, and silver, and store these commodities in vaults and warehouses. This was also disallowed by the SEC because of the problem of accurately pricing these materials and, therefore, determining a daily price for the fund.

The New Era Fund was launched in 1969. The previous year George A. Roche, a graduate of Georgetown University and Harvard Business School, had been hired from Proctor and Gamble as the second full-time analyst at Rowe Price Management, to focus on natural resources. George would prove to be one of Mr. Price's most inspired hires. Working mostly for the groundbreaking New Era Fund, he covered metals, mining, forest products, and precious metals. Later, George would become chairman of the New Era Fund Investment Advisory Committee and the fund's president. In 1984 he would become CFO of T. Rowe Price Associates, gaining the confidence of management with his careful and conservative oversight. He would become president of the firm in 1997.

Because of my background in science and technology, which was a major investment by the fund, I was also a member of the original New Era investment committee and a vice president of the fund. The New Era Fund was successful in quickly gaining assets from the beginning. The track records of the Growth Stock Fund and the New Horizon Fund were there for all to see. Only four years after inception, total assets for the New Era Fund totaled $200 million. As noted in its 1966 annual report, the Growth Stock Fund had taken more than 15 years to reach that level.

In 1968, Mr. Price offered to sell his controlling interest in Rowe Price Management to the associates. It was apparent that it would fit well into the future plans of the firm, which involved more new funds. Retaining the Price name within T. Rowe Price Associates was deemed to be critical. Again, there was much negotiation over price, particularly with the bargain price of the original firm now apparent to all. When Mr. Price threatened to bring in Lehman Brothers Holdings, Inc., as a buyer, the small staff of Rowe Price Management threatened to quit en masse, effectively ending that possibility. These outside negotiations ceased when Walter Kidd pointed out to Mr. Price that the firm had the right of first refusal in a sale of Rowe Price Management.

In the end, the firm agreed to pay Mr. Price $1.5 million for his majority ownership of Rowe Price Management. The deal was consummated in 1968, with the first closing in 1968 and the second in 1969. Mr. Price resigned as president and chairman of the New Horizons fund. Rowe Price Management was merged into the parent company in 1973 to simplify management. Mr. Price put $1 million in cash from the sale into the Equitable Trust Bank in recognition of the $5,000 line of credit, which had been so important to the young organization many years before. The rest went into his new model "inflation" fund, which still consisted of 50 percent in reserves, with the rest in natural resources, business services, and science and technology.

In line with his increasing concern about inflation and its ultimate potential impact on the stock market, the economy, and even society itself, he physically visited both the Mercantile-Safe Deposit and Trust Company and the Maryland National Bank vaults before deciding which offered the most protection for his bond and stock certificates.

In April 1970, Mr. Price wrote an important memo, which turned into a booklet, "The New Era for Investors" to his clients and the firm stating, "Our balance of trade has worsened and our gold reserves are inadequate to meet the claims of other nations. Total debt of the U.S., including its citizens and corporations, has more than tripled since the end of World War II to $1.7 trillion. Interest rates are higher than they have been at any time in the past 100 years and the liquidity of corporations and banks is critically low."

The "number one problem," he continued, "is accelerating inflation. The Full [sic] Employment Act of 1946 insures that inflation will continue. We cannot have full employment without inflation. Minimum wages have been continuously adjusted and insure that labor costs and its prices will escalate."

He notably stated one of his favorite themes: "Even the richest nation in the world cannot continue to spend more money than it collects without going broke. It is only a question of time." In no uncertain terms, he warned of the coming apocalypse: "Uncontrolled inflation creates ever larger booms and busts. There is no turning back once it is entrenched into society. Ultimately, there will be a very serious business depression that will create social revolution and confiscation of property of the Haves by the Have Nots. Destruction of the wealth of those that have created it will be by taxation, devaluation of the paper currency and confiscation of property." He was forecasting a return to the 1930s and worse. The employees and clients of T. Rowe Price were certainly warned what he thought their future held, in his opinion.

In Mr. Price's view, the best indicator of inflation was the U.S. Department of Labor's Consumer Index (CPI). The annual rate of increase in the CPI tripled to 6.2% between 1965 and 1969. Mr. Price felt that no future government could be elected that sought to control an inflation of this magnitude. He concluded his memo by insisting, "control of inflation can only be achieved by balanced budgets and increased savings. Such [unpopular] measures slow the economy and add to unemployment."

Mr. Price foresaw that profits would suffer for most corporations. Prices for labor and raw material would rise faster than corporate sales. Moreover, the government would raise taxes to pay for the increased cost of government services, and this would also negatively impact corporate profits. It would be doubtful that the majority of consumer stocks would give an investor enough protection again inflation.

To deal with the increasingly "dark new era" that he foresaw, he suggested raising the percent of a portfolio invested in natural resource companies to more than 30 percent. Such companies were certainly not growth stocks. They were mature, and in some cases not managed in an overly astute manner. Their natural resource holdings of timber, raw land, oil, gold, and silver, however, should substantially benefit from inflation. Gold and silver, in particular, were increasingly favored by Mr. Price, as the decade of the 1970s progressed.

He was very selective about the growth stocks that he thought were appropriate for this environment of accelerating inflation. He believed that their return on invested capital should be significantly higher than had been the norm for many growth stocks in earlier low inflation years. To make a real profit in a world where rampant inflation might exceed 10 percent, a company's return on invested capital must also exceed 10 percent. He favored faster-growing companies much earlier in their life cycle, such as were included in the New Horizons Fund. His model portfolio for the environment of the 1970s that he foresaw was structured very differently than the T. Rowe Price Growth Stock Fund and the portfolios of most of the firm's clients. As the list of growth companies with high ROIs narrowed in this new era, Mr. Price felt that there would be increased investor demand for those companies that still qualified. Continuing care would have to be exercised not to overpay as these companies rose in value.

The price of natural resource stocks indeed began to rise and was based on the value of their assets and not current earnings, as Mr. Price had forecast. In fact, he believed that such companies might not have any earnings under some conditions, but sell as highly valuable commodities in the market. "Throughout history," he wrote in the same April 1970 memo, "precious metals, such as gold and silver, have been a haven for people with wealth desiring protection against the ravages of inflation and the depreciation of paper money." For many years, Swiss bankers had recommended that their clients hold at least 5 percent of their assets in gold bars. With inflation relatively low since World War II, this had not been a profitable strategy. After 1968, however, the worm began to turn as inflation increased. Precious metals holdings began to be quite profitable. The price of gold rose first due to the declining dollar, and then with accelerating inflation, as Mr. Price had anticipated.

With the New Era Fund successfully launched and a new management in place, Pete Colhoun became president of the New Era Fund. Mr. Price and Marie Walper both officially retired from T. Rowe Price Associates on April 30, 1971; Isabella Craig retired at the same time. But Mr. Price was like the Cheshire Cat in Lewis Carroll's *Alice's Adventures in Wonderland,* slowly beginning to disappear, but then reappearing, while raising philosophical and baffling issues. Ultimately, all that would be left was his grin.

■ Chapter Fourteen ■

DARK NEW ERA, 1971–1982

After retiring his positions at the New Era Fund, Mr. Price disappeared from the financial stage to take care of his beautiful roses, enjoy being free of the constraints of business, and explore new countries with Eleanor. What became of his gloomy forecast?

The day he retired – April 30, 1971, as he noted in his journal – the Dow Jones Industrial Average was 942. It rose irregularly until January 11, 1973, when it closed at a high of 1052. This level was not exceeded for the next ten years, during which the market stayed most of the time well under 700, creating one of the worst bear markets since World War II. At this level, the stock market had shown no progress since October 1962. Mr. Price's conservative position, with 50 percent of his assets in highly liquid short- and intermediate-term Treasuries, turned out to be well justified. The Treasury notes produced more than an 8 percent yield throughout this entire time period.

He was also correct that the long postwar business boom was over. It came to a slow grinding halt during the decade following his retirement, in concert with the market. There were two official business recessions in the 1970s. The major expenses of establishing a home and raising the huge number of baby boomers were now behind the army of young men and women who had come marching home from World War II. Their outlays were no longer boosting the economy. As Mr. Price pointed out as early as September 1964 in "Notes on the Economic Trend and Investment Policy," "Rising debt, particularly consumer debt, has reached dangerous levels." The increased interest rates had made this debt even more painful. Moreover, "building construction, automobiles and most other durable goods industries have caught up with demand." Europe had fully recovered its manufacturing capability following the war. The U.S. balance of trade tipped deeply into the red, subtracting from our economic growth. As Mr. Price had pointed out, we had created our own competition. In 1971, the total U.S. trade deficit was $2 billion. By January 1978, the U.S. Treasury Department reported it had grown to $27 billion.

Richard M. Nixon had been elected president in 1968, replacing Lyndon Johnson, who chose not to run because of his enormous unpopularity, chiefly due to the Vietnam War. Unfortunately, exchanging a liberal Democrat for a conservative Republican did little to help the country's budget deficit: in 1970, the deficit was $3 billion, but by 1978 it was up to another record peacetime peak of over $70 billion. Americans continued to enjoy the butter, while buying guns and armaments for the Vietnam War and handing out welfare checks to its poorer citizens. In the same September 1964 memo, Mr. Price pointed out that even government expenditures for the Vietnam War and defense generally "had reached their peak and were headed downward." To pay for trade deficits, as well as budget deficits, the U.S. Treasury began to print money in increasing quantity. In 1971, the U.S. money supply, as measured by M2, grew 10 percent. (M2 is a measure of the total amount of cash, checking deposits, and time deposits in the U.S. economy. When M2 grows faster than the economy, surplus paper dollars are created, diminishing the value of the dollar and creating the risk of inflation.)

The following brief history of gold in the U.S. economy should help in understanding its role in the 1970s. In 1933, Franklin Roosevelt proposed that all citizens turn in their gold and gold certificates to the Treasury, in return for a flat payment in paper dollars and coins of $20.67 per troy ounce. The United States formally went off the gold standard. Roosevelt's advisors believed this move was necessary because individuals and companies, panicked by the bank failures, had been converting dollars into gold, thus rapidly drawing down the United States gold supply, causing deflation. By eliminating the restraints of the gold standard, the government was free to increase the supply of paper dollars at will, which, in turn, created inflation but stopped the run on its gold supply. England had successfully followed this same path two years before. The price that the U.S. government would pay for an ounce of gold was increased to $35 in 1934.

In July 1944, as the war in the Pacific was still raging, delegates from 44 countries met at the Mount Washington Hotel in Bretton Woods,

New Hampshire, to design a better system. Under the ultimate Bretton Woods system, the signatories would settle their international balances in dollars and, in turn, U.S. dollars would be convertible into gold at $35 an ounce. It was up to the U.S. government to keep the price of gold at $35 by controlling the supply of dollars. The United States dollar effectively became the world's currency.

As the United States' debts began to mount in the late 1960s, and the supply of printed dollars grew concurrently, it was obvious to the Bretton Woods signers that, just as Mr. Price had forecast in 1966, the dollar was becoming increasingly overvalued against gold. He had pointed out that the United States then held $14 billion in gold, but only $3 billion of that was available to cover its international obligations. Foreign banks held $14 billion in paper dollars that potentially could be converted into gold. Recognizing the situation, several nations began to ask that they be paid in gold instead of dollars. As these demands increased, the United States was, in effect, being subjected to a run on the dollar. It became obvious that the Treasury didn't have enough gold to satisfy the demand.

President Nixon went on television the evening of August 15, 1971, to announce that the United States would temporarily suspend the convertibility of the dollar into gold. As Mr. Price told George Roche, who was then an analyst and vice president of the New Era Fund and would later become the president and chairman of T. Rowe Price Associates in 1997, "Nixon, in effect declared national bankruptcy that evening." The following day, the Dow Jones rose over 30 points. Hard assets, such as the shares of profitable corporations, were worth more in terms of the suddenly cheaper dollar. This was particularly true of the shares of large international growth companies with high returns on capital, such as IBM. By the end of the year, the dollar was down 8 percent in terms of gold. Later, during 1973, the price of gold more than tripled to $126. The metal was rapidly gaining favor over the dollar.

In 1970, most of the world was being supplied with cheap crude oil from the Organization of the Petroleum Exporting Countries (OPEC), at a price of $1.21 a barrel. OPEC raised the price to $1.70 in 1971 to compensate for the decline in the dollar relative to gold. In 1973, Egypt and Syria invaded Israel, the beginning of what would be called the Yom Kippur War, in which the U.S. and several other nations supported Israel. Before hostilities ceased on October 26, OPEC retaliated by raising the price of oil by 70 percent to over $5 per barrel, and declaring an oil embargo against the United States and the other countries that had sided with Israel. OPEC also cut oil production back by 5 percent per month, and threatened to continue to cut back unless Israel moved out of its newly occupied territory. By the end of 1973, nominal oil prices were up to $15 a barrel.

With inflation escalating, the economy in a tailspin, the market hitting new lows, and the value of the dollar collapsing, these were tumultuous, dark times by any definition. The T. Rowe Price firm, however, did very well in the early years of this dark new era, although many of its competitors had a hard time in the weak stock market. At a number of mutual funds, shareholders were selling more shares than they were buying, causing net redemptions, or an actual shrinkage of the assets of these mutual funds. Some firms were being forced to merge and disappeared altogether. In 1971, the three equity mutual funds of T. Rowe Price took in an astounding 54 percent of the industry's net sales that year, yet they accounted for less than three percent of the industry's assets. Profits of the firm in 1971 hit a record of $1.8 million, as reported in the April 1972 issue of *Fortune*. As usual, Mr. Price had sold too soon but, as he had once noted in a client mailing, "It is always better in such situations to be a bit early than late."

Lines of cars began to stretch out for miles to buy gas. What had been 10-minute fill-ups of gasoline at American pumps could now take more than an hour. Many gas stations completely ran out of petroleum products. Various forms of gas rationing were quickly established at the state and local levels. The increased price of petroleum spread throughout the economy, adding to the inflation already created by the decline in the value of the dollar. The Consumer Price Index went up 7 percent in June 1972, and then rose 11 percent more the next year. All around the industrialized world inflation began running at double-digit rates. Again, Mr. Price's forecast came true, although even he could not have anticipated the "help" from OPEC.

Rapidly rising prices were, in effect, a tax on U.S. consumers. This caused another recession, beginning in November 1973 and lasting until March 1975. Industrial production fell 13 percent and unemployment rose to 9 percent, the highest recorded level since the Great Depression. In this environment, consumers were suffering the worst of all possible economic worlds. The prices of goods and services were rising at a rapid rate because of persistent inflation, which, coupled with high unemployment, created a stagnant demand in the economy. This condition was called "stagflation" by the press.

In the firm's April 1973 revision of the brochure on the Growth Stock Philosophy, the basic definition remained the same, but "should rise at a rate faster than the rise in the cost of living to offset the expected erosion in the purchasing power of the dollar" was added. It was important that the growth be real, after adjusting for inflation. Sales growth and return on invested capital would have to be well above the inflation rate.

"Long-term growth" was added explicitly in 1973. Normal business cycles can cause a company's growth rate to vary. Increasing profit margins can also cause a company to appear temporarily to be a growth stock. Sales growth is a much better indicator of long-term growth than growth in earnings per share.

Though he had first publicly defined a growth stock in 1939, Mr. Price was reluctant at that time to ascribe a specific expected growth rate. There were many internal and external factors to consider in determining such a number. Expectations were so low in the 1930s that even a modest growth rate would have seemed overly optimistic. By 1973, after long experience with his own model accounts, the outstanding performance of the Growth Fund, and with a bit of morale help from his more optimistic young associates, of which I was one, he would finally establish a numerical goal. "A portfolio of growth stocks," he would write in this brochure, "should double in earnings over a 10-year period. It is believed that market value would follow earnings and also double in a 10-year period." He would also return to his warning that "only careful research could separate the effects of the business cycle from the underlying growth of the company."

With its new hires, the firm had an excellent cohort of investment professionals, many of them experienced, over a number of years, in the Growth Stock Philosophy. In truth, T. Rowe Price Associates had not been a "one-man firm" for many years. When Mr. Price retired, he had not attended a Growth Stock Fund Investment Committee meeting for eight years, or a meeting of the New Horizons Fund for three years. His attention had been solely focused on the New Era Fund, his model accounts, and a few of his long-term personal clients.

The firm had then operated for at least a decade with the committee system, a majority vote carrying the decision. The fund investment committees operated in the same manner. They were made up of three to five voting members from both the counsel and the research divisions. At the weekly meetings, several other research analysts were also in attendance to discuss specific buy/sell decisions. Stock turnover remained low for all three funds.

Investments continued to be made with a projected time horizon of more than five years. In an article published in the April 1972 issue of *Fortune*, Cub Harvey, the president of the New Horizons Fund since 1969, told "How T. Rowe Price Does It": "Although I might wander across the floor to get a quote from the trading department, I could just as easily wait until the next morning and read the quote in the paper." Very few, if any, so-called performance funds were managed in such a relaxed manner in 1972. Most were run by a single superstar who spent his or her harried day in the trading room, selling stocks that appeared weak and buying those that seemed to be in an early uptrend.

Walter Kidd, an original founder and long-term head of research, retired in 1972. By then, he had thoroughly instilled the T. Rowe Price method of performing research into all the analysts. This included at least annual on-site visits with the top executives of the twenty or thirty companies for which an analyst might be responsible, phone calls to discuss important changes and new quarterly reports, and continuous monitoring via trade publications and brokerage reports. The analyst would also schedule visits with competitors. Although the companies might be located in pleasant cities like Atlanta or San Francisco, trips to visit them, as I well remember, were anything but pleasurable with Walter in command. Heavy leather-strapped briefcases were carried for each company to be visited. These contained all the annual and quarterly reports since the last visit, SEC filings, selected financial data kept by the firm's statisticians, carefully clipped and filed items from newspapers and trade journals, and reports by Wall Street analysts. Walter even insisted that analysts include a 100-watt bulb to replace the usual 20-watt bulb in the hotel lamps of the cheap hotels we analysts were permitted to stay in. These powerful bulbs allowed us to properly absorb all this information late into the nighttime hours and develop a written agenda for the next day's meeting with management.

No more than two meetings would be scheduled per day. The evening before, it was always an early dinner, with the 100-watt bulb still on after midnight. For most analysts, it was like preparing for a final exam at college in a tough subject. Questions were carefully written out and strategically placed in notes for the interview so that key points were asked different times from different directions. The focus was not only on financial projections, but also included an in-depth discussion of products and sales and any important changes in management, what the CEO thought about when he woke up at three in the morning (still a favorite question, according to recently retired firm president and CEO James A. C. "Jim" Kennedy).

Meeting the top people was important, although the first meeting might be with the analyst's normal contact, such as the vice president of finance. Another key executive, such as the vice president of sales, would often be included later. Meeting the key decision maker, or CEO, at least annually, was often difficult due to his (CEOs were usually men at that time) busy schedule, but was a top priority of Mr. Price. As T. Rowe Price Associates grew larger and better known as an important shareholder with an excellent reputation for thorough preparation, it became easier for the research analysts to set up these interviews with top executives. Between clients and the funds, the firm's total position in a company's stock might exceed 10 percent of the total capitalization. Such large positions were quite common in the New Horizons Fund, where the companies were smaller.

These meetings were then written up for internal consumption in considerable detail. Patents were monitored and often discussed in these write-ups, occasionally with the actual drawings. The last paragraph of a report was a carefully considered buy, sell, or hold recommendation, with the reasons spelled out in detail. The focus was, of course, on the longer term, with a poor short-term outlook often a good reason to recommend buying the stock as it declined in price. These recommendations were an important consideration at bonus time.

While this in-depth research did not change with the departure of Mr. Price or Walter Kidd, the major problem the firm had in the early 1970s was finding suitable growth companies selling at reasonable prices. The New Horizons Fund was closed, as mentioned, to new investors for nearly three years because of the inability to find suitably priced small companies for investment. Cub Harvey told *Fortune* in the same

April 1972 article mentioned above, "If we had a sharp drop in the stock market, we would be in great shape." In a speech Charlie Schaeffer gave in the summer of 1970 called "The Laser Beam Effect," he predicted this overvaluation of growth stocks. Like atoms being squeezed in a strong magnetic field and rising to higher energy states, a relatively small supply of growth stocks would be squeezed to higher levels of valuation by the force of huge sums of money funding the rapidly increasing appetite of pension funds.

The deep recession of 1973–1975 temporarily cooled inflation. In 1976 the Consumer Price Index was "only" up 5 percent – still quite high compared to the 1960s. In 1976, in reaction to the weak economy, the Watergate scandal, and inflation, Jimmy Carter was elected to replace Gerald Ford as U.S. president. In July 1979, in a revolution sponsored by supporters of the Shia Muslim cleric Ayatollah Khomeini, the Shah of Iran was overthrown and forced to flee to Egypt. Partly in retaliation for Carter allowing the Shah's subsequent entrance to the U.S. for treatment of advanced lymphoma, a group of Khomeini supporters stormed the U.S. Embassy in November, taking more than 50 Americans as hostages. In response, Iran's oil shipments were cut off by the Carter administration. Although this only affected about 4 percent of the U.S. oil supply, it caused oil prices to rise to 90 dollars per barrel over the following 12 months. Consumers, remembering the oil embargo of 1973, again began to form lines at gas stations and to hoard petroleum products in tanks at home.

All of this contributed to the industrial world's focus on the weak American dollar. From the sidelines, in articles and memos, Mr. Price had been strongly recommending gold, and the metal climbed rapidly again, peaking on January 21, 1980, at $850 an ounce, a record that would hold for 26 years. Inflation around the world began to ramp up again. By March 31, 1979, the increase in the CPI was back into double digits, with a 10-percent increase. A year later to the day, the CPI rose a record 14.8 percent.

Consumers began to anticipate inflation in their buying decisions. This created a positive feedback loop that drove inflation even higher. The actual cause for inflation in the 1970s was not well understood at the time, and even many years later there is considerable debate among economists. To Mr. Price, however, the reasons were not mysterious. He had written about them extensively. Fundamentally, he believed that the

U.S. government was, once again, printing too much money. To him it was plain common sense (horse sense). It was obvious to him that printing dollars at a rate faster than the real growth of the economy will inherently cause the value of the dollar to decline and the CPI to commensurately increase. When Milton Friedman, the Nobel Prize–winning economist, wrote in his 1970 book, *The Counter Revolution in Monetary Theory,* "Inflation is always and everywhere a monetary phenomenon," Mr. Price would likely have agreed, though there is no mention of Friedman in his writings.

These surplus dollars were created by out-of-control government spending. This caused a huge budget deficit of $74 billion in 1976 ($327 billion in 2018 dollars), a postwar record. As Mr. Price well understood, when faced with choosing between inflation or higher unemployment, the Fed would always choose the former. However, Arthur Burns, chairman of the Fed throughout most of the 1970s, noted: "'Maximum' or 'full' employment, after all," he said, "had become the nations' major economic goal – not stability of the price level." M2 money growth again accelerated to double-digit rates, reaching an 11 percent growth in December of 1983, based on the Board of Governors of the Federal Reserve System, "Money Stock and Debt Measures."

Jimmy Carter was swept out of office in a landslide vote for Ronald Reagan. The Californian assumed the presidency in 1981. Carter's popularity had been badly affected by the runaway inflation, but it was his weak performance in attempting to gain the release of the American hostages, during which eight American soldiers died, that also undermined his term (their eventual release occurred some months into Ronald Reagan's first term).

Carter, however, should get a lot of credit for appointing Paul Volcker as chairman of the Federal Reserve. Strong actions were needed and Volcker proved to be the individual to take them. On October 6, 1979, he began to rein in runaway inflation. Overnight, he switched Fed policy from targeting interest rates to focusing on the root cause of the inflation – money supply. The days of easy money quickly turned to the days of expensive credit. Loans at the prime interest rate carried an interest rate of more than 20 percent, 30-year mortgages cost over 18 percent in interest, and 10-year Treasuries paid a 15.8-percent yield during 1981, according to the U.S. Treasury Department. Mr. Price was certainly not suffering with 50 percent of his money still in reserves at such interest rates.

The economy began to slow and unemployment to rise. Mr. Price had written in a September 1971 internal memo, "Current Beliefs about the Future, or Interpreting Current Events," that voters "will not support any government in the near future which puts the control of inflation ahead of full employment and continued prosperity." He was proven absolutely correct. None did, but when Volcker took such measures as an unelected academic, Mr. Price opposed his actions in "Economic Trends and Current Investment Policy" (July 20, 1981). It was not because he didn't believe this was what was needed to end inflation, but rather he thought that Volcker might be stepping too hard on the brakes. He felt that the economy would be seriously affected by 20-percent-plus interest rates. Business could not operate at such high interest levels – which were well above the return on capital for most companies. It is uncertain if inflation could have been stopped with a lighter touch, but clearly something had to be done quickly to stop what was rapidly becoming an uncontrollable situation.

Volcker came under tremendous criticism at the height of the resulting economic setback. Unemployment went back over 6 percent. The construction industry stalled, with rates for construction loans at more than 19 percent by October 1981. The House Majority Leader, James Wright, a Democrat, called for Volcker's resignation, and even President Reagan's Treasury Secretary, Donald Regan, directly criticized the Fed's position.

By paying no attention to the Employment Act of 1946 or to the 1978 amendment to that act, known as the Humphrey-Hawkins Full Employment Act, Volcker had stopped the United States just short of the cliff. Inflation had peaked in March 1980, and began to decline into a long period of low inflation. The Dow Jones Industrial Average turned up in July 1982, with smart investors beginning to understand and appreciate Volcker's miraculous rescue. He set the stage for a vibrant economy that lasted nearly twenty years and ultimately put millions of Americans back to work.

It was clear to those of us who worked with him that Mr. Price had little use for economists generally. He particularly objected to the English economist John Maynard Keynes. He believed that his theories of deficit spending to stimulate the economy had done much to lead the UK and the United States down the path toward greater socialism, but had offered little to pull their economies out of recession. This was discussed in Chapter 9, and particularly in Mr. Price's memo "State Capitalism." In a speech at a 2003 conference at the Federal Reserve Bank of Dallas, Ben Bernanke, the Fed chairman who would go through the financial crisis beginning in 2007, referred to Friedman's eleven key monetarist propositions. He pointed out that the efforts by economists to reduce unemployment by accelerating money growth "contributed significantly to the Great Inflation of the 1970s … after the Great Depression, the second most serious monetary mistake of the 20th century." Bernanke noted that "the Great Inflation would simply not have been possible without the excessively expansionist monetary policies of the late 1960s and 1970s." Mr. Price would have agreed.

Chapter Fifteen

THE GRIN DISAPPEARS, 1972–1983

Mr. Price in his seventies was still full of ideas. He enjoyed watching His forecasts of the runaway inflation begin to come true and basked in the resulting good performance of the New Era Fund, the even better results of his own model inflation fund, and the increasing income his conservative portfolio was generating. But he couldn't stay silently on the sidelines. The enjoyment for him was the challenge of new investment concepts. Once a new strategy was proven, it was time to move on.

As his health had returned, there were vexing ideas and advice still to be passed on by the Cheshire Cat. It was impossible for him to stop thinking about the world of investing, which had been his life's fascination and his occupation for more than fifty years. A little more than a year after his official retirement in 1972, he wrote Charlie Shaeffer a letter, with a bulletin attached called "The New Era for Bond Investors." In it, he pointed out that the accelerating inflation he had forecast would have a profound effect on bonds as well as stocks:

1. It [inflation] significantly reduces the proceeds on both income and principal. A 5 percent inflation rate, for example, would reduce the purchasing power of today's dollar by 39 percent in 10 years and at the end of 30 years, it would be down 77 percent. The money supply (M2) in early 1972 was increasing at an 11% (annual) rate.

2. The United States government was generating a deficit that was increasing. In addition, many states and local governments

were near insolvency and heavily dependent on taxes to stay afloat. The tax burden of United States citizens was bound to increase.

3. When the money supply and interest rates are controlled by the government, the old economic laws no longer apply [also very true today]. Normally, interest rates rise and bond prices fall when the economy is booming. On the other hand, when the economy is in the doldrums, interest rates fall as demand for credit declines. In this environment, bond prices rise. This normal fluctuation in the price of bonds allows investors to efficiently manage their bond portfolios. In recent years, however, bond prices continue to decline simply due to the accelerating government-created inflation, without regard to the economy. Long-term bonds not only lost money for investors, due to the decline in the purchasing power of the dollar, but also because of their greatly increased supply. Tax-exempt bonds with a 20-year maturity dropped 37 percent from August 1, 1968 to May 1970. Corporate long-term bonds suffered even worse, declining 53 percent over the same time period. Bonds, in other words, were behaving like stocks in this new era. Clearly, bond portfolios could no longer be put away and forgotten as they had in the past. In this new environment bonds must be intensively managed.

4. Bonds and fixed income securities remain an important component of investment portfolios, despite their poor recent performance. Bonds are needed by investors to pay regular income and to pay living expenses. For institutional investors, the yield from bonds is required to pay operating expenses. In 1972, the yield on tax-free bonds was more than five percent, when the yield on large growth stocks was only one percent. Bonds, therefore, yielded more than five times the yield of stocks. For investors who were in a 50-percent tax bracket this increased to seven times.

To effectively manage bonds in this new era Mr. Price suggested that much more attention be paid to maturity schedules, with continued trading necessary to keep maturity schedules short and losses to a minimum.

In addition, more research was required, particularly in the important tax-free area, given the declining financial health of states and municipalities. As he said in "The New Era for Bond Investors," "Investors should place much less emphasis on past and current credit ratings."

Up until this time, the firm had not actively managed their clients' fixed income portfolios. If such a portfolio was quite large, as it might be for a pension fund, it was typically turned over to a bank trust department to maintain. For most clients, the firm had simply followed the normal path, at the time, of staggering maturities of bonds so that the risk of loss was minimized. (When a bond portfolio is staggered, the portfolio is divided into, perhaps, four parts. Each part is invested in comparable bonds, but with a different maturity – such as two, five, seven, and ten years. This reduces the risk of interest changes and balances the yield between the higher long-term rate and the lower short-term rates. Unfortunately, it doesn't work well in the environment of accelerating inflation that the firm and its clients found themselves in during the 1970s.)

After carefully reviewing Mr. Price's memo, Charlie agreed. Mr. Price had once more provided the firm with an important new business opportunity. Carter (Toby) O. Hoffman, who had joined the firm in 1961, was then acting informally as the head of what would become the Fixed Income Department, giving advice on this investment area to the other counselors. He came to the firm with a background in accounting and was able to thoroughly analyze a balance sheet or a report by a municipality to determine whether the bond might be indeed repaid at maturity, the most important consideration in buying any bond. His analysis was considered, in-house, to be more reliable than the more superficial credit ratings provided by Standard & Poor's Financial Services, Moody's Investors Service, or Fitch Group. Toby, however, was primarily a counselor, with a number of large clients. As bond performance became more important, Toby could not manage both his own clients and the firm's bond portfolios. When approached by Charlie to be the leader of the new Fixed Income Department, he chose to remain as a counselor. The firm went on a search for a bond manager.

The field of fixed income was and is much larger than the equity market. A bond department would have the potential of adding a significant new earnings center for the firm and, at the same time, help existing clients. Active management of client bond portfolios would protect and enhance the return from client's fixed income portfolios, particularly in the current economic environment. Skillful trading could also produce significant additional capital returns.

Because it had provided little real management of client's fixed income accounts, the firm had not charged much in the past for administering and managing them. A reasonable fee for active bond management could easily be justified in this new volatile environment. There was also the opportunity to create specialized bond funds for both individuals and pension funds.

In the stock market, commissions and trading profits by 1970 were razor thin, prices were publicly available, and commission schedules were published. Bond trading, however, took place in a freewheeling over-the-counter market where spreads could be relatively wide. Traders often were a bit "careless" in their pricing of bonds, and there was no central market to determine accurate current prices, such as existed for stocks on the New York Stock Exchange. Innocent amateurs were often eaten alive by professional Wall Street bond traders. Even today, there is still no central bond exchange where prices are openly quoted and bids and offers are transparent. Tom Wolfe gives an entertaining portrayal of this market in his 1987 book, *The Bonfire of the Vanities*. Michael Lewis was hired as a bond salesman at Salomon Brothers, fresh out of Princeton, and his *Liar's Poker,* published in 1989, is more accurate and gives a lively, nonfictional account of the bond trading market and some of the characters that populated it almost thirty years ago. That market is not as flamboyant today, and profit margins have narrowed significantly, but on occasion, like the recent bust in 2008, it can seem like the Wild West again.

Right in Baltimore, Charlie and Toby found their person, George J. Collins, to run the bond department. He was working for a large local insurance company, the United States Fidelity and Guaranty Company. Thirty years old, he had started his career as a catcher for a semiprofessional baseball team, but left when he decided he had no chance to rise to the major leagues. After a four-year career in the Air Force and a one-year stint as an analyst at a small local brokerage firm, he had joined USF&G as a trader in the bond department. He had done very well in that hectic, competitive world. After three years, he was considering more lucrative offers from Wall Street when he was approached by T. Rowe Price Associates. The opportunity to build an entirely new business in fixed income from the ground up won him over, despite the firm's comparatively modest compensation strategy. He joined in 1971.

Mr. Price was involved in the search process. He met George before he was hired and took an instant liking to him. He wrote to Charlie, "I have had several talks with George and think he is an outstanding bond man and is doing an excellent job. I hope his department will be enlarged, so that the firm will become expert in this important field." He and George subsequently established a very comfortable personal and working relationship, which was rare for Mr. Price – but then maybe he was getting a little older and more relaxed in retirement. Plus, George's knowledge of Mr. Price's personal holdings, relatively obscure bonds, cemented their relationship.

Initially, George's blunt manner and manic pace mystified many in the T. Rowe Price organization. He was isolated with his credit analysts and traders on a different floor with what George claimed were World War I desk chairs and Civil War desks left by Union soldiers when they departed Baltimore. He had a view across a narrow alley to a brick wall.

The bond world is indeed very different from that of equities, but George's success began to win converts. His first major account came at the end of 1972, when he secured the bond portfolio of Northwestern Bell's pension fund. It began as a $25 million account, not to be sneezed at even in those days of larger and larger accounts. The bond portfolio of the Baltimore County pension fund came soon afterward.

That was just the beginning. In 1973, Charlie authorized the creation of the New Income Fund. This was a balanced maturity, fixed-income fund. Rather than run it in the traditional manner of staggered maturities, George managed it based on the concept of total return. That is, profits could be generated by making money from buying bonds at a good value and then selling them for higher prices, without waiting for them to mature. The bonds could be sold either when the value inherent in the bond was recognized by the market, or when interest rates fell and prices rose in value. The client made money through capital gains from the sale of the bond, as well as from the income generated by the yields on the bonds themselves. The investment program also included preferred stock and a limited amount of common stock.

In order to uncover hidden value in bonds and thoroughly examine their credit risks, a good research department was required, similar to what existed at T. Rowe Price on the equity side. As Mr. Price had discussed in the memo "New Era for Bond Investment," there would be less emphasis on past credit ratings and more emphasis on detecting opportunities in changing markets through research. Developing superior trading strategies, and often simply being more aggressive, were also key strategies. Most importantly, George and Mr. Price agreed that inflation would dramatically accelerate in the 1970s. As a result, George followed the philosophy of early recapture of capital. He kept all the bond portfolios relatively short-term, primarily buying short and intermediate bonds, or those close to their maturity dates. He often opportunely sold them early, recapturing his capital as inflation drove interest rates ever higher and bond prices commensurately lower. As the results proved, following this strategy, he performed far better than his competitors, who bought many of the same bonds, but held them longer, even to maturity.

Like two of the three original equity mutual funds, the New Income Fund was a slow starter. When interest rates soared in the mid-1970s, however, it took off. By 1977, it had reached $284 million in assets and became the third-largest corporate bond fund in the country. By then, George was clearly winning over the equity side of the firm. Like the Cheshire Cat, Mr. Price just smiled benignly.

The fixed income markets were changing dramatically, and T. Rowe Price's bond department was leading the way. In 1976, Congress passed legislation permitting tax-free municipal bond funds, and the firm was quick to seize the opportunity. Before this legislation, tax-free income went through the corporate shell of a mutual fund and became taxable. This was eliminated under the new law. In the first five months of operation, according to George, the new Tax-Free Fund accumulated $75 million in assets. It had grown to $215 million in assets by 1978 and was again the third-largest fund of its type.

In 1976, George persuaded the firm to start the Prime Reserve Fund. Though the Federal Reserve System regulated the interest rates that banks and savings and loan associations could pay to their depositors, there was no such limit on mutual funds. On the other hand, the public initially viewed money market funds with considerable suspicion. Unlike bank deposits, money in short-term money market funds, like the Prime Reserve, was not insured by the U.S. government. The Prime Reserve Fund also had a slow start, chiefly because of this "trust" factor. When interest rates reached double digits, far above the 5.5 percent level that banks were allowed to pay, the Prime Reserve Fund finally took off. Such rates proved to be irresistible to corporations and, eventually, to the public as well, even without insurance.

The Prime Reserve Fund was important to the firm in another way. It provided a handy parking space for investors in the company's equity funds. When some of these investors became nervous about the stock market, they could seamlessly move their money from an equity fund to the Prime Reserve Fund. The firm continued to get a fee from managing the Prime Reserve Fund, although at a lower percentage rate than an equivalent amount in an equity account. Most importantly, when someone sold his or her equity fund, the client did not vanish, perhaps forever, into a bank savings account. He or she could instead easily move money back into the market when the time was right.

Reserve funds, such as the Prime Reserve Fund, also increased investors' interest in the mutual fund industry as a whole. As George mentioned, many shareholders of Prime Reserve had never owned an equity mutual fund before. The fluctuating trendless stock market of the 1970s convinced many investors that their own instincts, and those of their brokers, were not to be trusted. Once they had put their toe into an investment in the Prime Reserve Fund, it was simple to move over into an equity fund managed by professionals, which produced much better results and allowed them to sleep at night.

By 1983, according to George Collins and *The History of T. Rowe Price Associates, Inc.*, only twelve years after Collins had joined T. Rowe Price the Fixed Income Department was managing more than $2.2 billion in private counsel accounts. The tax-free bond fund had $673 million in assets and the Prime Reserve Fund, despite its slow start, had amassed $2.7 billion. In total, the Fixed Income Division accounted for nearly half of all of the assets under supervision by T. Rowe Price Associates, with a similar percentage of the earnings. This was a remarkable feat in a new business that Mr. Price had initiated and George Collins had executed. There was no surprise when George was made president and CEO of the firm in 1984, at 43 years old.

With 20/20 hindsight, it was fortunate for the firm that it started the Fixed Income Department when it did. The equity environment changed after 1972 – and particularly for T. Rowe Price Associates. One minute it seemed that the world was its oyster, with growth stocks outperforming the market, and both the Growth Stock Fund and the

New Horizon Fund leading all competitors for their first ten years. In 1971, the Growth Stock Fund rose 30.4 percent, with the Dow Jones up only up seven percent. But it all changed quickly. As investors might have noted in the annual reports, during the next 10 years the Growth Stock Fund only beat the market in one year. The New Horizons Fund did better, but its record over the next decade fell far short of its first ten years.

Mr. Price and Eleanor continued to avoid the damp, cold Baltimore winters at the Hillsboro Club near Pompano Beach, Florida. Following his retirement, the Prices generally arrived after Christmas and stayed through until April, returning only so as not to miss the lovely Baltimore spring and the rebirth of his roses. A casually elegant club that has been in existence for more than eighty years, the Hillsboro Club catered largely to East Coast families who enjoyed soaking up a week or so of warm southern Florida weather there in the winter. Friendly and comfortable, it was more relaxed than many clubs in the Palm Beach and Naples areas, with wicker furniture in tasteful pastel colors, and a large 1,000-foot private beach. Tennis was a major sport at the club, which Mr. Price played into his seventies. The club also offered world-class croquet for the less active members. There was plenty of social activity for the young, and comfortable dining and sitting around for the older members. It was just the kind of place for Mr. Price and Eleanor in their retirement years.

When I visited the club in 2014, a member heard that I was writing a book about Mr. Price. She came over during the cocktail hour and told me about meeting him at the club in the mid-1970s. She had her nine-year-old niece with her, and they were seated near the Price's dinner table. At that time, the club still used finger bowls, with a separate, round doily napkin. Her niece had never seen a finger bowl before. Her husband showed her niece how to transfer the bowl properly to the doily, and then put her fingers into the water. There was a subdued burst of laughter as Mr. Price doubled over at the sight. She suddenly saw his human, nonbusiness side. He had just been another fussy old man, but now he became "Uncle Rowe."

When he was in Baltimore, Mr. Price regularly visited his office at One Charles Center. He mostly worked on his family portfolios and those of old friends and charities. He also occasionally interacted with the young professionals, as well as members of the New Era Fund, where he still made suggestions on new investments.

Another story about Mr. Price was told by M. David (Dave) Testa in an interview with Steve Norwitz, who was hired in 1971 and later became a director and senior member of management. His office was only two doors down the hall from Mr. Price. Several times a day Mr. Price would walk by on his way to the Quotron machine, a popular electronic device which displayed stock quotes, to obtain quotes for the stocks in his model portfolios. After about a month, Mr. Price stuck his head in the door and then came in and stood there. He asked Dave how he was doing, and Dave said that things were going very well. Mr. Price stood there and looked at Dave for a while. Then he asked if he was learning anything. Dave replied that he was "actually learning quite a bit." Mr. Price looked at Dave some more and then asked him, "What is a growth stock?" Dave had just been reading all of the marketing material on that subject. He regurgitated all of the various definitions and qualifications for a company to be a growth stock. "You haven't learned a thing," Mr. Price said, and turned around and left.

For a new employee and a fresh Baker Scholar from Harvard Business School, this put-down was a cold shock. When Dave got back from lunch later that day, he discovered a brochure in the middle of his desk from 1950, written by Mr. Price. It included a reprint of his 1939 *Barron's* article in which he first defined the Growth Stock Philosophy. Mr. Price had underlined a passage that stated, "A growth stock is a company whose earnings and dividends grow at a rate faster than the economy and inflation." And that's it, Dave recalled thinking. Straightforward, to the point, with no wasted words. The best philosophies are often the simplest.

Mr. Price would also occasionally meet with the counseling and research staff to discuss performance, his favorite topic and, he believed, the key to the firm's past success. He would often also talk about the firm's history, the personal attributes that made it tick, and its simple focus on what was best for the client. He taught the young professionals his core belief that the payoff for being honest, straightforward, and loyal to the client would not only produce a continued flow of fees, but it would also build the firm's business over the longer term through references from satisfied clients. As he pointed out, a good relationship with the client would even take you over the rough patches of short-term weak performance.

In 1975, the firm moved to its current home at 100 East Pratt Street in Baltimore Harbor. Once more, it had outgrown its quarters, with offices on four floors at One Charles Center and the elevator, once more, a major inconvenience. Mr. Price was not included in the move. According to George Roche, this was because someone had not included an office for Marie Walper. Mr. Price, therefore, decided to stay with her at One Charles Center. Based on a number of reports from mutual friends, the oversight hurt him deeply. He was particularly disappointed that the young associates, whom he enjoyed interacting with so much, didn't seem to want him around. It was this slight that probably gave rise to some of Mr. Price's critical comments to the press in the latter 1970s, although, in the opinion of those who knew him, Mr. Price was never a man to carry a grudge.

The present T. Rowe Price Group Headquarters in the foreground on the Baltimore Harbor, with the original offices at 10 Light Street in the background. Photo by the author.

It is unclear how this seeming oversight occurred. It was certainly not intended as such by the firm. It was probably an unfortunate error caused by all of the thousands of details surrounding the move. After all, Mr. Price had officially retired from the firm in 1971. Someone on the administrative staff must have assumed that he meant it.

T. Rowe Price Associates did continue to pay for his offices at One Charles Center, and Marie kept her office next to his. They had made the full circle in a sense. The firm had begun in 1937, when Mr. Price and Marie opened the door into a two-room suite at 10 Light Street.

In the early 1970s, Mr. Price noticed that Eleanor was becoming increasingly forgetful. When Mr. Price went with her to see their family doctor, concerned about her loss of memory, his doctor assured them that she was fine. As recounted by Dr. Rabins (see the next paragraph), there was then a dangerous episode at the Hillsboro Club when Eleanor stepped into a steaming hot bath, having forgotten to turn on the cold water. She was badly burned. Mr. Price went to two additional doctors for second and third opinions. They also failed to detect a problem. One weekend, after they were back in Baltimore, he was working outside in his yard at the same time as his neighbor, Dr. Richard S. Ross, Dean of the Johns Hopkins University School of Medicine, was in his adjoining yard. When Mr. Price described Eleanor's condition and his difficulty in convincing any of her physicians that something was wrong, Dr. Ross suggested that they visit Dr. Paul R. McHugh, who was then the director of the Department of Psychiatry and Behavioral Sciences at Johns Hopkins, and an expert in memory loss.

A Dementia Research Clinic had been established there and was sponsoring a geriatric psychiatry program, led by Dr. Peter V. Rabins, MD, the program's founding director, and later the first holder of the Richman Family Professorship of Alzheimer Disease and Related Disorders in the Department of Psychiatry and Behavioral Sciences of the Johns Hopkins University School of Medicine. Eleanor was diagnosed with Alzheimer's. Dr. Rabins's group schooled them in the care that she would need and what to expect as the disease progressed.

Looking back on his experience and the difficulty he had getting a correct diagnosis – even in a sophisticated medical community like Baltimore – Mr. Price recognized that many others might be in a similar situation. According to Dr. Rabins, late in 1979 he decided to gift $250,000 in securities to endow the T. Rowe and Eleanor Price Teaching Service, located in the geriatrics section of the Johns Hopkins

Department of Psychiatry and Behavioral Sciences of the Johns Hopkins University School of Medicine. Its mission was "the training of doctors and nurses in the causes and treatment of loss of memory and the associated general dementia," according to Dr. Rabins.

Mr. Price had always enjoyed working with intelligent young people, and he was impressed by Dr. Rabins. In turn, the doctor found Mr. Price to be polite and never condescending. However, he said that Mr. Price was not one to tolerate suppositions. He insisted that if Dr. Rabins did not know the answer to a question, he say so. As others had discovered, Mr. Price valued honesty and frankness. Mr. Price spoke with Dr. Rabins every three months or so over the course of the several years of Eleanor's treatment. Ultimately Dr. Rabins was named the Director of the T. Rowe and Eleanor Price Teaching Service of the Department of Psychiatry and Behavioral Sciences.

According to Dr. Rabins, Mr. Price's private goals in regard to the service were three-fold: 1) to ensure that physicians, nurses, and all health care providers were taught about Alzheimer's disease and related dementias, because little was known about them at that time; 2) to provide this information for both the person with dementia and for the family caregiver; and 3) to find a cure.

Dr. Rabins remembers Mr. Price explaining that "before he invested in a stock, he always thoroughly investigated all aspects of the company. He carefully studied its business as well as its finances." This was the approach that Mr. Price wanted Dr. Rabins to take in his research into Alzheimer's. He wanted the group to thoroughly study all the known science at the time in an effort to better understand the disease.

Nancy L. Mace, MA, a consultant to and member of the board of directors of the Alzheimer's Association and an assistant in psychiatry, was hired as coordinator of the T. Rowe and Eleanor Price Teaching Service. Working with Dr. Rabins and a nurse, Mary Jane Lucas, she set up the Alzheimer's Association Chapter of Greater Baltimore, which held monthly meetings with patients, their families, and caregivers to discuss issues and solutions.

Minutes were kept of these meetings and distributed to the participants and other interested parties. These notes were mimeographed and stapled together. The package of notes grew significantly in size over time. They were finally edited by Dr. Rabins and Nancy Mace and were originally published in 1981 and are still in print in a sixth edition under the title *The 36-Hour Day: A Family Guide to Caring for People Who Have Alzheimer's Disease, Related Dementias, and Memory Loss.* According to Dr. Rabins, more than three million copies have been sold, the largest number for a book title ever sold by Johns Hopkins Press. It has become the bible for the care and treatment of Alzheimer's, and has been translated into multiple languages. The book now discusses all the potential treatments that might lead to a cure of the disease.

When Mr. Price died, his gift would be increased to $1 million dollars under his will. Although Alzheimer's research is more substantially funded today, when Mr. Price made his initial and subsequent donations, very little money was being spent in the United States on the study of the disease. This made his contribution even more significant at the time.

As Eleanor's memory loss worsened, it became impractical to continue to live in their beloved Guilford home. They moved late in December 1974 to the Warrington Apartments on North Charles Street in Baltimore, which housed a number of Mr. Price's old friends in large, comfortable apartments.

On May 3, 1981, his wife and lifelong partner died. He and Eleanor had a true and beautiful partnership. In describing their relationship following her death, he alluded to their shared love of gardening, saying, as quoted in her obituary, "I raised the flowers, she put them in beautiful arrangements, and together we won many awards." This metaphor was quite poetic for a man whose speech was usually concise and businesslike. He rarely spoke of personal issues. His allusion to a garden and her beautiful bouquets suggests that he credited Eleanor for creating a warm, colorful environment for the two of them. Because she so ably tended to the domestic needs of the couple and their boys, Mr. Price was able to focus on building his business and establishing a preeminent reputation in his industry. It was a true partnership of equals and Eleanor was his lifelong love. Thomas Rowe Price IV, Mr. Price's grandson, said his grandfather told him that whenever he was in the hospital, he always had a picture of her looking like the day he married her.

Following Eleanor's death, his younger sister, Gahring, who then lived in Lancaster, Pennsylvania, often came down to take care of him. His older sister, Mildred, who had guided him so often to his new schools, had died some years before. It was still a close family.

Mr. Price continued to write and publish his investment bulletins privately throughout his retirement. These were distributed to key members of the firm. He also remained intensively competitive, publishing the results of his model accounts and comparing them with the performance of the firm's mutual funds. The competition was congenial and the intent was a good one: to keep the firm and the funds focused on performance and always trying to do better.

Mr. Price also retained his long habit of intense concentration and need for privacy. Although his office before the move to 100 East Pratt Street was in the middle of the counsel floor, he always kept his door shut. He was definitely not the open-door type of leader. Everyone had to have an appointment to see him, with a precise time to begin, and Marie Walper was the strict gatekeeper.

Pete Calhoun tells a story of knocking on Mr. Price's door one day and there was no answer from within. Nevertheless, Pete went in, saw that Mr. Price was deep in study, and sat down in front of his desk. Mr. Price didn't look up. Pete kept sitting there. Finally, Mr. Price said, "You know how irritating I find it when people come in at the wrong time?" Pete said he knew that. Mr. Price asked, "Is your watch working today?" Pete said that it was. Mr. Price said, "Do you know how annoyed I get when people ignore my privacy?" Pete said that he did. After several similar questions and answers, Mr. Price said, "Well then, would you please get out of here!" in a loud voice. Pete got up and went to the door. In leaving, he turned and said, "Mr. Price, you will be the last person in this building, and the building is on fire." With that, Pete left. Mr. Price looked out of his office and saw that the firemen were indeed occupying the floor.

Mr. Price, as noted, did continue to pay particular attention to his youngest "child," the New Era Fund. He realized that, though the concept of growth stock investing and his outstanding long-term record was well-established and accepted, the New Era Fund's performance, with its unique investment strategy aimed at profiting from inflation, would be significant to his legacy. Even though he attended no more meetings of the Fund's investment committee after 1973, he did regularly contact its chairman, Bob Hall. The committee made all the purchases and sales of stocks in the portfolio, controlling its performance. Often Mr. Price's call to Bob would be on Sunday morning and he would begin teasingly with, "I know you are probably not in church." Then he would begin a review of the fund's performance, its purchase and sales of stocks, and Mr. Price's general outlook for the economy and the market.

All of this could easily take an hour or more. What Bob had expected to be his breakfast time often became brunch. This was how Mr. Price remained an integral part of the New Era Fund, even in absentia.

Often these conversations became a bit contentious when Mr. Price sensed that Bob was not in total agreement. Bob remembers saying (under his breath), that he was always held accountable based on Mr. Price's high standards. Which meant that your standards were always being raised, of course.

Bob also remembers that Mr. Price could be very generous and thoughtful to those with whom he worked closely. "When my father died, "he said, "he called me up and even wrote me a letter. I don't know how he even knew about it. He was retired and vacationing at the time. But he kept track and went out of his way to offer his condolences."

During the late 1960s and early 1970s, as referenced in Chapters 13 and 14, Mr. Price had begun to significantly build up his position in gold stocks in his model accounts and, through his strong urging, the New Era Fund had followed, although to a lesser degree. He had first established a small initial position in gold in his Model Inflation Fund in 1967. He added to these holdings in 1970 and early 1971. When President Nixon took the country off the gold standard in 1971, Mr. Price aggressively bought gold stocks, which appreciated sharply during the 1973–74 market break. By the first quarter of 1974, gold accounted for over 30 percent of Mr. Price's total model equity portfolio. As was his custom after such an appreciation, he sold enough of his gold holdings to cover 80 percent of his total costs, plus the capital gains taxes. The gold stocks in his account had risen over 700 percent between 1972 and 1974. Gold promptly declined sharply, as inflation ebbed in 1975 and 1976. Mr. Price switched back to the buy side and bought aggressively once again. For the first time since his early thirties, he became an active trader and this time much more successfully. He believed rightly that inflation was far from over and that gold remained the investor's best protection against it. Although an oil or timber company could conceivably be a growth stock for five or 10 years, this was not true of a highly volatile gold company, where earnings were relatively meaningless and management was usually very thin. As he often told Bob Hall, "Gold stocks could not be just bought and held."

His program of aggressively buying gold again in the mid–1970s bore fruit as gold hit a record price of $850 in early 1980. Because it was even more heavily invested in gold stocks, Mr. Price's model inflation fund did even better than New Era. Winning this little match between his model fund and the New Era Fund brought Mr. Price great satisfaction.

As *Forbes* commented in "Why T. Rowe Price Likes Gold" in the October 15, 1975, issue, "Some of his rivals [other money managers] are studying the trees. Others study the forest. But Price tries to take in the whole landscape. With … almost uncanny perspicacity."

On July 30, 1975, he wrote a final memo on "Better Performance" to the firm's professional staff. At the end he wrote, "Like Mohammed [sic] Ali, I believe in retiring a winner. God knows because of my age and poor health, it is time to stop competing!" He did, however, introduce one more new investment concept, a salvage and recovery fund. At a meeting of the firm's investment professionals in 1969, he had suggested that T. Rowe Price Associates consider a mutual fund based on this idea. No action was taken, and in 1970 he started a small model account of his own to invest in such companies to test out the idea. He quickly determined that one needed intimate knowledge of the securities in question and unlimited patience. In "Fertile Fields in the Eighties," an article he wrote for the November 9, 1981 issue of *Forbes*, he suggested putting "25 percent of a new cash account into the building and construction industry," which had been decimated by the high interest rates and weak economy of the previous decade. Many such companies were indeed selling at well under book value. More than a year later, on December 6, 1982, *Forbes* reported in the article "Stocks for the Mid-80s" that this final recommendation by Mr. Price had "raised eyebrows" at the time, as the companies he suggested were "in almost total disfavor on Wall Street. They had, however, made a spectacular recovery, far outperforming the market."

He explained in an article in the *Baltimore Sun* that the place to look for investment opportunities for a salvage and recovery fund was in industries that had been declining for a number of years, and that the opportunities were greatest when the country was in a recession. Buying had to be done gradually, with many more shares purchased as the stocks declined under book value. He warned that these investments should be sold quickly when earnings recover.

With rapid inflation, high interest rates, and weak business conditions, the environment indeed seemed to be ripe for such a fund. The firm's Investment Policy Committee made a visit to his apartment, after the article was published, to discuss the concept. Mr. Price discouraged the idea for the firm at that time. He had discovered, with his model salvage and recovery portfolio, that there was just not enough liquidity for big institutional accounts or a mutual fund on the scale of the firm's other funds.

It turned out that the firm actually did adopt a version of this concept a few years later when it entered the field of value investing, which was strongly promoted by James (Jim) S. Riepe who was hired then to direct marketing as well as other important areas within the firm. (This is discussed in detail in the Epilogue.)

In the December 1982 *Forbes* article, Mr. Price also recommended, for the first time in nearly 20 years, that investors buy bonds. Specific bonds were not named, but a longer maturity was implied. Assuming that the investor bought long-term Treasuries, then a favorite of Mr. Price's, he would have had a total compound return on his capital of 14 percent over the following decade, far better then the 10.8 percent for the Standard & Poor's 500 Index. Mr. Price recognized that Volcker's strong medicine had stopped the country's inflationary spiral that had so concerned him 15 years before, and that the economy would soon begin to prosper. *Forbes* reported that his recommended list of "stocks for the' 80s were already up 24 percent versus 14 percent for the market."

As he might have reminded his audience: "Change is the investor's only certainty."

In November 1982, he fell ill again and, as his doctor was trying to put him back into the hospital, he reportedly told friends that he had so many ideas – and opportunities – that there weren't enough hours in the day to talk about them all.

Late on a Friday afternoon in April 1983, Henry H. Hopkins, the firm's chief legal counsel, got a call from Mr. Price, who was at the Greater Baltimore Medical Center (GBMC). "Henry," Mr. Price said, "I would like you to update my obituary and bring it out for me to check over. I need it right now." As recalled by Henry to me, he was about to leave for his home on Gibson Island, an hour's drive away, but he quickly called a member of the Communications Group. Henry explained that Mr. Price wanted his obituary revised and updated quickly. He said,

"I can't. We are going out to dinner. When do I have to have it ready?" Henry said "You and I had better review it and you should take it out to him tonight. Tell your wife you will meet her wherever you are going. You will be late." "Okay," he said, reluctantly. "I'll stay."

Henry read the Sunday paper carefully, but there was no obituary. There wasn't one on Monday either. Monday night, Henry played tennis doubles. One of his tennis partners was a general surgeon at the hospital and Henry asked him, "I heard Mr. Price was dying. He is at your hospital. Have you heard if he did die?" The surgeon replied, "How did you hear that?" When Henry explained it to him, the doctor said, "Friday night, when I went by to see him. I would have bet one million dollars that he was going to die. That he was on his deathbed. He had major stomach issues. His stomach was just disintegrating. I thought I was going to get a call that night, but I didn't. Saturday morning early I went in to do my rounds. I walk into Mr. Price's room and there he is sitting in his chair all dressed in his suit and necktie." Mr. Price said, "I decided not to die. Check me out. I want to leave now. Right now!" The doctor added, "That was one of the major miracles of my practice." Henry replied, "Mr. Price, indeed, is known to change his mind on occasion."

And change was indeed in the air and it remained the only certainty for Mr. Price. In his last bulletin, "Outlook for 1983 and Beyond," August 1, 1983, he said, "Stocks are statistically cheap. This will be the biggest Christmas in many years. We are on the verge of the biggest bull market in a long time." He suggested that investors have 70-plus percent of their portfolio in stocks, which was his position at the time and which, for him, was extremely aggressive. None of the stocks he recommended were resource stocks and the great majority were true growth stocks, both big and small. One could imagine his old partner, Mr. Ramsay, saying "But Rowe!" as he would when Mr. Price abruptly changed his mind.

Bob Hall visited him during this period, at home in his apartment. "He was a very sick man by this point," Bob recalled. "He was surrounded by nurses and sipping water. He looked at me and laughed that the nurses all thought he was drinking water. Then he cupped his hand and in a loud whisper said, 'It's really gin.' Naturally, it wasn't," Bob continued, "but there was a person with a very sunny, optimistic disposition behind that tough, gruff exterior. Even at the worst of times, when he was at the end of his life, he was able to poke fun at himself."

When Mr. Price turned bullish on the stock market in his last investment bulletin to clients, the Dow was 1,194. January 2018 it hit a new all time high of 26,617, up more than 21 times.

Mr. Price died at home from a stroke on October 20, 1983. He was 85.

Part Four

MARKET ANALYSES

Chapter Sixteen

INVESTING FOR THE DECADE, 2017–2027

This chapter falls outside of the period of Mr. Price's lifetime and is based entirely on the author's and Bob Hall's' speculation as to how Mr. Price and his investment concepts might approach today's markets.

Mr. Price had two distinct advantages over most other investors. He was an innovative visionary and a gifted soothsayer. In addition, he was extremely focused on the business of investing, literally reading reports and studies on that subject from the time he woke up at four in the morning until he went to bed at nine-thirty in the evening. During his prime, before he retired from the firm, he only took time out from these studies for meals, occasional dinners with good friends, and preparation for and participation in meetings with clients and mutual fund advisory committees.

In the 1930s, he had the vision and foresight to develop the Growth Stock Theory of Investing. Described in more detail in earlier chapters, this was the concept that one might achieve superior investment results with a program based on the commonsense concept of buying and holding only the stocks of companies that had the ability to sustain superior earnings growth over the long term. This was far ahead of his time. In the years immediately following the Great Depression, the emphasis was not on investing for the future, but on the preservation of one's remaining capital.

Even today, many investors put their money into stocks that they believe will quickly go up, rather than in companies that should produce longer-term superior growth in earnings. "Longer-term" for Mr. Price typically meant ten years. The time horizon for most current investors is six months or less. Because of this very different focus, there is actually less competition for superior growth stocks today than during much of the past 40 years. Particularly during the seventies, growth stocks became popular, and, hence overpriced, largely due to the firm's widely advertised outstanding success.

Mr. Price also had the rare ability to foresee crucial changes in world sociopolitical and economic trends, and to understand how these changes would impact the investment environment. Typically, his clients would be fully invested years before others recognized that the market environment had changed. In modern-day financial parlance, he had the ability to foresee the "black swans." This is a concept, first postulated in Roman times, for rare, significant events. In his 2007 book, *The Black Swan: The Impact of the Highly Improbable*, Nassim Nicholas Taleb discussed how black swans impact the financial markets. He defined a black swan event as "an outlier, as it lies outside the realm of normal expectations ... [and] carries an extreme impact."

Mr. Price demonstrated the amazing ability to anticipate major changes in financial markets consistently over a long period of time. His advice to invest at the end of the bear market, in the blackest days of the 1930s; the forecast to his clients of a bull market beginning in 1942, following the rapid march of German troops through Europe and the equally quick Japanese victories throughout the Pacific; his positioning of his clients' portfolios in 1950 for the greatest business boom in history, while his peers were still concerned about another depression; and his early forecast in 1965 of the ruinous Great Inflation of the 1970s were all black swans.

Bob Hall and I worked for Mr. Price for more than a decade. Bob's excellent investment record is discussed in the foreword. We got together recently to consider how Mr. Price might adjust his investment outlook in the current environment.

He certainly would have a keen insight into prevailing issues, such as the artificial, very low interest rate structure engineered by the Federal Reserve System, the trend today toward national identity, and the liberalizing of Generally Accepted Accounting Principles (GAAP earnings), which make reported earnings virtually meaningless, or take "companies into an alternate reality," according to a February 24, 2017, article in the *Wall Street Journal*.

In the dialogue that follows, we will not attempt to match Mr. Price's unique ability to forecast the future. We will merely outline the present social, economic, and political environment, as he defined them in 1937 in his first bulletin, "Change: The Investor's Only Certainty," and discuss the various currents at work in this environment, as he did every five years or so over his long career. We will probably miss the next black swan, should one be lurking in the reeds.

We do believe, as he did, that it is quite possible to construct an investment program that can produce a superior return over the long term, even without this forecasting. We observed that, in the midst of dramatic change, Mr. Price's own portfolio was always well over half invested in a diversified list of growth companies. By simply following his basic principles of superior investment research, focusing on the quality of a company's management, and carefully analyzing the important financial trends within the company and the industry in which it operates, it has continued to provide highly competitive results for its clients.

The first goal of my meeting with Bob was to review the currents and tides at work in the world and then to develop an investment program for the next or 10 years or so, incorporating any major changes from the forecast outlined in Mr. Price's last article in the December 6, 1982, issue of *Forbes* titled "Stocks for the Mid-'80s."

We both agreed that the major long-term currents, which Mr. Price had identified in 1937, hadn't changed direction over the centuries – and certainly not over the thirty-six years since the 1982 article, because they were based on the fundamental nature of mankind. These currents, however, could be substantially modified by the "tide," as he discussed. There was no question in 1937 that the tide was running in a direction favoring the progressives, toward more government control of the economy. We believe Mr. Price would point out that such tides can and do run their course and eventually change their direction.

"The major force behind the long-term current towards liberalism," as he wrote in his 1937 "Change" memo, "was the rise of the masses to power over the past century." According to Mr. Price, this trend had been propelled by better and faster communications. The telephone exponentially accelerated communications around the turn of the century. The radio followed, with the ability to communicate instantly with millions of people. After World War II, commercial airplanes facilitated travel throughout the world in days instead of weeks or months. Television provided the transmission of pictures in the 1950s, adding a whole new dimension to the power of radio. Suddenly, the average person was able to easily visualize his or her situation and compare it to that of others around the world and see firsthand the impact of major events.

The most important recent innovation in communications has been the Internet, which reached commercial scale after the birth of AOL in 1983. Billions of individuals are now connected every day online, cheaply and easily able to instantaneously communicate their thoughts with pictures and movies, either to individuals or simultaneously to millions of others. The Internet was credited with amplifying the Arab Spring that began in 2011 and, while it is still in an early phase of technical and social development, it will no doubt continue to create more political change around the world.

In 1937, the world's economy had stalled after a very slow recovery from the severe financial collapse during the Great Depression. Real unemployment in the great majority of countries remained at high levels throughout the 1930s. Governments depended on deficit financing to keep up even a modest growth, just as is true today. Socialism was on the rise around the world and there was much political ferment, particularly in Europe.

Mr. Price believed that this rise of the masses, or the "Have Nots," as he termed named them in the 1930s, was also true of nations. He identified the U.S., Britain, France, and Russia as the "Have" nations, and Germany, Italy, and Japan as "Have Not" nations. Today, the U.S., the EU, and Japan are the obvious major "Have" nations, with China and Russia the major "Have Nots." China, economically at least, has been rising rapidly in recent decades, allowing its population to achieve a better life. GDP per capita in China, however, is still only $16,000, less than a third that of the U.S. Politically, it remains a socialist republic run by the Communist party. After a brief experiment with U.S.-style capitalism and open elections, following the collapse of the Berlin Wall in 1989, Russia has become more centrally controlled.

Mr. Price also said that the rise of the masses in a democratic society meant bigger government with increasing regulation of business and more resources allocated to the Have Nots with higher taxes on the wealthy to pay for it. He predicted that as the trend toward socialism gains power in this environment, it will take over more control of those industries that impact basic human needs such as agriculture, transportation, water, heat, and social benefits such as health, education, and insurance. In the last ten years, steps toward universal health care have been introduced, there has been a partial takeover of the funding of college education with the government now controlling the student loan programs, and the attempted regulation of the Internet by the FCC under the old telephone regulations with Net Neutrality, which has been lifted.

Another of Mr. Price's major concerns has always been the depreciation of the dollar through inflation. This has not been a factor for more than ten years, as measured by the Consumer Price Index, but that could change quickly in an improving economy.

Much of the industrial world's economy is currently operating under capacity. In the last decade, China has been an important factor behind the world's economic growth, but China's growth has been decelerating. Each Chinese child will very soon support nearly four grandparents and two parents, as well as his or her own family, due to the impact of the one-child program. China's production costs are rising, impacting exports. China's total debt load, as a percent of GDP, has surpassed our own level and is still increasing, according to the Bank of International Settlement. The EU is also suffering declining populations, due to declining births, as well as heavy debt loads. The EU debt at the end of 2017 was approximately equal to the U.S., while the Japanese government was saddled with an unpayable total debt load of more then 300 percent of GDP, according to many economists and a December 11, 2017, *Forbes* article, "When Will Japan's Debt Crisis Implode?"

Due to the inflow of more than one million legal immigrants per year, the U.S. population continues to slowly grow, despite a declining birth rate, but its total debt load, including government and non-financial corporation debt, has reached a high of 250 percent of GDP. The U.S. budget has only been in balance four years since Mr. Price's death, more than thirty years ago. Government debt has, therefore, increased in most years. In human terms, the U.S. debt of more than $20 trillion is equal to more than $200,000 per household, more than doubling the $150,000 of debt already burdening the average household from a mortgage, credit cards, and educational loans.

The addition of all this debt has helped to keep the industrialized world's economy growing since 2008, but this will eventually reverse as the rate of debt creation declines and, ultimately, as countries are forced to begin repaying it. No nation, as Mr. Price said in "The New Era for Investors," published April 1970, "can continue to spend more then it earns; it's only a question of time until it catches up to them." The day of reckoning has been temporarily postponed as the world's central banks dropped interest rates to some of the lowest levels in history. As interest rates eventually return to normal levels, more and more countries, companies, and individuals will find it difficult to afford their debts. As Mr. Price would surely point out, this huge and increasing debt, plus the trillions the Fed and other central banks have generated to keep interest rates low, is a combustible financial mixture. It can be ignited quickly into inflation if the economy accelerates. Like Milton Friedman, Mr. Price believed that inflation is created when money is printed at a rate faster than the growth in the economy, as discussed in Dr. Bernanke's address at the Dallas Federal Reserve Bank on October 14, 2003.

The replacement of the eight years from 2009 to 2016 of increasing taxes, business regulations, and government intervention under President Obama, with a more business-friendly, growth-oriented government, will help, and might even temporarily turn the tide, leading to a faster-growing U.S. economy over the next five years or so. Mr. Price believed that elections could be indicators of change, but do not in and of themselves create change. The fundamental factors of high debt and slow population increase in the industrialized world will continue to impact longer-term growth.

Given Bob's and my fairly gloomy long-term outlook, reflecting what we believe would be Mr. Price's views today, an investor nowadays might properly ask whether he or she should buy stocks at all. We believe, as Mr. Price certainly did, that ultimately the investor's best financial protection is the ownership of shares of companies with fine managements, excellent balance sheets, working in fertile fields with projected above-average growth and a high return on capital.

Mr. Price also felt that it was very important for a new investor in the stock market to perform a careful, honest inventory of his or her own financial condition before actually putting any funds to work. A new investor should create an investment program in writing and stick to it. For example, a relatively young person in her late thirties or early forties with an existing portfolio of stocks containing some capital gains would be fast approaching the high earning years of her career, so she should have excess cash to invest. We will assume that this younger investor has a mortgage, but her other debts are modest, allowing her to build up her investments from her own savings and earnings. If she had accumulated a lot of debt, or if she was older and much closer to retirement, there would need to be more attention paid to capital preservation and current income. A good way to obtain diversification at the outset would be by buying an equal amount of two mutual funds. One would feature high-quality growth stocks, and the other would offer worldwide equity and fixed income diversification.

For our young client, we would only have a maximum 10 percent actual cash reserve, and we suggest that it be in a fund of short-term fixed income securities. International diversification would add to its safety. These reserves would be for buying stocks on a large market dip or, most important, to provide some cash for an unforeseen cash emergency.

The investor who would like to build her own stock portfolio, perhaps initially as a supplement to the funds, should reread Chapter 9. She should take a hard look at her own portfolio of stocks to determine if any are true growth stocks. For those that aren't, she ought to set sales prices and get rid of them. It's always better to do selling and buying over a minimum of several months. The investor should identify any large capital gains and spread them out over two years. At current federal and state taxes, it's easy to get a tax hit of 20 percent of the gains. On the other hand, it is always worth biting the bullet and paying the taxes to switch into a superior company with a better outlook, than continuing to hold one over several years with subpar prospects. It's easy to forget that the great fortunes were made by long-term investors in companies like DuPont, 3M, Merck, and IBM that remained great growth stocks through thick and thin for more than seventy years and rose thirty or more times in value, as described earlier. These are the kinds of premier growth stocks that our investor should ultimately invest in, if she decides to invest some of her money herself. It doesn't take a genius, as Mr. Price pointed out, to buy and hold shares of well-managed companies in growing industries, which will ultimately produce superior growth in market value – just a little common sense and patience.

But what are the great growth companies of today? For most investors who are working hard in their jobs, or who just don't have the time or inclination to do all the required homework, the best answer is to stick to the above mutual funds and let the experts discover these companies. For those with the time and inclination to begin to manage a portion of their own portfolios, after investing perhaps 60 percent of their assets in mutual funds, and who have absorbed and believe in the lessons of this book, we would suggest that they look carefully at the portfolios of the mutual funds that have won the Morningstar annual awards. An investor might get an idea of which companies these managers believe to be the best growth stocks by examining their top ten holdings. Because these positions are subject to change from actions of the portfolio manager, it would be wise to check in each quarter to see if all of these companies are still on the list.

In managing a portfolio, it is well to remember Mr. Price's advice to gradually take profits, as a company becomes a large percent of a portfolio, and certainly when it becomes excessively overvalued. His goal was to recover his original capital by selling a portion of such holdings as they rise and depositing the funds in a quality income fund mentioned above. He would retain the remaining shares as long as the company remained a growth stock. Bob would politely disagree. He does not sell because of temporary overvaluation. He points out that the best companies do grow faster than the pack. By allowing this to occur without any pruning, the best stocks automatically grow relatively larger, creating faster overall growth for the portfolio. Moreover, there are no capital gains to pay. Having personally experienced, as president of the Growth Stock Fund, the long slow recovery of growth stocks from their overvaluation in the early 1970s, I am probably more in Mr. Price's camp. We leave the reader to make the choice between the two strategies.

To build a retirement account over several decades, an interested investor with extra time might want to become more venturesome. He or she might begin by adding shares of companies that are familiar through a job or from a consumer standpoint, again using the basic concepts for picking growth companies discussed in Chapter 9. Financial data can be obtained online or through a subscription to a service such as Value Line. Managements often speak at investment forums around the country or at annual meetings, where they can be individually questioned. *Fortune* magazine produces many well-researched articles that focus on the managements of exciting companies

On the other hand, the investor might decide that sleeping at night is much easier when his or her assets are safely in the hands of professionals, such as those who are successfully running the mutual funds. Several companies today have created "target" funds, which set a target date for retirement or college and manage a portfolio of funds with this specific date in mind. If the investor has accumulated assets of $3 million or more, he or she might consider turning their portfolio over to a professional.

Chapter Seventeen

WEAK PERFORMANCE OF THE GROWTH STOCK FUND, 1970s

T his chapter includes discussion of the present and the author's investment advice.

T. Rowe Price, as a firm, has produced good long-term stock market results over many years and is continuing to do so. The only lengthy period of time when this was not true was during the decade of the 1970s. During that time, based on the Growth Stock Fund's annual results in its annual reports, which generally reflected the Councilor Division, the Growth Stock Fund only outperformed the Standard and Poor's 500 Index annually on four occasions, and ranked near the bottom of mutual funds with a goal of equity growth with income secondary. This was quite a comedown from being the number one fund in the country in its category for its first ten years.

Largely because of the outstanding results of the T. Rowe Price funds and the firm's pension clients in the 1960s, however, T. Rowe Price Associates began to take on a disproportionate share of new business in the early 1970s, as discussed in the April 1972 issue of *Fortune*. Competitors' clients began to demand exposure to growth stocks. Many investment firms responded by investing in the same growth companies that were publicly displayed in the Growth Stock Fund and New Horizons shareholder reports. The larger growth companies in the Growth Stock Fund were even given a special name in the financial press: the "nifty fifty." Soon, the pension funds and fund portfolios of competitors began nearly to mirror the holdings of the Price funds. This copycat behavior caused a large inflow of capital into a relatively small part of the stock market over a short period of time, in what Charlie had called a "laser beam" in his forecast that this would happen a decade before, as discussed earlier. This phenomenon pushed growth stocks to high relative valuations.

This overvaluation was recognized by the firm and discussed in the shareholder reports of the New Horizons Fund and the Growth Stock Fund in the late 1960s and early 1970s. The stock market did break sharply in 1973, initiating a bear market that continued throughout 1974, with growth stocks leading the way in the decline. The readjustment of the high valuations of growth stocks caused them to decline in value, despite their continued superior earnings growth. The New Horizons Fund dropped a heart-stopping 42 percent in 1973, and followed with another 39-percent decline in 1974. The Growth Stock Fund dropped 26 percent in 1973 and 34 percent in 1974, far worse than the Dow Jones Average. The counsel accounts generally followed the performance of the Growth Stock Fund.

As mentioned earlier, this was not the first time that large growth stocks had a period of poor relative performance. In the years immediately following the Growth Stock Fund's launch in 1950, the fund only beat the Dow Jones Industrial Average once in its first three years. The investment committee, in an attempt to achieve better short-term market performance, reduced their holdings of large growth stocks modestly, and added high-dividend-paying, low-priced "value" companies, such as those in the fire and casualty business and paper industry. Fortunately, after a pause of several years, growth stocks resumed their good relative performance. The committee quickly switched back to better growth stocks.

In the early 1960s, growth companies again became extremely overvalued, with a number of the firm's favored growth companies selling for more than fifty times earnings. Again, the committee bought some lower-priced, slower-growing companies, such as airlines, but the market break in growth stocks lasted only a few years. Growth stocks again recovered and the nongrowth stocks were sold, impacting the fund's recovery only to a modest extent.

In looking back on these two episodes, it could be argued that switching from higher-priced growth companies to cheaper, slower-growing growth stocks had not been a good move. Simply holding higher-growth stocks through these temporary periods of overvaluation would have been the better strategy.

Growth stocks did recover in 1975, and the Growth Stock Fund and New Horizons Fund temporarily did better than the market averages, based on the GSF and NHF annual reports. The adjustment in the value of large growth stocks, however, turned out to be far from over. Following this short rebound, growth stocks entered a long period of relative underperformance. New Horizons did better, particularly in the later years of the decade. Its decline had been sharper at the outset, and the rapid growth in earnings of the small, resilient companies that made up its portfolio caused New Horizons to recover much faster than the Growth Stock Fund.

With the initial expectation that the poor performance of growth stocks would once again be brief, it was decided to stay with them in the 1970s. Closing the fund was impractical, as the Growth Stock Fund and counsel accounts shared basically the same investments. Switching to nongrowth stocks seemed to make no more sense than it had proven to be in the past. Most clients had chosen T. Rowe Price because of its success with growth stocks, and this was what they wanted. The Growth Stock Fund had been specifically bought by its shareholders because of its portfolio of growth stocks. Its emphasis on the Growth Stock Philosophy was clearly spelled out in the prospectus. The research department, except for a few analysts connected to the New Era fund, was well versed in growth companies, but had little experience with nongrowth companies. In the counselor division, individual clients had huge gains, which would be very expensive to liquidate.

In the end, the firm did modestly raise some cash reserves, but continued to very selectively purchase growth stocks, as they became better values. After all, these were still the best-managed companies in the world, operating in very fertile fields longer term.

Unfortunately, unexpected international events and high inflation continued to create a poor environment for growth stocks. Oil stocks, which represented a large percentage of the value of the stock market, were doing very well, with political events and accelerating inflation rapidly increasing the price of oil. By 1977, this poor relative performance of growth stocks had become a major issue with clients and the shareholders of the Growth Stock Fund. Many of the firm's competitors were beginning to publicly question its Growth Stock Philosophy and to promote "value stocks."

John Boland, in the November 8, 1982, issue of *Barron's*, probably said it best: "That year [1973] marked the last gasp of the growth stock frenzy. It also ended the long trend of rising fortunes for the Growth Stock Fund's Investors, who saw the value of their shares plunge more then 50% over the next two years. By the end of the decade 'Nifty Fifty' was a byword of ridicule, a reminder of Wall Street's follies. A bear market and a decade of inflation had crushed the premium price-earnings multiples."

The article "Identity Crisis at T. Rowe Price," in the November 1982 issue of *Institutional Investor* magazine, begins with a T. Rowe Price associate "rather testily" saying, "If pension funds were on the ball, they would know we're not just growth stocks." The author continued, "Plagued by poor equity performance, T. Rowe Price has … moved away from growth stocks." Others accused the firm of falling in love with its investments and not seeing the infirmities and other blemishes that had infected their beloved large-growth companies.

With his legacy in question, Mr. Price began to accept interviews with newspapers and other publications. He would point out the excellent performance of his own model growth fund portfolio, buoyed by better-performing small growth companies, as well as by very large positions in gold and other natural resource companies, which were responding very well to the inflationary environment.

The stock market stayed in a funk, without any clear direction, throughout the late 1970s. The relative decline in the valuation of large growth stocks continued to negatively impact the performance of Growth Stock Fund and counsel accounts.

However, the world turned again, and the stock market soared on the back of the "Volcker Market." In what would prove to be his last memo, "The Overlook for 1983 and Beyond," on August 1, 1983, Mr. Price's first sentence read, "The outlook for 1983 is favorable for business and the stock market." Later in this memo, he said that as of June 30, he had "71% of his portfolio in common stocks and convertible bonds," up from 51 percent in his prior memo. The bear market for Mr. Price was over. All of the recommendations in the article were traditional growth stocks.

During the decade of poor performance there had been much criticism that T. Rowe Price, the firm, had lost its way. It was claimed that it was investing in mature companies that were no longer growth companies. To respond to these concerns, we have analyzed three of the Growth Stock Fund's portfolios: 1960, when the fund had a superb first ten-year performance, beating all other U.S. equity funds with similar objectives; 1972, which marked the twenty-year period where it enjoyed a very good performance compared to other large growth equity mutual funds, as indicated in the April 1972 issue of *Fortune*; and 1980, when it was ranked by Wisenberger fifth-sixth out of fifty-nine large long-term growth funds with the worst decade of relative performance in its history.

We looked at three key statistics of these portfolios: five-year sales growth, which is the best indicator of underlying growth, assuming no acquisitions; five-year per share growth, which defines the performance of a growth stock; and return on equity, which is the key financial parameter used by Mr. Price in identifying a true growth company. A company's long-term growth is ultimately tied to its return on equity.

Comparable Annual Portfolio Statistics

	1960	1972	1980
5-year sales growth	10.7	15.3	15.7
5-year EPS growth	7.2	14.5	19.3
Return on equity	13.8	15.1	18.5
Price/Earnings	26.9	54.4	14.6

This table was created by Karen Malloy, retired TRP fund statistician.

A review of this table indicates that the 1980 portfolio had a very good mix of growth companies, which, if anything, were performing financially better than the two earlier portfolios. There is no indication that the firm had suddenly stopped identifying and investing in vigorously growing companies. As can also be noted, the price to earnings ratio was 54.4 in 1970 but had dropped to 14.6 in 1980. This cut its appreciation by nearly 75 percent and was the real reason for the fund's poor performance.

Could this happen again? In the sixty-eight years of the Growth Stock Fund's existence, this long under-performance has only happened once. There are so many different ways that money is managed and invested today that it seems doubtful that a majority of the country's investors would once again suddenly descend on growth stocks and push their relative prices to such heights.

If a period of substantial overvaluation should reoccur, however, we would hope that the readers of this book would recognize it, based on Mr. Price's advice for calculating fair value and, perhaps, do some selective trimming of the most overpriced stocks, but continue to hold the great majority through the episode. One thing remains certain, that the government will demand its percentage of any realized gains.

For those who prefer more diversified portfolios, T. Rowe Price now offers more than one hundred mutual funds, with many different investment strategies and the ability to easily switch among them. Well-known, excellent mutual fund companies offer many others.

◼ Epilogue ◼

T. Rowe Price Today

f Mr. Price miraculously arrived one pleasant summer morning in 2018 at 100 East Pratt Street in downtown Baltimore, the global head-quarters of T. Rowe Price Group, what would he find that was famil-iar? What would be new? How had the company that he, Charlie, Walter, Marie, and Isabella founded in 1937 with so much effort and sacrifice fared over the 35 years since his death? What is the working environment at the company like now? Would he still be proud to have his name on the masthead?

Standing on the southwest corner of East Pratt and Light Streets, he would discover that the exterior of the original building had changed very little. It is the same handsome, modern concrete structure that Pietro Belluschi designed for IBM, the building's first major tenant. T. Rowe Price Associates had moved there in 1975, also as one of the first tenants. Baltimore Inner Harbor to the south would be beginning to bustle with tourists. East Pratt Street traffic would seem the same – heavy. He would notice a twenty-eight-floor tower attached to the rear of the original ten-story building. The tower added 110,000 square feet, bring-ing the total interior square feet for all tenants to 653,000. Mr. Price would soon discover that the firm had also expanded, far beyond the three floors that it had occupied in the original building in 1983, the year that he died. The T. Rowe Price Group now fills the entire original building, plus an additional three floors of the new tower.

When he opened the familiar glass door on the front of the building, facing the harbor, instead of the old banks of brushed chrome elevator doors, he would find that the lobby is now two stories high. T. Rowe Price associates would be wearing photo security badges, which opened the gates leading up to the steps to the second floor.

Once Mr. Price had entered the offices and taken the elevator to a higher floor, he would have felt very comfortable. There are light gray cubicles in the center of each floor, with functional offices grouped around the periphery. Wall-to-wall carpet keeps the noise level down. Each of the first 10 floors was expanded, of course, with the addition of the tower. If he wandered around the eighth floor, he would note with satisfaction that the current executives had given up the big original corner offices of the early 1980s, and now occupied small offices, some with just a glimpse of Baltimore Inner Harbor. The office of the president and CEO, Bill Stromberg, is only slightly larger than any other. He would also have noted that the best space on the floor was occupied by large conference rooms, with great views of the harbor. These rooms were good places to meet with clients or other associates. If he walked back to the elevator lobby and went to the ninth floor, he would have found on the northern side of the lobby a comfortable grouping of modern furniture in which he could rest for a minute from all the walking around. There would be several years of the firm's annual reports on a table comfortably near his chair. He might decide to check out a few of these reports to see how his old firm was doing. Several items in these reports would catch his eye.

Seeing the first paragraph of the 2013 annual report, Mr. Price surely would break into a grin and maybe even a dry chuckle as he read, "Client confidence in T. Rowe Price is based on the expectation of excellence and reliability. We deliver on that expectation by consistently adhering to our core principle – CLIENTS COME FIRST." He would surely have thought, "By God, those young men did learn what I preached for so many years, and passed it along to the current generation. I couldn't have said it better myself. This is what the firm has always been all about."

He would notice that the 2014 report was also on the table. "Earning our clients' confidence starts with delivering consistently excellent investment results and outstanding service," it read. "But it doesn't end there. Confidence also comes from knowing that every associate at T. Rowe Price embraces the view that our firm's success follows from the success of our clients." Seventy-four percent of all the company's funds across their classes outperformed their comparable Lipper Average on a total return basis for three years, 80 percent for five years on the same basis, and 88 percent for ten years. Mr. Price had always focused on the long term, or ten years.

In the 2015 report he would see that ten of the funds were closed to new investors because demand had outstripped the ability of management to find suitable investments at reasonable prices for these funds. He would have smiled in approval. This was similar to the firm's action in the late 1960s, when the firm had closed the New Horizons Fund for the same reason. It was all part of putting your clients first.

Convinced that things were going well and that the current management was looking at the right things, he might open the 2016 annual report to the page on performance and be startled to see that 94 percent of the firm's U.S. Equity Funds had outperformed their Lipper Average over the last decade, an amazing 100 percent for five years; these numbers are based on the same criteria as the 2013 results above. "Wow," he might have thought, "the firm is hitting on all the cylinders! As I always preached, great performance is the key to success in the investment business."

Reading these reports, Mr. Price would have also learned that his old company had gone public in 1986. In the summer of 1982, the stock market started a historic climb, ending the long doldrums of the 1970s. Business picked up dramatically for T. Rowe Price. The company began to expand its investment offerings and to take in-house many fund administrative functions. It significantly increased its investment in the technology for fund administration and portfolio management. It began to market its products in new venues. All of these functions increased its need for capital.

Over the years T. Rowe Price had been approached by many firms seeking to acquire it. Under the concept of creating a financial supermarket, there were some banks and investment firms that felt T. Rowe Price would fit nicely into their corporate structure. The problem was that after a few years, the acquiring company would typically begin to change the acquired company's business practices in an effort to improve profits. This usually destroyed the acquired firm. Something needed to happen, however, beginning in the early 1980s, as T. Rowe Price had little permanent capital, with most of its earnings used to buy the stock of retiring executives.

The board of directors decided to find a solution to this problem. George Roche was asked to devise a program to solve what was a complex issue. The firm not only had its own current shareholders, but also a large group of former shareholders (almost a hundred) who had recapture rights under the shareholder agreement.

The management agreed that the firm should remain independent. It had a strong culture, and management feared that a new owner would tamper with it. It had hired a number of very able individuals in recent years, many of whom might leave after an acquisition. The investment results for the clients were very strong. The firm's reputation for always doing the right thing for its clients placed it among the most respected firms in the business. The overall investment environment was good, and the firm's efforts in client service, marketing and technology were proving successful. The firm could continue to sustain itself and grow profitably as an independent entity. But there was little room for an unexpected large cash drain. What was missing was the insurance policy of a strong balance sheet.

George determined that the best course of action was to take the company public. This would solve the capital problem because the firm would have substantial permanent capital after the offering. It would also place a more realistic valuation on the stock than the private company valuation. Finally, it would leave the company as an independent entity managed by its current team, retaining its unique culture and controlling its own destiny. His public offering program provided a fair but workable compromise between the old and new shareholders. Its brilliance was that it gave the former shareholders immediate cash by selling some shares of what had been an illiquid holding. The program, however, also permitted old shareholders to retain part of their stock, so that they could benefit from the company's future growth. The associate shareholders could continue to hold their shares and options with less potential dilution than had existed under the original stockholder agreement. The offering was assisted by the old shareholders selling some of their shares in order to create a reasonably sized public offering. Otherwise, the company would have had to sell corporate shares, causing dilution.

George proved to be a good salesman of this complicated deal. Some important blocks of stock had fallen into the hands of heirs, some of whom did not have as much financial sophistication. He did an excellent job of negotiating with this large, diverse group. In the end, 100 percent of all the shareholders, new and old, agreed with the program. The firm went public on August 11, 1986, and has remained as an independent entity with a very strong balance sheet ever since.

George told the story of inviting one of the older shareholders to lunch at a New York club during these negotiations. He had forgotten to mention the actual reason for the lunch in his invitation. When George began to discuss the financial situation of the firm and the possibility of a public offering, he noticed that this individual's attention began to wander. He really didn't have any interest in George's spiel. He had long since sold all of his shares and was enjoying his new life of retirement in Florida. He obviously didn't remember the recapture agreement. When George explained that by selling some of the shares generated by the recapture agreement in the offering, he would receive a very tidy sum, this elegantly dressed gentleman let out a whoop and poured salad over his mostly bald head – to the astonishment of the waiter and his nearby club mates!

The public offering proved to be a very good idea, in ways that could not have been predicted in 1986. By 1990, the firm's net worth had increased to $100 million ($192 million in 2018 dollars). In that year a real estate company, Mortgage and Realty Trust (MRT), went bankrupt. T. Rowe Price had a significant position in this company in the Prime Reserve Fund, as well as in client accounts. The firm decided to buy in the underlying debt of MRT held by the fund and its clients to protect them from any risk or the need to write down their portfolios. The cost to do this, by the company, according to George Roche, was approximately $67 million, or two-thirds of the firm's capital. It required several years of difficult negotiations, but eventually the firm did recover almost all of its capital.

Ten years later, on April 11, 2000, the firm's international investment partner, Robert Fleming Holdings, Ltd., agreed to be acquired by Chase Bank. The joint venture had been formed between the two companies to be Rowe Price-Fleming International, Inc., which managed all of the T. Rowe Price international mutual funds and clients. Under T. Rowe Price's agreement with Robert Fleming, it had right of first refusal should Fleming desire to sell its shares. T. Rowe Price management felt that it was important to acquire Fleming's 50-percent ownership in the joint venture. Because many of the clients and shareholders had joined because of T. Rowe Price, it was believed that they should be protected. In addition, it was held that the international funds and money management business would fit well with the company's future plans. The firm made a $700 million offer, which was accepted, and T. Rowe Price assumed total ownership of Rowe Price-Fleming International. Again, this constituted two-thirds of the firm's then net worth and could not have been accomplished without the cash from the public offering.

In the company's 1986 prospectus, by 1983 assets under management had reached $16.5 billion dollars, with revenues of just under $60 million. The Growth Stock Fund alone had reached more than $16 billion in assets.

In the thirty-four years between 1983 and 2017, Mr. Price could have calculated on a scrap of yellow paper that revenues at $4.8 billion had grown an amazing 80 times, and assets under management were now over $1 trillion. The Growth Stock Fund had reached $46 billion! Total employment in 2018 approached 8,000 individuals. A large part of this increase in personnel was due to bringing in-house all of the mutual fund services.

When Mr. Price realized how large the firm had grown, he might have felt a sense of awe, as he recognized that not only had it grown far beyond his wildest dreams, but also well beyond his ability or interest to manage, much less to control. He would have felt the admiration and pride that a parent feels when his small child grows up to be a mature, highly accomplished adult. He had always preferred a small group, but he would have respected those who had the ability to carry his original investment concepts to such great heights – particularly as he realized that management had accomplished this by adhering to his original philosophy of providing the client with outstanding service and superior performance.

If he got up from the chair and wandered further down the hallway, he would have begun to pass the offices of the investment professionals. The analysts and portfolio management offices were along the exterior walls, with their assistants working in adjacent cubicles in the center of the floor. Looking in, he would have seen none of the piles of paper reports that had occupied the floors and visitors' chairs of the analysts and portfolio managers in 1983, or copies of the current *Wall Street Journal* that were must-reading by all professionals when he retired in 1971. Instead, the occupants were monitoring large computer screens, where such information would be stored.

If Mr. Price had stepped into an analyst's office, such as that of Kennard (Ken) W. Allen, who manages the Science & Technology Fund and leads its technology research team, he would have met an impressive, outgoing young man. Ken earned his B.A. from Colby College and has been with the firm for eighteen years. Mr. Price would also have learned that all current news and financial information, both published and in-house, was now instantly accessible not only on those computers, but also on Ken and his colleagues' omnipresent iPhones and iPads. It could be easily reasoned over and communicated anywhere in the world at the touch of a button. In fact, technology's ability to manage information had become much more important throughout the investment process by 2017. With the dominance of the Internet, the problem had become too much information. As Ken would have emphasized, the skillful analyst at T. Rowe Price maintained superior performance in 2018 in part by understanding which information was important to the companies that he followed and which was not, and deriving insights from that which mattered. The firm was greatly aided in this process by continuing to focus on the longer-term outlook, ignoring much of the noise of short-term data so emphasized today by the hedge funds and most mutual funds. This unique focus remained a major competitive advantage.

Typical TRP analyst's office. Photo by the author.

In 1983, there had been 21 equity portfolio managers (counselors), but only 26 equity analysts, all located in the U.S. Mr. Price would have discovered that according to the 2017 annual report, there were 71 equity portfolio managers, more than triple the number in 1983, despite assets under management rising almost 50 times. The use of computers to manage and properly distribute assets had made managing money much more efficient. In addition, much of the increase in assets had gone into existing funds, which were far easier and less time-consuming than clients. The total number of equity analysts had increased almost six times to 148.

The job of a portfolio manager had been greatly refined by 2018. In 1983, the portfolio manager was called an "investment counselor." He or she was hired directly for that position from business school or another financial institution. As I observed, no counselors in 1983 other than the fund managers had ever been research analysts. A counselor usually first worked under a senior counselor on a team. As he or she gained experience and a good performance record, he or she would eventually graduate to become a senior counselor and head of a team. Counselors in 1983 had a mix of many different clients, including pension funds and individuals. A high percentage of their time involved counseling individual clients to buy or sell specific industries and companies in order to meet their specific personal objectives. The more senior counselors, with good performance records, would be invited to serve on one of the four equity fund advisory committees, along with selected research analysts. The funds, however, were just another client, an adjunct to the counselor's or analyst's other job commitments. The actual responsibility of managing the funds was shared by all the members of the advisory committee, although the preponderance of the responsibility fell on the chairman.

Had he continued along the corridor, Mr. Price might have met Brian Berghuis. Brian manages the Mid-Cap Growth Fund with the very able assistance of John Wakeman. He would have learned that they had won the prestigious Morningstar Fund Manager of the Year Award in 2004 for domestic equity funds. Brian graduated from Princeton with an A.B. degree and from Harvard Business School. He would have explained that the committee system, with its advantage of developing ideas from several sources, and its ability to facilitate debate on investment decisions, had been retained for each fund, but in an abbreviated form. It could be called upon as needed by the portfolio manager, but the final decision to buy, sell, or hold a stock was strictly his. The committees were only advisory. On an overall basis, however, Brian would have stressed that both research and portfolio management remained a highly collaborative team effort. Communication had actually improved over 1983, although the number of people now involved was much larger, because of the technology and the emphasis on communication by management. Despite the importance of a team effort, a major effort had been made to prevent "group think." As Mr. Price would have discovered in these conversations, there were no shrinking violets. Everyone was encouraged to speak their mind and disagree when the facts, in their opinion, called for it.

In this conversation with Brian, Mr. Price would have learned that he was a very well-informed investor, had an impressive intellect, and was both pleasant and professional. He would also have learned that the path to becoming the manager of a fund in 2018 was long and challenging. A research analyst might come straight out of a business school with a master's degree, or as an associate analyst who would be hired for a limited time, such as during the summer before entering business school. The new MBA would have the goal of becoming an analyst, but not the promise. His or her inexperienced recommendations would be subject to careful oversight and consideration for the first two or three years. He or she would be assigned a mentor who would work closely alongside. Finally, after this probation period, if his or her recommendations were beginning to make money, he or she could become a full-fledged analyst.

Mr. Price would also discover that analysts are judged today by far stricter standards than they were in 1983. With the assistance of custom software, the analyst at T. Rowe Price in 2018 is measured by how much money his or her recommendations actually make for the firm. The job involves closely following thirty or so stocks, writing reports with specific buy, sell, or hold recommendations, supporting those conclusions in weekly investment committee meetings, and then making the rounds of the portfolio managers to answer any questions and to give them a nudge to act on the recommendations. He or she must not only generate good investment ideas but, to merit a good bonus, sell them to the portfolio managers. All portfolio managers now come out of research positions, but the decision to transition to a portfolio manager is not made by every analyst, as it wasn't in 1983. A successful analyst today can make as much money or more than a portfolio manager, although the average pay for a portfolio manager is more. It is similar to the decision made by many engineers when deciding between management and engineering for their career. Some analysts enjoy delving into the depths of a company and coming up with great new investment ideas, more than running a diversified portfolio, which crosses into economic sectors beyond their specialty.

James A. C. Kennedy, the firm's president and CEO until he retired in 2016, received his undergraduate degree from Princeton and his MBA from Stanford. He recalls that he turned down the first six offers to become the Director of Research, far preferring to remain an analyst. Of course, the seventh offer proved to be the one that was irresistible and he took the job – but still with a touch of regret. Jim took the job because he realized that it is the analysts who come up with the ideas that can make a real difference in performance. For the good of the firm, he had a responsibility to try to maximize the analyst's important role.

Today, most of the portfolio managers at T. Rowe Price are responsible for billions of dollars of assets. A portfolio manager of an equity or bond fund is focused only on that fund. His or her time is not diluted by other accounts. He or she knows intimately all the companies in the portfolio and visits on a regular basis with management. The firm has even developed an app for portfolio managers for use on their iPhones, which contains the most recent financial and portfolio information on each company in the fund, together with its current market price. They can issue buy and sell orders to the trading desk from their mobile phones anywhere in the world. Of course, such orders are well verified and double-checked.

Mr. Price would have applauded this total focus by the fund managers on their funds. It was the way he ran the New Horizons and the New Era Funds when he phased out of managing most of his individual accounts in the late 1960s. In 1983, as noted in the prospectus issued prior to the company going public, institutional and individual accounts totaled about $8.3 billion of the firm's assets, or about half of the total assets under management. Since that time, there has been an enormous shift in pension funds from defined benefit to defined contribution, as discussed in Chapter 11.

According to Brian Rogers, the nonexecutive chairman of the board, this shift has caused managed pension fund assets to drop under 20 percent of total assets under management today. Mutual funds have simultaneously increased, as they became the investment vehicle favored by most employees for their retirement accounts. Traditional investment counseling to individuals in 1983 was still about 20 percent of the firm's total assets under management. Today, individual accounts with assets of more than $3 million are still managed very capably by Mark Weigman and his team, but they represent only $3.7 billion total, or less than 0.4 percent of total assets under management.

In 1983, there were eighteen portfolio managers and traders in the fixed income department and six credit analysts, managing five funds and a number of institutional accounts. Today, there are seventy-seven portfolio managers and traders and seventy-six research and credit analysts. They manage seventeen mutual funds, totaling $105 billion. Mr. Price would have noted with satisfaction that about half the investment professionals today are research or credit analysts. From his days of running the Mackubin, Legg bond department in the 1930s, he well remembered that outside credit analysts cannot be relied upon. He and George Collins, the first head of fixed income at T. Rowe Price, agreed that thorough in-house credit analyses were at least as critical in managing bonds as excellent equity research was in managing stocks.

The great majority of all public and private debt is still rated by the big three – Standard & Poor's, Moody's, and Fitch. These are the same three firms that totally missed the warning signs of the coming financial collapse in 2007 and 2008. In fact, they were instrumental in creating it by awarding very high credit ratings to the structured financial notes, which were built on dubious mortgages generated by the housing boom in 2006 and 2007. In return, these three rating agencies received large fees from investment banks like the Goldman Sachs Group, Inc., and Morgan Stanley. Banks and other institutions then created and sold the structured products for large commissions to the public and other institutions. The day Lehman Brothers failed and went into bankruptcy, the notes of Lehman, whose assets largely consisted of such highly leveraged paper, were rated triple A by these agencies.

This house of cards imploded during April 2007, when nearly two trillion dollars of structured notes were written off. This ultimately caused the bankruptcy of large brokerage firms like Bear Stearns Companies, Inc., and the collapse of the stock market. Several large banks, as well as AIG, a large insurance company, had to be rescued by the federal government. General Motors, which had to be rescued by

DuPont early in Mr. Price's career, fell into default and was also bailed out by taxpayers.

The T. Rowe Price Group went through this credit crash largely unscathed. Walter Kidd first saw to it that, once T. Rowe Price became profitable in 1949, by assuring that not only did it stay profitable, but it also began to build up a strong balance sheet. George Roche continued this tradition during the years that he was chief financial officer. When the company went public in 1986, it reported, before the offering, that cash and liquid securities were $18 million, more than enough to pay off all of its current liabilities and debt. By the end of 2017, according to the firm's annual report for that year, liquid assets had grown remarkably to $4.1 billion in cash and marketable securities. Liabilities in 2017 were only $717 million. As George was fond of saying, "A good balance sheet doesn't matter until it matters, and then that is the only thing that matters."

Soon after he was elected president of T. Rowe Price at the beginning of 2007, Jim Kennedy moved his desk into the fixed income area. He knew little about it, having focused on equities during his long career at the firm. "One of the most important benefits [of this move]," he said, "was getting to know a young analyst named Susan G. Troll." She had received her Bachelor of Science degree from Drexel University, and was a Certified Public Accountant. If Mr. Price had met Sue during his tour, he would have found an energetic woman who talked in rapid-fire phrases, her mind moving quickly through complex issues. She had become skeptical of the forecasts made by so-called fixed income "experts" at places such as the Goldman Sachs Group, Inc. and Morgan Stanley, when their ideas clearly did not reflect the reality that she found in the marketplace. After thoroughly studying the condition of the mortgage market in 2006, she became convinced that it was going to implode. Credit spreads were tightening, while fundamentals were deteriorating. It made no sense. Thanks to her warnings, which earned her the nickname of the "Duchess of Doom" on Wall Street, the firm's fixed income department eliminated nearly all of its subprime mortgage exposure, which was not assured of being paid off in the near future, as well as the small number of complex structured notes it held, which were then still highly rated. It was a year early but, as Mr. Price often said, in such situations it was far better to be early than late.

Susan Troll, Associate Portfolio Manager at the T. Rowe Price Group. TRP archives; photo owned by Peter Hunt.

The Prime Reserve Fund had always been very conservatively managed, as it continued to be during this entire period. Near the bottom of the credit crisis in May 2008, the fund had only one structured note, equal to 0.2 percent of its portfolio. It was one of the very few such notes that would pay principal and interest owed, on time, two months later. The Prime Reserve Fund had none of the problems of maintaining the one-dollar share price faced by many of its peers.

Managing a fixed income portfolio in the 2006–2008 environments was extremely difficult. A fixed income fund's performance is based on its total return on capital and income to its shareholders. Typically, higher-yielding securities are the riskiest. It seemed that in 2007, you could have your cake and eat it too, with the high-yield structured notes ranked highly by the credit agencies. Many of the firm's competitors took the bait, and for a short time performed much better on paper. By taking the contrary course and staying away from the tempting higher yields, the T. Rowe Price fixed income funds ultimately performed strongly relative to their peers, according to Ted Wiese, the head of Fixed Income, and suffered none of the large write-downs of other funds during this period.

Mr. Price would probably have ended his visit to his old firm at East Pratt Street and not gone out to its new campus in Owings Mills. His major interests were always the investment process, the firm's investment performance and its attitude toward its clients. The administrative details had never been a strong focus of his, although he had always believed that they should be in capable, knowledgeable hands, beginning with Walter Kidd in the office and Eleanor on the home front.

T. Rowe Price Group offices at the Owings Mills, Maryland, campus. TRP archives.

The administrative function had also changed and grown considerably since his death. There were many new mutual funds, and the number of shareholders had expanded substantially. The State Street Bank and Trust Company had been running the funds' back office in 1983, but there had been growing concern that T. Rowe Price should begin to deal directly with its mutual fund shareholders. Client service was too important to leave in the hands of a third party. The top management members at T. Rowe Price were excellent managers of financial assets, but no one had much administrative experience, other than that learned on the job as the firm expanded.

In 1981, Edward (Ed) J. Mathias, a vice president and director of the firm, suggested that his fraternity brother from the University of Pennsylvania, Jim Riepe, might be the person to fill this requirement. Jim had spent the last twelve years of his business career at Wellington

Management and the Vanguard Group, where he was the executive vice president reporting directly to John C. Bogle, the firm's founder and CEO. Vanguard at that time managed the country's first index fund for retail customers. An index fund is run by a computer and mirrors an index. Costs can be quite low because the expense of a research department and portfolio managers can be eliminated. The downside is that the portfolio cannot do better than the index. Vanguard's original computer program mimicked the Standard & Poor's 500 Composite Stock Price Index. Today, Vanguard is a giant in the investment management business, with more than $5 trillion under management in many different index funds. In 1981, shareholder relations, administration, sales and marketing, and finance at Vanguard all reported to Jim. Not only did he have the administrative experience needed at T. Rowe Price, but he was also personable and fit in well with the existing management of the firm. He was also well known in the mutual fund industry. T. Rowe Price was fortunate to be able to hire Jim in 1981.

He immediately became a member of the management committee and the board of directors. He assumed responsibility for a number of important areas in the Mutual Fund Division, including sales, marketing, distribution, client service, and the important technology involved in properly serving millions of shareholders. As Jim said, from a marketing perspective, the firm didn't have a single mascot or logo identity. Each fund had its own favorite. Jim settled on the large bighorn sheep for its wisdom, independence, and strength. It had been the symbol of the Prime Reserve Fund since 1976. He also established the motto "Invest with Confidence." Both are still used today in T. Rowe Price's promotion and advertising.

In 1984, in this first move to build up the fund's back office, Jim brought in-house the funds' important calls division from State Street and the firm began to handle all the fund shareholder telephone calls from Baltimore. In those days, this was the primary way of communicating with shareholders. In 1991, the transition from State Street was completed when the last elements – the processing of fund data and fund accounting were largely brought in-house. Fortunately, the tower at 100 East Pratt Street had been completed, so most of this large increase of administrative staff could easily be housed. Jim also brought many new services to the firm's mutual fund shareholders.

He put in place over the next several years the computer technology that allowed the firm to communicate on a one-to-one basis with its shareholders using computers and, later, cell phones. Distribution channels were expanded and new channels were opened for both mutual funds and private clients. Despite the huge growth of fund operations under Jim's leadership, he was also able to greatly improve the quality of these services for the mutual fund shareholders and clients, at a lowered price.

Although T. Rowe Price remains committed to the basic growth stock philosophy, with the Growth Stock Fund still its largest equity fund today, Jim realized shortly after his arrival that it would be important for the firm's future growth to diversify its product. When he arrived in 1981, 90 percent of the firm's equity assets were invested in just the single category of growth stocks. The only nongrowth stocks were in the New Era Fund and a few specialized accounts.

Another reason for diversification was to better serve the large market that was rapidly unfolding in the "defined contribution" plan business, discussed in Chapter 11. In a defined contribution plan, employees took over the responsibility of saving for their retirement from their employers. At that time, this was done primarily through 401(k)s, tax-deferred vehicles into which employees deposited funds that were deducted from their salary. Most often these were supplemented by additional funds donated by the employer. The human resource departments usually approved a range of mutual funds in which the employees could invest. Selected funds generally provided full services, offered diversification, and had a good reputation. Both equity and fixed income funds were made available so employees could structure their own portfolios depending on their age and income.

This was a very different process than the firm's principal business of managing corporate pension funds. In managing a "defined benefit" pension fund, the customer was usually the chief financial officer; the account was managed by a counselor. Performance in managing pensions was very important, because it directly impacted the company's bottom line.

Riding on the back of this defined contribution trend, it was evident to Jim that mutual funds would rapidly grow and become much more important to the firm in the future. Modernizing the back office was essential, but so was diversifying the product. By 1981 the long decline in the relative performance of growth stocks, as their high valuations in the 1960s unwound, was just coming to an end, but this was not yet apparent to the investing public. A category that had done relatively well in the past decade was value stocks. Jim felt that to be successful in the retirement market, it was important for T. Rowe Price to have funds that offered both capital appreciation and dividend income, which a portfolio of value stocks would do.

A value stock is generally defined as a stock that, after careful analysis, is worth more than its current market price. This is often due to unrecognized assets on its books, but it can also be for a variety of other reasons that push it out of fashion, such as a cyclical downturn in business, the market's concern about the current management, or a temporary slowdown in earnings growth. Such a stock generally sells for a low relative price-earnings ratio and price to book value. It often has a relatively higher dividend because of its low price. Classical value stock investing grew out of the academic work of Benjamin Graham and David Dodd at the Columbia Business School beginning in 1928. They published the seminal text on this subject in 1934, *Security Analysis*, which became mandatory reading in college business courses. It remained in print through six different editions, with the last published in 2008. Warren Buffett was undoubtedly their most famous pupil.

As Jim was looking around for a portfolio manager in this area, he met L. Gordon Croft. Gordon was considered a bit of a maverick, an independent thinker, at T. Rowe Price. He had an uncanny ability to see behind a company's current weak financials and poor management to see a much better future. He had an excellent performance record of investing in such value stocks during the volatile 1970s. However, such companies were quite different than the growth stocks that the firm had featured since its inception. With no other immediate candidates, Jim decided to give Gordon a crack at running the company's first value-oriented fund. After considerable arm twisting, because this fund would clearly be at variance with the firm's traditional growth stock investments and Gordon himself was a bit controversial, the other members of management finally agreed to name Gordon as the new fund's first president.

The Growth and Income Fund was launched in 1982. It performed well and was well received by investors. After several years another value-oriented fund was launched in 1985, called the Equity Income Fund, run by the team of Thomas (Tommy) H. Broadus and Brian C. Rogers. Brian is currently nonexecutive chairman of the board of

T. Rowe Price. The fund was an offshoot of an account that they had run for Duke University, whose guidelines specified that both yield and quality were important. This account emphasized good companies that were undervalued for what appeared, after careful research, to be temporary reasons. After Tommy retired, it continued to have an outstanding performance under Brian during the difficult early years of the twenty-first century. The fund, chiefly because of its record, was extremely popular, and briefly became the largest fund at T. Rowe Price in the early 2000s.

This was quickly followed by the Small Cap Value Fund in 1988, which employed the same basic concepts used in the Equity Income Fund but with New Horizons–sized companies. Over the following decade, five more value-type funds were launched by the firm. Overall value stocks gave the firm's earnings much the same needed boost in the early 2000s that bonds did in the decade of the '70s, as growth stocks faded in popularity in both time periods. As Bill Stromberg, president and CEO of T. Rowe Price Group, said, "Value stocks offer a great investment offering to our clients and provide good balance to the firm, as they tend to lead at different parts of the economic cycle than growth stocks. Having strong offerings in both areas reminds all of us that no investment style dominates in all seasons and diversification is important."

In the late 1990s and the early years of the twenty-first century, new accounts began to be drawn into T. Rowe Price, attracted by the continued excellent performance of these funds. T. Rowe Price ultimately coined the term "GAARP" for its particular style of investing in the value area, which translated to "Growth at a Reasonable Price." At the end of 2015, GAARP-oriented mutual funds accounted for $84 billion. A number of "sector" funds were launched, offering portfolio management opportunities for equity analysts and providing greater diversity of product. A sector can be an industry such as New Era's emphasis on natural resources or a geographic area. New industry funds were opened in areas such as health care and science and technology. After the firm bought out Fleming, its overseas partner, in 2000, Jim and the investment group also expanded the line-up of international mutual funds.

As existing funds continued to grow in size and new funds were added, mutual funds became the firm's major business, as Jim Riepe had foreseen in 1981. This also created continued strong growth of the investment staff, as well as fund administration. Once more, the firm outgrew its quarters and new space had to be found. After considerable search, the firm decided to build a corporate campus in Owings Mills, Maryland.

Currently, about 3,500 associates work at Owings Mills, and the six buildings encompass over one million square feet on the 72 acres. Portions of finance and accounting, legal, human resources, technology, and other functions are all located there, as is the group that serves the funds' shareholders. This operation is supported by a large, complex computer/communication system, fully backed up offsite.

As the back office gained in sophistication, certified professionals began to help mutual fund shareholders with their overall investment programs, and particularly their retirement funds. An outgrowth of this individual service was "target date funds" These funds "target" a specific year that represents a time when money will be needed for such events as retirement or college entry. The balance in the fund between equity and fixed income reflects the length of time until the target date. The firm handles all the administration and mix of investments, which changes gradually as the target date approaches. T. Rowe Price today is one of several mutual fund groups that can offer clients such in-house full service, including client service, administrative expertise, and investment management.

In 2003, there was a mutual fund scandal involving a number of well-known funds. The transgressions involved such things as "late trading" by favored shareholders, who were allowed to buy or sell shares of the fund after hours, at the prior day's price, thereby profiting from any changes in the market after the close. Another transgression involved "front running," in which some clients were told of planned trades by the fund, so they could trade first, and profit from the change in market price from the sizable transactions by the fund. T. Rowe Price was not involved in any of this, and Jim Riepe became a spokesman for the industry in criticizing and ending such practices.

By 2018, the T. Rowe Price Group had expanded far beyond Baltimore. It now controls 31 acres and 245,000-square-feet of office space in Colorado Springs. In Tampa, Florida, the firm rents a 70,000-square-foot building, also principally for shareholder services and fund sales. Globally, the company now has offices in Amsterdam, Copenhagen, Dubai, Frankfurt, Hong Kong, London, Luxembourg, Madrid, Melbourne, Milan, Singapore, Stockholm, Sydney, Tokyo, Toronto, and Zurich. In the U.S., in addition to Colorado, Florida, and Maryland, the firm has offices located in New York, Philadelphia, and San Francisco.

Bill Stromberg became the next president and CEO, following Jim Kennedy's retirement in 2016. Bill graduated from Johns Hopkins, majoring in mathematics, and earned his MBA from the Amos Tuck School of Business Administration at Dartmouth. He has served at the firm for nearly thirty years in a variety of positions, beginning as an analyst, covering environmental and industrial companies. He initiated the concept of what became the very successful Dividend Growth Fund, and was its first portfolio manager. This fund identified companies that paid solid, rising dividends, and, after careful analysis, promised to continue to do so. He was most recently head of the Global Equity and Global Research Groups. His performance in this role is mirrored in the outstanding investment results that the firm has enjoyed during his tenure. The T. Rowe Group is well-positioned for the new century with its excellent record of performance, its great diversity of product, global exposure in both products and research, a strong team of experienced professionals, its in-depth management group, an outstanding customer service department, its extremely strong balance sheet, and the more than $1 trillion that the firm manages, as of April 2018.

Mr. Price could end his visit with the knowledge that his name is indeed safe in the hands of management. The firm is set to grow and will undoubtedly continue to be respected for the performance, ethics, and high quality of service that it provides to its clients. He can rest easy.

Sources

GENERAL

Many of the facts and information contained in this book were derived from the private files of the T. Rowe Price Group and interviews conducted by the author. These are not available to the public.

PRIVATE JOURNALS: For over forty years of his adult life, T. Rowe Price kept a journal. After his death six journal volumes were made available to the T. Rowe Price Group and quotes were used for a private corporate history written for the firm's fiftieth anniversary in 1987 but they were never published. They were also made available for an article, "The Diaries of T. Rowe Price," published in the August 1987 issue of the now-defunct *Warfield's* magazine, a semi-monthly Maryland business periodical published from 1986 to 1991. All six journal volumes were lost over the intervening years. Recently, however, one of the journals, covering the years 1943–1950, was discovered, viewed by the author for this book, and is now privately held by T. Rowe Price Group.

A second important source for this book was *The History of T. Rowe Price Associates, Inc.* The author, Edmund L. Andrews, was a professional writer who later became an economics correspondent for the *New York Times*. He had access not only to Mr. Price's journals, but also to two of the founders, Charlie Schaeffer and Walter Kidd, as well as to all of their records and notes, which have also vanished over the years. The book was intended for the company's fiftieth anniversary in 1987, but was never published. Its 144 pages nevertheless contain a wealth of information about the firm's history.

Also important to this book were the more than twenty years the author spent at the firm, ten of these in close contact with Mr. Price. His positions included analyst; member of the investment committee of the Growth Stock Fund, the New Horizons Fund, and the New Era Fund; president of the Growth Stock Fund; and chief financial officer. Committees chaired were the Long-Range Planning Committee and the Compensation Committee. After leaving T. Rowe Price, the author became a general partner of New Enterprise Associates, a venture capital partnership in which T. Rowe Price was an original limited partner. He held this position for twelve years before retiring.

PRIVATE CORPORATE PAPERS: Mr. Price was a prolific writer over the course of his investment career, including investment advisories for his clients and papers for his employees. Having spent twenty-two years at the firm, the author has copies of a number of these papers. Copies of these client advisories and internal memos and papers are privately held by T. Rowe Price Group and were made available to the author.

ECONOMIC: General economic statistics are based on the author's research from outside sources, some of which are listed below in the sources for specific chapters, and a T. Rowe Price economist, Richard Wagreich, who is mentioned in the acknowledgments. All referenced in-house T. Rowe Price information, data, and analysis have been kindly furnished to the author by various internal sources, or from the author's position as a former T. Rowe Price executive, fund president, and CFO. External T. Rowe Price data was obtained from their annual reports, their Form 10-K reports, mutual fund reports, and recent analyst reports that give a comprehensive summary of a company's financial performance. Information was also drawn from the Investment Company Institute's *2016 Investment Company Fact Book* (https://www .ici.org/pdf/2016_factbook.pdf) and from Nikki Ross, *Lessons from the Legends of Wall Street: How Warren Buffet, Benjamin Graham, Phil Fisher, T. Rowe Price and John Templeton Can Help You Grow Rich* (Chicago: Dearborn Publishing, 2000).

QUOTES AND INTERVIEWS: Quotes by Mr. Price that are not attributed to a source (e.g. *Barron's, Forbes,* his private journal, or an individual) came from private, in-house T. Rowe Price Group files that are not available to the public, and through interviews conducted by the author with the following past or present executives with T. Rowe Price: Preston G. Athey, Grace W. Beehler, Edward C. Bernard, Andrew Brooks, Howard P. Colhoun, George J. Collins, M. Jenkins Cromwell Jr., Austin H. George, Robert E. Hall, Curran W. Harvey Jr.,

Henry H. Hopkins, Hal B. Howard Jr., James A.C. Kennedy, Dorothy B. Krug, Alan D. Levenson, Edward J. Mathias, Steven E. Norwitz, Francis C. Rienhoff, James S. Riepe, George A. Roche, Brian C. Rogers, William J. Stromberg, William B. Thompson, Susan G. Troll, Richard B. Wagreich, and Clive M. Williams.

Interviews with family members, friends, and others consisted of the following: James D. Hardesty, James Harvey, Martha Healy, Ann D. Hopkins, Ann Shaeffer Mackenzie, Rose Mooney, Margaret Herrera Moore, Ann B. O'Neill, Thomas R. Price III, Dr. Peter V. Rabins, Truman T. Semans, Charles W. Shaeffer, Jr., and Eleanor Healy Taylor.

Note: The use of some of the above-named sources particularly applies to quoted material in Chapters 12, 13, 15, 16, and 17.

Foreword

Mutual fund information came from Arthur Wiesenberger, *Investment Companies* (New York: Arthur Wiesenberger & Co., 1958).

Chapter 1

In addition to interviewing Mr. Price's son Thomas Rowe Price III regarding details of the early family history, standard methods of genealogical research were employed to produce genealogical reports and pedigree charts for T. Rowe Price, Jr.'s paternal and maternal ancestors and family. Using Family Tree Maker and Ancestry.com, a family tree was created and appropriate records (e.g. census, birth, marriage, death) were attached as sources and as the creation of source citations. Searches of newspaper archives included Newspapers.com and in particular the *Baltimore Sun* and the *New York Times*.

Information about the family home and Mr. Price's early years in Glyndon, Maryland, came from Maryland property records, as well as *Glyndon: The Story of a Victorian Village Historic Glyndon* (Glyndon Community Association, 2010). Information about Mr. Price's high school and college years were obtained from his Franklin High, Reisterstown, Maryland, 1914 yearbook and the *Phoenix* and the *Halcyon*, Swarthmore's college newspaper and yearbook, respectively.

Ann O'Neill and sisters Martha Healy and Eleanor Healy Taylor from Historic Glyndon, Inc. were interviewed and provided valuable insight

236 ■   SOURCES

into the early life of T. Rowe Price, Jr. and family. Additionally, Margaret Herrera Moore, the widow of Mr. Price's nephew Rowe Price Moore, shared her late husband's recollections and collection of photographs of the Price family.

Chapter 2

Richard Phalon's 2001 book *Forbes Greatest Investing Stories* (Hoboken, NJ: Wiley, 2004, Chapter 3) provided additional background information for this period of Mr. Price's life. Historical information about DuPont and General Motors came from the DuPont company website history section. Additionally, articles from 1923 and 1924 in the *New York Times* and the *Washington Post* provided details of the criminal case against Smith, Lockhart & Company.

Chapter 3

Facts regarding Mr. Price's early years at Mackubin, Goodrich & Company came from the unpublished private corporate history of T. Rowe Price Group and a July 25, 1999, article by Bill Atkinson in the *Baltimore Sun*, "Legg Mason Reaches 100." Information on George Clement Goodrich (G. Clem Goodrich) was obtained in part from *Baltimore: Its History and Its People* by Clayton Colman Hall (1912).

Eleanor Gherky's engagement to Mr. Price was reported in the *Baltimore Sun* on December 27, 1925 ("Goucher College Senior Who is Engaged to Wed").

Extensive biographical research on Eleanor Gherky's father, William D. Gherky (also known as William D. Gharky) included the following sources: *Who's Who in Engineering: A Biographical Dictionary of Contemporaries 1922–1923* by John William Leonard (John William Leonard Corporation, 1922); American *Electrician, volume 11* (1929); *The Electrical World and Engineer, volume 24,* (November 10, 1894); and his obituary published in the *New York Times,* January 18, 1937. Details of Mr. Gherky's extensive inventions and patents were obtained from various editions of the *Official Gazette of the United States Patent Office; Electricity: A Popular Electrical Journal,* and *American Electrician.*

Finally, the sources of the value of William D. Gherky's estate were his will and other probate documents provided by the City of Philadelphia, Register of Wills.

The author interviewed Mr. Price's son Thomas Rowe Price III, and reviewed interviews conducted by the firm of him and his son, Thomas Rowe Price IV, who had shared their memories of Mr. Price and their mother, Eleanor Gherky Price.

Chapter 4

A key source for this chapter was John Kenneth Galbraith's book *The Great Crash 1929* (New York: Mariner Books, Houghton Mifflin Harcourt, 2009; first published 1955), which provides an economic history leading up to the 1929 stock market crash. Another important source was David E. Kyvig's book *Daily Life in the United States, 1920–1940: How Americans Lived Through the Roaring Twenties and the Great Depression* (New York: Ivan R. Dee, Rowman & Littlefield Publishing Group, 2002). Facts concerning both national and local Baltimore events beginning with Black Thursday, October 24, 1929, through the end of that October were obtained from the issues of the *Baltimore Sun* published on those dates.

The discussion of Mackubin, Legg is based on the *Baltimore Sun*, "Legg Mason Reaches 100," July 25, 1999; interviews with Truman Semans, who has spent his career in management positions at Baltimore financial firms and is currently vice chairman of Brown Investment Advisory & Trust Company; and interviews with Jim Hardesty, former executive vice president of Mercantile Bank, founder of Hardesty Capital, and known as a student of the history of Baltimore financial scene.

In addition to an interview with Mr. Price's son Thomas Rowe Price III, standard genealogical and biographical research was conducted for Marie Walper, Isabella Craig, Walter Kidd, and Charles Shaeffer who formed Mr. Price's first team at Mackubin, Legg & Company and who spent nearly fifty years with him. Finally, details of the amount bequeathed to Eleanor Gherky Price were obtained from William D. Gherky's estate documents from the City of Philadelphia, Register of Wills.

Chapter 6

Details of the 1937 birth of T. Rowe Price & Associates came primarily from the unpublished company history written for the fiftieth anniversary in 1987 and private papers belonging to both Mr. Price and the firm. Biographical research conducted for Charles W. Shaeffer included sources such as the December 21, 2004, obituary in the *Baltimore Sun;* his 1927 William Penn High School (York, Pennsylvania) yearbook; the 1932 yearbook for Penn State college; and interviews of Mr. Schaeffer's son, Charles W. "Pete" Shaeffer Jr., conducted by the author.

Chapter 7

The author's privately held copy of Mr. Price's first article, "Change: The Investor's Only Certainty," written in February, 1937, served as the primary source for this chapter.

Chapter 8

Mr. Price wrote a number of client advisories during the firm's early years and in World War II. Sources of information in this chapter were the following privately held client advisories: "State Capitalism" (February 17, 1938); "Why We Advocate Greater Liquidity at the Present Time" (October 1939); "War on Capitalism and the Investor's Battle for Survival" (May 15, 1940); "Why Buy Stocks Now?" (May 22, 1941); "The Investor Faces War, Peace and Inflation (1942), and "Looking Toward a Post War Economy" (June 1942).

The famous series of *Barron's* articles from 1939 mentioned in this chapter are completely cited in the source notes for Chapter 9, where they are discussed in detail. Mr. Price did author a January 6, 1942, article in *Barron's* entitled "Growth Stocks in War Time Markets."

Chapter 9

A series of five articles fully defining Mr. Price's Growth Stock Theory of Investment were written by Mr. Price, published in *Barron's* in 1939, and form the core of this chapter. These articles were "Picking 'Growth'

Stocks: Corporations, Like People, Have Life Cycles; Risks Increase when Maturity is Reached" (May 15, 1939); "Picking 'Growth' Stocks: Measuring Industrial Life Cycles; The Fallacy of Investing for High Current Income" (May 22, 1939); "Picking 'Growth' Stocks: Procedure of Selection Applied in Three Fields; Factors to Consider" (June 5, 1939); "Picking 'Growth' Stocks: How to Detect the Change from Growth to Maturity, Chrysler vs. General Motors" (June 12, 1939); and "Using 'Growth' Stocks: 'Stable' and 'Cyclical' Types Permit Flexibility in Portfolio Management" (June 19, 1939).

An additional source was Mr. Price's April 1973 brochure, "A Successful Investment Philosophy Based on the Growth Stock Theory of Investment."

Chapter 10

Two privately held client advisories penned by Mr. Price were referenced for this chapter: "Follow Up of 1945 Forecast," written just days before the first atomic bomb was dropped in August 1945, and the second advisory in May 1946, "Opportunity Versus Accomplishments."

Biographical and genealogical sources were studied for information on John B. Ramsay Jr. and family, including the 1922 Princeton University *Bric-a-Brac* yearbook and a 1988 obituary from the *Baltimore Sun*.

Chapter 11

Peter F. Drucker's *The Pension Fund Revolution* (1976; republished by Transaction Publishers, 1995), provided information on General Motor's pension plan changes spearheaded by Charles E. Wilson in 1950.

Barron's invited Mr. Price to update his 1930 articles on Growth Stocks. He published two articles with the same title, "Picking Growth Stocks for the 1950s," on February 6 and February 20, 1950. He followed that up with two additional articles in *Barron's*: "Picking Growth Stocks for the 1950s" (June 18, 1951), and "Fifty Growth Stocks for the 1950s: 1953 Revision" (October 1953).

The author referenced the following publications for statistics regarding the amount of pension assets managed and the percentage of equities invested in those pension plans: "Private Pension Plans, 1950–1974" by Alfred M. Skolnik (*Social Security Bulletin* 39, no. 6, June 1, 1976); "Private and Public Pension Plans in the United States" (National Bureau of Economic Research, 1963); "The Pension and Retirement Markets: Composition and Growth of U.S. Pension Assets" (U.S. Department of Labor); "Private Pension Plan Bulletin Historical Tables and Graphs 1975–2015" (U.S. Department of Labor, February 2018); "Employee Benefit. Plans, 1950–1967," by Walter W. Kolodrubetz (*Social Security Bulletin* 32, April 1969); and "Historic Study of Private and Public Pension Plans 1968-89" (Goldman Sachs, 1989).

Biographical and genealogical research was undertaken for background on E. Kirkbride Miller and John Hannon.

Chapter 12

Historical information came from Martin Walker's *The Cold War: A History* (New York: Henry Holt &Co., 1994).

Chapter 14

Remarks by Ben S. Bernanke on October 24, 2003, at the Federal Reserve Bank of Dallas Conference on the Legacy of Milton and Rose Friedman's *Free to Choose*, Dallas, Texas (www.federalreserve.gov/boarddocs/speeches/2003/20031024/default.htm).

Chapter 16

The following sources were consulted for this chapter: "The Government Takeover of Student Lending" (*Forbes,* May 11, 2010); "Net Neutrality a Go for Internet Providers" (*US News & World Report,* February 26, 2015); "A Political Opening for Universal Health Care?" (*Atlantic,* February 14, 2017); and Nassim Nicholas Taleb, *The Black Swan: The Impact of the Highly Improbable* (New York: Random House, 2007).

Index